More than
Half the Sky

This is a facsimile edition of the book first published in 1996.

mc **Marshall Cavendish**
Editions

This facsimile edition published 2009
Cover design by Lock Hong Liang
Cover art: Helena Beumer (rose), Marta Dehnel(ink bottle)

Published by Marshall Cavendish Editions
An imprint of Marshall Cavendish International
1 New Industrial Road, Singapore 536196

Other Marshall Cavendish Offices
Marshall Cavendish Ltd. 5th Floor 32–38 Saffron Hill, London EC1N 8FH • Marshall Cavendish Corporation. 99 White Plains Road, Tarrytown NY 10591-9001, USA • Marshall Cavendish International (Thailand) Co Ltd. 253 Asoke, 12th Flr, Sukhumvit 21 Road, Klongtoey Nua, Wattana, Bangkok 10110, Thailand • Marshall Cavendish (Malaysia) Sdn Bhd, Times Subang, Lot 46, Subang Hi-Tech Industrial Park, Batu Tiga, 40000 Shah Alam, Selangor Darul Ehsan, Malaysia

Marshall Cavendish is a trademark of Times Publishing Limited

National Library Board Singapore Cataloguing in Publication Data

More than half the sky : creative writings by 30 Singaporean women / edited by Leong Liew Geok. – Singapore : Marshall Cavendish Editions, 2009.
p. cm.
ISBN-13 : 978-981-261-893-1
ISBN-10 : 981-261-893-7

1. Singaporean literature (English) – Women authors. 2. Short stories, Singaporean (English) – Women authors. 3. Singaporean drama (English) – Women authors. 4. Singaporean poetry (English) – Women authors. 5. Women – Singapore – Literary collections.
I. Leong, Liew Geok.

PR9570.S52
S823—dc22   OCN319113437

Printed in Singapore by Utopia Press Pte Ltd.

Contents

Leong Liew Geok	*1*	Introduction
Rasiah Halil	*23*	Doors
Suchen Christine Lim	*24*	Bandong; *from* Bit of Earth
Wee Kiat	*47*	Pearls on Swine
Agnes Lam	*61*	Satin flowers
Ho Poh Fun	*62*	existential
Stella Kon	*64*	*from* Dragon's Teeth Gate
Verena Tay	*78*	Prosperity
Lin Hsin Hsin	*84*	A Woman's Place
Eng Wee Ling	*86*	*from* Wing Tips & Shoulder Pads
Amy Sobrielo	*103*	War Poems
Lesley Yeow	*112*	Women at Odds
Nirmala PuruShotam	*123*	tongues
Angeline Yap	*124*	Memo
Rebecca Chua	*125*	*from* Separate Lives
Ovidia Yu	*153*	*from* The Mother and the Muscle and the Making of Love
Rasiah Halil	*164*	Letters
Lai Ah Eng	*165*	Rachel, Her Parents, My Mother and I
Leong Liew Geok	*178*	First Aunt's Solitudes
Nalla Tan	*181*	*from* Pink Kisses
Mary Loh Chieu Kwuan	*190*	Rice
Claire Tham	*197*	David's Story

Theresa Tan 202 *from* Kaleidoscope Eyes

Lee Tzu Pheng 213 Under the Bell Jar

Ho Poh Fun 215 in the proximity of humans

Heng Siok Tian 217 The lady to her scholar

Leong Liew Geok 218 China Girl Not Picture Bride

Geraldine Kan 220 The Matchmaker

Angeline Yap 229 For Tze, July 1993

Denyse Tessensohn 231 Kumari

Lin Hsin Hsin 237 Till Bankrupt Do Us Part

Eleanor Wong 238 *from* Exit

Rosaly Puthucheary 259 The Rap

Lee Tzu Pheng 260 Not All Babies Have Endearing Faces

Elizabeth Su 261 Gareth's Room

Heng Siok Tian 282 Quartet: Grandmother's bun

Agnes Lam 284 On bare feet

Nirmala PuruShotam 285 daddy loves me

Rosaly Puthucheary 286 A Reel

Tan Mei Ching 287 Never Mind Father

Minfong Ho 291 Turning Thirty

Leong Liew Geok 307 *Glossary*

Leong Liew Geok 311 *Selected Bibliography*

326 *The Contributors*

Contents
(arranged by genré)

Drama

Eng Wee Ling 86 *from* Wing Tips & Shoulder Pads
Geraldine Kan 220 The Matchmaker
Stella Kon 64 *from* Dragon's Teeth Gate
Theresa Tan 202 *from* Kaleidoscope Eyes
Verena Tay 78 Prosperity
Eleanor Wong 238 *from* Exit
Ovidia Yu 153 *from* The Mother and the Muscle and the Making of Love

Fiction

Rebecca Chua 125 *from* Separate Lives
Minfong Ho 291 Turning Thirty
Lai Ah Eng 165 Rachel, Her Parents, My Mother and I
Suchen Christine Lim 24 Bandong; *from* Bit of Earth
Mary Loh Chieu Kwuan 190 Rice
Amy Sobrielo 103 War Poems
Elizabeth Su 261 Gareth's Room
Tan Mei Ching 287 Never Mind Father
Nalla Tan 181 *from* Pink Kisses
Denyse Tessensohn 231 Kumari
Claire Tham 197 David's Story
Lesley Yeow 112 Women at Odds
Wee Kiat 47 Pearls on Swine

Poetry

Heng Siok Tian   *217*   The lady to her scholar

  282   Quartet: Grandmother's bun

Ho Poh Fun   *62*   existential

  215   in the proximity of humans

Agnes Lam   *284*   On bare feet

  61   Satin flowers

Lee Tzu Pheng   *213*   Under the Bell Jar

  260   Not All Babies Have Endearing Faces

Leong Liew Geok   *178*   First Aunt's Solitudes

  218   China Girl Not Picture Bride

Lin Hsin Hsin   *84*   A Woman's Place

  237   Till Bankrupt Do Us Part

Nirmala PuruShotam   *123*   tongues

  285   daddy loves me

Rasiah Halil   *23*   Doors

  164   Letters

Rosaly Puthucheary   *259*   The Rap

  286   A Reel

Angeline Yap   *124*   Memo

  229   For Tze, July 1993

Introduction

Prelude

Why women? A (male) friend had wondered when told that I was working on an anthology of creative writings in English by Singaporean women.

A good question.

Why not?

Humanity entirely is of woman born. Women comprise half the human race; Singaporean women represent nearly half the nation's population.[1] Constituted differently from men, women are likely to be shaped by different kinds of experience, probably perceive things differently from men, and consequently, probably place different emphases on living. For these reasons, what women are thinking and writing today may provide valuable insights into the issues which affect us all in our lives. They are of interest and significance not just to women, but men as well.

Genesis

The twenty-nine writers (excluding myself) I invited to participate in this project had no brief except that their work be 'previously unpublished', of 'reasonable length' and in English. They were free to write whatever they liked in poems, plays or stories, and were not required to address themes of perceived or apparent interest to women. Unfortunately, several others whom I also invited either had no 'previously unpublished' work, or did not write in English. Regrettably, they do not appear. I have not included translations of non-English works: there being no dearth of works by women writing in English, there seemed little need for translations (which would themselves have created potential problems of accuracy and imaginative validity with reference to the original works) to augment voices already present.

The three genrés of drama, fiction and poetry are represented in the works of seven dramatists, thirteen fictionists and ten poets.

In the anthology proper, the entries are arranged by thematic interrelation and difference rather than in generic categories. But for ease of reference by the reader, a separate page following the Contents lists the forty entries and their thirty authors under their respective genrés. In the anthology, while the twenty poems easily appear in their entirety, completeness has not been possible for drama and even fiction. Three of the thirteen entries in prose fiction are excerpts from longer works, and five of the seven dramatic pieces are excerpts from plays. Nevertheless, each can stand on its own and does not depend on a knowledge of the larger work. In some instances, background notes have been provided by the playwrights themselves.

As anthologies go, *More than Half the Sky* makes no claims to being exhaustive of women writing in English in Singapore, but since more women writers have been included than excluded, a certain representativeness may be claimed for it. What has emerged from this collective enterprise testifies to the presence, variety and richness of women's voices in Singapore, and the resourcefulness with which these thirty women have turned experience, observation, ideas, arguments and skirmishes to creative and literary use. Ranging in age from twenty-seven to seventy-four, they represent a wide spectrum of lived experience, and address a wide range of issues with seriousness, wit, humour, flair and subtlety.

Women's Work; Women's Minds
More than Half the Sky is of course an allusion to Mao Tze Tung's prescription for the men and women in the People's Republic of China where the sexes were to be seen and treated in a communist state as equal: 女人能顶半边天 . Women (in China at least) hold up half the sky; the other half, men presumably hold up in an admirably equitable division of labour and responsibility. For most of us who live outside the purview of myth and theory, in nations communist, socialist, democratic or mixtures of these, the practical truth is no match for ideal or equitable states. In Singapore in fact, women are likely to hold up *more* than half the sky than only one half of it. As traditional gender roles overlap with new realities, many women find themselves doing a double shift, bearing the brunt of domestic

responsiblities even as they work outside the home.

Women's work is in the home; men's in bringing the bread home. In an urban and modernising society like Singapore's, the facts of living may belie the fictions of apparent tradition. The traditional dichotomy of a gender-based division of labour can no longer be presumed in Singapore, where two-income families are rapidly becoming the norm rather than the exception.[2] Increasingly, families benefit from the purchasing power a dual income brings; increasingly, in Singapore, as more women join the workforce, out of national and economic necessity,[3] and more women move up the educational ladders of qualification and attainment, traditional gender roles will inevitably be subject to revision and redefinition. Just as the traditional role of the husband as the sole (or primary) provider, and the traditional function of the wife as beneficiary of that largesse are changing, so too are women's perceptions of their role in the household, and their part in the world outside it.

When the Great Marriage Debate raged in Singapore more than a decade ago, one of the discoveries (already known to women) made by (male) political leaders worried about the phenomenon of educated, marriageable women who were not marrying although there were large numbers of marriageable men at large, was that Singaporean women had changed far more than their male counterparts, particularly in their expectations of marriage and the sharing of housework and parenting.

In another example of the acknowledged disparity in expectation and awareness among the sexes, a recent survey[4] of young Singaporeans by the Social Development Unit showed that while most male graduates would like to have three children, most women graduates settled for two. It is not difficult to account for the difference in preference. Women *know* that quite apart from conception, pregnancy and parturition, the responsibilities and burdens of parenting are seen as still primarily theirs. This assumption, integral to the classic demarcation between men's work (on their careers) and women's work (on their children and in the home), is less than tenable in a modern urban society, and is very likely to change in time. It is at these crossroads[5] between the traditional and the evolving, between what men currently expect women to do and what women's own expectations of themselves are, and vice versa, and within the context of modern urban living that *More than Half the Sky* can be placed.

Engagements

This is the third anthology of women's writing in Singapore to appear. The first, *The Sun in Her Eyes: Stories by Singapore Women*, edited by Geraldine Heng, was published by Woodrose Publications in 1976, and comprised sixteen short stories contributed by Rebecca Chua, Stella Kon, Teresa Lim, Tan Lian Choo and Nalla Tan. The second, *Playful Phoenix: Women Write for the Singapore Stage*, was edited by Chin Woon Ping for TheatreWorks and published in 1996. Four of the six plays collected here are by Singaporeans (Dana Lam, Tan Mei Ching, Eleanor Wong and Ovidia Yu); the remaining two by the Malaysian, Leow Puay Tin, and the Malaysian-born Chin, now an American citizen.

What does *More than Half the Sky* show and tell about thirty Singaporean women's thoughts? Without claiming for it the status of being representative of the concerns of Singaporean women in particular, or women in this part of the world, what emerges from forty contributions in all is a spectrum of preoccupations and interests, not all of which are linked exclusively to women. Not surprisingly, a good number of the entries focuses strongly on women, without excluding men, a predominant number of writers being engaged with the sites and spaces where men and women interact or compete or confront each other, at home and at work. Others however, attempt to locate the position of women in relation to their community and society, from the past to the present. Childhood, and parent-child relationships, are explored. Then too, issues of individual and political freedom are debated. The materialism of Singaporean society is demonstrated. The carelessness and callousness of men and women towards non-human life are judged. The bonds of family, friendship and our common humanity are affirmed. These thematic clusters are played out in scenarios which engage mothers and daughters (far more often than mothers and sons); fathers and daughters (rather than fathers and sons); children; grandmothers (rather than grandfathers); men and women, husbands and wives, women and women, the individual and his or her community, and the individual and the state.

In 'Doors,' the opening poem, Rasiah Halil asserts for herself a gypsy freedom and an opening out suggestive of the defiance of limits, discovery of experience and disclosure of the new. The poet departs from closing doors in favour of the opening of new doors to life's fresh possibilities. In marked contrast is the sense of claustrophobic closure that 'Under the Bell Jar' communicates, as Lee Tzu Pheng reimagines the sufferings of Sylvia Plath's 'broken life' which led to her suicide. Though sympathetic, the poet moves away from the negation of Plath's death to affirm in this bleakness, the *redemptive* power of the helplessness (which Plath might have experienced) which Lee would see as a proper function of poetry. In these two poems, the voices are distinctly those of contemporary women who, refusing to enter the doors of death, independently work out more positive solutions for themselves.

Their predecessors were not so lucky. In Suchen Christine Lim's dramatic narrative, women were commodities to be bought, sold and abused by men as well as their own kind. The narrator of 'Bandong,' Wong Tuck Heng, an immigrant newcomer to the tin-mining Bandong settlement in the Malay Peninsula, witnesses the persecution, torture and drowning in a pig basket of a young woman, by the Cantonese community of men and women who punish her for adultery with a man from the rival Hakka clan, 'mirroring brutal nature herself like the mother cat devouring its own young because it was tainted by the odour of an enemy.' Inter-clan hostility between the Hakkas and the Cantonese combines with public punishment for a sexual transgression despite mitigating circumstances: the woman had been bought from a brothel to be wife to an idiot man-boy who had kicked and beaten her in rejection. A woman's fate was a simple matter then: the end of her young life was marriage; the end of marriage was children, and for the Chinese, particularly sons; the end of later life was becoming the powerful and feared (if not respected) mother-in-law and finally, a mellower (perhaps) grandmother.

Under the old dispensation, 'a mother-in-law is the sky and we daughters-in-law are the earth. You can do anything to her as long as she's under your roof.' Compare the fate of this unfortunate woman in Bandong during the early decades of the twentieth century with that of her contemporary 'successor,' Beverly, whose working-class mother-in-law negotiates between her, a middle-class English-educated daughter-in-law with whom she scarcely communicates, and her own son, a Cantonese-speaking, English-educated lawyer. In Minfong Ho's 'Turning Thirty' as well as in Lim's 'Bandong,' the problematic relationship between mothers-in-law and daughters-in-law exemplifies a classic characteristic of Chinese family relationships. Where the earlier Ah Lai's mother is an utter bully bent on the exercise of a mother-in-law's authority and power, the Old One is portrayed by Ho as a woman whose heart for the Filipino maid wins the day over the head of her daughter-in-law, who has threatened to sack Rosa unless the video camera (which Rosa has pawned to raise money for a bank mortgage at home) is returned in time for her husband's thirtieth birthday party.

A third story, 'Separate Lives,' by Rebecca Chua shows little, if any, tension between Lindy and Irene, her daughter-in-law—the author here being primarily interested in the relationship between a divorced mother and her children. Perhaps too in this case, the generational gap is bridged by the common English education and the modernity of both women: Lindy is closer to Irene's time in outlook and attitude than Minfong Ho's the Old One (the honorific already conveying official distance) to Beverly, or in Suchen Lim's 'Bandong,' Ah Lai's mother to her alienated and maligned daughter-in-law.

The woman as victim—of injustice, misunderstanding, ill luck, or her own cattiness—is a motif that runs through the other stories concerning mothers and daughters and their attempts at mutual communication and understanding. In 'Women at Odds,' Lesley Yeow shows how the friction between Fang and her mother is caused not only by the latter's disappointment that Fang, with an Honours degree in Business Administration, would work for a pittance as a full-time Christian worker, but also by the religious divide between a 'spirit-worshipping' woman of the old school and a 'born-again' Christian daughter:

... a life of abstinence and deprivation. What a waste of education! Let those who did not finish school become priests. Not her daughter with the glowing future. Was this what she worked and fought for? To see her child struggling to make ends meet when her peers were executives and reaping all the benefits for which their education had primed them?

(p. 114–115)

Beneath these differences, the bond between mother and daughter runs deep and strong, where the relationship between mother-in-law and daughter-in-law is altogether different, a sensitive matter that cannot, it would seem, weather domestic fissures of disagreement or protest. Here, one party (mother-in-law or daughter-in-law) would treat the other (daughter-in-law or mother-in-law) as The Other, with a formal politeness that excludes intimacy or friendship.

The mother-daughter bond is again demonstrated in the scene excerpted from Theresa Tan's 'Kaleidoscope Eyes,' where Clare's mother demands to know the cause of Clare's barrenness after one and a half years of marriage. Clare is forced to confess that her husband is gay, and has left her for another man. Whereas Clare has learnt to come to terms with the sexual proclivities of her husband, her mother, stunned by the revelation, makes no attempt to hide her feelings. And in Rebecca Chua's 'Separate Lives,' Sharon, a lesbian, regards her mother, Lindy, as 'of that generation that didn't believe that life was complete without a man. They couldn't do anything without one.' Danny too sees his mother as an upholder of the status quo: 'Continuity was what kept them going. Family. Familiarity. For the sake of his father. For the sake of her children. That was how his mother had organised her life, along lines he and his sister had never been raised to recognise or accept' (p. 152).

In contrast to Lindy, who sacrifices a legal career for motherhood and parenting (and whose daughter feels has lead a wasted life), perhaps inadvertently killing her marriage through adherence to a domestic routine which cuts her off from the 'other' outside world, the widowed 62-year-old Margaret drawn by Ovidia Yu in 'The Mother and the Muscle and the Making of Love' is enjoying her friendship with a 29-year-old boyfriend who has the physique of a bodybuilder. Here, the relationship between the mother and May, the scandalised daughter, provides the dramatic centre of an excerpt which re-examines parental responsibilities and demonstrates how even if children are critical of their parent(s), they themselves are subject to their own prejudices and to their own social conditioning. May's reactions, and her brothers' less intense responses, create the taut humour that results from Yu's juxtaposition of the conventional with the outrageous.

Humour as a dramatic tool takes on a satirical edge in 'The Matchmaker,' Geraldine Kan's short play about a one-woman SDU, a matchmaker who runs a telepathic computer conference. She arrives at Susie's doorstep with a computerised file of three prospective partners for Susie to choose, recommending criteria such as PEP (potential earning power), academic background and IQ as important considerations for mate selection. But for Susie, 'There's just too large a gap between the way man and women here think. The men are just too damned conservative and chauvinistic.' 'The Matchmaker' is a tongue-in-cheek look at the highly educated unmarried woman of childbearing age. Hardly the traditional woman, Susie gives the self-appointed matchmaker a frustrating time; of the three suitors, she takes a keen interest in the man least likely to succeed, Singaporean style.

In her largely autobiographical 'Rachel, Her Parents, My Mother and I,' Lai Ah Eng uses the intersecting perspectives of childhood, adolescence and adulthood against the corresponding backdrop provided by her father's coffeeshop in Sentul, and Cambridge University. The adult narrator's journey into the past is triggered by an epiphanic recognition of King's College Chapel as the background of a photograph the family received many years ago from a young Englishwoman, Rachel Wenban-Smith, who had visited the family in Sentul when the narrator was eleven and with whom the narrator had enjoyed an outing. Twenty-five years after that meeting, the narrator (now a doctoral student in anthropology at Cambridge) successfully traces Rachel's whereabouts and visits the Wenban-Smiths in Brockenhurst.

The journey, a 'post-colonial' quest of the narrator's for her own (and her mother's) links with Britain in the colonial era, progresses by way of reminiscence of the narrator's mother as a washerwoman at the British barracks near their home, then a domestic employee of the Wenban-Smiths; and her uncle and aunt who (with their four children) followed their employer back to Britain as his butler-cook and domestic. It moves between the Malaya of the colonial past and the Britain of the present, towards the rediscovery—not only of Rachel's parents, but also that she and the narrator are coincidentally 'sister' social anthropologists, although the actual ending, a postscript, is the death of the mother who had first linked the two women.

Lai's recollections of a childhood richly spent in a squatter settlement on the outskirts of Kuala Lumpur may be compared with the loss of childhood evoked in Agnes Lam's poem, 'On bare feet,' where homeless, dislocated and helpless children—refugees from persecution—are grievously wounded, in more lasting ways than the merely physical. 'daddy loves me,' by Nirmala PuruShotam, catches another traumatising aspect of the dark, unhappy side of childhood. The ominous atmosphere reinforces premeditated physical abuse of another kind—that of a man incestuously forcing himself upon his own daughter in the space and shadows of the night. But when 'the body leaves / the cradle stolen,' the hypocritical 'daddy disguised in daylight / weaves crayonned coloured play / for his very good little girl.' PuruShotam's poem may also be read as a metaphor for the oppression women suffer at the hands of powerful, patriarchal men.

In this anthology, the appearances of fathers are few and far between, few writers being centrally concerned with men as fathers; rather, in the majority of these thirty writers, poetic, dramatic and fictive landscapes are largely presided over by women, present as well as absent, and 'non-fathering' men. That younger boys are seen in relation to a maid, or their mothers and grandmothers, is a reflection of the woman's traditional role as caregiver. Probably too, in this part of the world, in real life fathers do not play as important a role as mothers in women's and men's lives. Besides

Lai and PuruShotam, Tan Mei Ching uses the father figure as the traditional figure of authority, characterised by a cultivated aloofness and isolation, as if the role of a father demanded both, in a household that actualises the feminine space traditionally associated with it—the man has a wife and three daughters. Thus in 'Never Mind Father,' the young narrator views her father as 'an important man with a lot of responsibilities, and when he was home, he would want rest from the world, so we didn't want to bother him' (p. 288). The mother-father divide between the warm and approachable mother, and the distant, worldly father, provides the three sisters in the story with ways of approaching and anticipating either parent's reaction to their actions. But although it is their mother who scolds, and it is their father who punishes, the story eventually humanises the father: in a gesture of peace, he invites his hurt daughter to take a walk with him.

The Singaporean preoccupation with things material, prosperous and lucky features significantly in a number of contributions. In her story, 'Pearls on Swine,' Wee Kiat takes a sardonic look at the fads and fashions of the rich. A pet pig, Oon Oon, is acquired for Ralph Tan, the son of a Towkay, and to their chagrin, is looked after by the Towkay's various staff, each of whom has his/her own tale to tell. Ralph loses all interest in porky when at his 'My Pig and I' party, a finer pet is brought by a friend. The unsuspecting Oon Oon is promptly despatched to its original home in Jurong. A story that combines various points of view, 'Pearls on Swine' is palpable comment on the callous attitude some Singaporeans have towards pets which are bought, fussed over, and discarded when their master or mistress finds caring for them a chore. While not advocating keeping birds as pets, Ho Poh Fun's 'in the proximity of humans,' makes a case for a less oblivious human attitude to the feathered nature which has been driven out by the man-made 'crowd of high sky-scouring scenarios,' or upon colliding with the high windows of skyscrapers, is reduced to 'palpitating feathers / a beak shattered / a wing crushed.'

The tension between the pragmatic life and the ideal life, between compromise and principle, appears in Ho's 'existential,' a poem about the negotiations and compromises made between past, present and future. The poet sees children as pragmatically moulding the past that they inherit from their forebears, appraising what's still pertinent to the new, betraying fidelities in their mutable existentials, in the pragmatic necessity of adapting to change. On the commercial front, in the excerpt from Stella Kon's 'Dragon's Teeth Gate,' rampant greed motivates Freddie, owner of Jingqi Centre. Playing Mephistopheles to Freddie's Faust, the God Kuang Ho, God of wealth and prosperity, intends to multiply Freddie's wealth a hundred times in return for the souls of the workers who worship him during their after-work training sessions. He promises Freddie a regional chain of stores, immense wealth and material success. As Kon sees it, the acquisition of wealth, and more wealth is but inversely proportional to the moral health of the soul.

A similar materialistic excess informs 'Prosperity,' by Verena Tay, a play which gives the special-offer-bargain-hunting *kiasu* habit of certain Singaporeans a wicked twist. Mrs Tan finds herself besieged with *all* the unsold mandarins from the grocer's *entire* stock, which her husband has bought at a very special price. Now not only is their sitting room inundated with symbols of prosperity on Chinese New Year's Eve, the closet and bedroom are in a similar state of superabundance. In his passion for the special offer, Mr Tan has overlooked the overripe state of the *kum* which cannot be thrown out for fear of driving all the luck and prosperity out of the door of their corner flat in Toa Payoh …

The irresistible place the irrational impulse enjoys in the psyche of the ordinary man or woman is wittily shown by Lin Hsin Hsin in 'Till Bankrupt Do Us Part,' a poem which argues how twenty-four-hour-a-day armchair shopping, by cool courtesy of the Internet, 'will empower some and bankrupt others.' Denyse Tessensohn's 'Kumari' makes narrative use of shopping without paying, all for a greater good. With Ariff Mydin for accomplice, Kumari Govindran steals from the supermarket where she works, so as to help a dozen near destitute old people who do not make enough from collecting and selling discarded clothes to buy proper food for themselves. Although the thefts total a formidable $2278, all is forgiven when the motive is known and the press gives the human-interest story maximum publicity.

On the other hand, Agnes Lam would think of others not personally known or encountered, but wholly imagined through the contemplation of 'Satin flowers.' In the retrospective enumeration of the discrete processes of creation of the bouquet, the poet surmises that eight pairs of hands and the bits of several lives will be thrown away should she discard this present, now beginning to rust. Where Lam thinks of workers unknown, Rasiah Halil's open heart directs her letters to friends everywhere—in Singapore, Malaysia, Brunei, the United States, the United Kingdom, Canada. Just as her earlier 'Doors' is open to experience beyond the orthodox boundaries of gender and its accustomed spaces, 'Letters' affirms the transcending universality and freedom of friendship.

The subject of freedom and mobility is sardonically addressed in Lin Hsin Hsin's 'A Woman's Place,' which questions the limits on freedom conferred by both society and gender, and is critical of the traditional precedence granted to men:

> if a woman looks into a man's face
> man will return a gaze
> put her in her place
> & make her feel out of place
>
> (p. 85)

If women are restricted by the constraints of gender, the constraints of family, society and state often hamper the individual in her or his freedom to choose and create. And the freedom to name is similarly subject to precedent, as Nirmala PuruShotam's 'tongues' demonstrates. Here the resistance that the speaker meets from an already named world of things ('house. / stone. / road. / tree. / sky'), in her attempt to 'tutor' these terms according to her own rules, eventually leads to her failure. Similarly, the actor in 'A Reel' by Rosaly Puthucheary, is not his own man. He plays a role tightly controlled by director and film, his feelings and emotions staged in accordance with the script and director. And in the Trial scene from Eleanor Wong's 'Exit,' the tensions between freedom and control in the individual's relationship with the state are expressed within an absurdist-surrealistic political framework. The state forbids its citizens to live in another country:

> You. Chen Tze Wen ... committed the offence of treasonable disloyalty in that you wilfully harboured, singly or in consultation with another or others unknown, a prohibited intent, to wit, the intention to quit the country without lawful excuse, and have thereby committed an offence punishable under the Deportation Act of 1990.
>
> (p. 240)

In Chen's trial, the Defence Counsel argues that 'the prospect of life here was so intolerable, the accused had no choice, indeed, was compelled, to leave.' The picture painted by Wen himself is of an existence completely subservient to work, in furtherance of the ends of the state. Emotionally exhausted by the ruthless demands made on his time by the work ethic, Chen has bought a one-way air ticket out of his job, home and country. Ironically, the punishment for this treasonable act is deportation for life!

Other sites of conflict are defined by men and women contending for dominance and power. The male-female stereotypes of superiority and subservience, boss and secretary, leader and follower, man vs woman—at work, in the home, in love and marriage, or out of both—are played out in no fewer than eight of the forty contributions.[6] Placing women in dominant positions, Eng Wee Ling and Amy Sobrielo examine the results in their relations with subordinates and peers, in Act 1 of 'Wing Tips and Shoulder Pads' and the short story, 'War Poems' respectively. The battle of the sexes between Loh Keen Yin and Bob Lee in the dramatic excerpt is fought out in mutually competing oneupmanship so as to impress their boss. Bob, the new deputy junior trainee assistant manager and one of 'those who think women can only type, make coffee or answer the phone,' cannot accept the idea of reporting to a woman boss whom, on first meeting, he has already assumed to be 'Mr' Loh's secretary. Their power play and dirty tricks are in no small part caused by the circumstances of having a female as boss and the male her subordinate. The truce that they subsequently observe is prompted by the necessity to unite to see an important presentation through. Even then, Bob's gender prejudices are difficult to shed, and continue to encroach upon their professional relationship. When Keen Yin invites him to lunch as his boss, he involuntarily declares that he never lets a woman pay for him.

In 'War Poems,' the insufferable superiority of Jacqui Loh, Literature teacher in Dover West Secondary School, takes a beating at the hands of her Philistines, the (male) science teachers. On the pretext of wanting to improve himself, Philistine Lim invites her to identify a war poem which—as the dénouement reveals—is a clever collage of Wilfred Owen and James Joyce. Poor Jacqui is told too late, why she could not identify it. The (male) revenge masterminded by Lim is an unmitigated success, the irony being that the instrument of revenge should be a poem borrowed from two well known poems in English literature. The fury of these men at Jacqui Loh's loud insults is far more controlled than that which appears in Rosaly Puthcheary's poem, 'The Rap,' where the anger, horror and violence of the rapper's 'acoustic rumble' is given effective rhythmic shape in four measured and taut stanzas, although the nature of their source is unplaced.

Where professional relationships deal with the politics of the office or the politics of cultural difference in the Staff Common Room, relationships from love, romance and marriage are not spared the machinations of power. Leong Liew Geok's 'China Girl Not Picture Bride' reprises the old story of marriage as an agent of upward mobility for a pretty woman who marries a much older Singaporean in China to give herself and her mother a better life in Singapore, and who uses her youth as a bargaining tool with her indulgent husband. Not so 'The lady to her scholar,' Heng Siok Tian's poem. Too shy to declare her love, the subject must pine in muteness and lovesickness for her oblivious scholar. As Heng clearly sees it, the state of pining, stripped of its poeticizing symbols, is a sickening one. Where 'China Girl not Picture Bride' asserts the woman's ambitions and desires, Heng's lady, reminiscent of an earlier era, must suffer the propriety of mute silence. Suffering of another kind, borne as a result of the forces of history, is the subject of Leong Liew Geok's narrative poem, 'First Aunt's Solitudes,' where a tragic fate dogged the lives of her aunt and uncle whose original separation from their families as a result of the Japanese invasion of China in the late '30s, was turned by subsequent political and geographical circumstances into a life-long one.

Three generations of women present in 'Quartet: Grandmother's bun'—the speaker (daughter), mother and grandmother—demonstrate the bonds women share in the family.[7] The speaker observes the careful routine of her grandmother unravelling and reshaping her bun in a favourite corner of the kitchen, in gestures which epitomise preservation and perseverence:

> as you let your hair down
> you put away stray strands
> beneath benign bun
> like pain
> neatly tucked away
> camouflaged with black pins:
>
> (p. 282)

In a parallel scene, the speaker's mother is discovered in this same corner, 'hunched over rubbing her aches / with the sour-black ointment / you gave her.' Subtly, Heng speaks of the aches and pains that women receive; their retreat to a quiet corner to recover speaks of women's power to accommodate and endure.

The modern and contemporary woman is unlikely to hide her feelings, assume modest silence or suffer mute pain, as demonstrated by 'Pink Kisses,' 'Rice' and 'David's Story.' In the first, which is part of a longer work-in-progress, Nalla Tan portrays a wartime romance set in Ipoh, between Juniki Utago, a married Japanese officer, and Tamar Raghavan, the sister of a recruit in his training school. Utago has fallen passionately in love with the young girl; the sense of wartime uncertainty only intensifies the blossoming relationship between the lovers even as B29s are flying overhead on reconnaissance missions, and in Europe, the military conflict has swung in favour of the Allied forces.

This romance between native and invader during the Japanese Occupation of Malaya and Singapore has a successor in the marriage between local and expatriate in 'Rice,' by Mary Loh Chieu Kwuan. The strains in the domestic relationships which precede the narrator's romance and marriage, cluster around the symbolic aspects of rice as the dietary staple of the Chinese family, the source of life. When in a quarrel, the narrator's mother leaves her father, she nevertheless allows herself to be persuaded by her daughter to return to her husband, the breadwinner, the supplier of rice. The narrator learns the art of cooking rice from her mother; knows that the serving of rice by her mother to her father is a ritual acknowledgement of his place as head of the house. The family is expelled from her paternal grandmother's house after the narrator's sister accidentally breaks grandmother's rice bowl. Naturally she grows up disgusted with the ritualistic excess of rice, but Loh provides no escape from cultural baggage, despite marriage with an Englishman. On their return from an Italian honeymoon, Brian Worth, seemingly a 'bangers and baked beans' bloke, asks of his wife, a first home-cooked meal of 'one or two Chinese dishes … and a bowl of rice.'

Where 'Rice' uses culture and symbol for meaning and impact, Claire Tham's 'David's Story' works independently of cultural location or dislocation. The intense triangular relationship between Li, Wai Keong and David, the narrator-usurper, is played out in Oxford, London and Calais. David, who is after and gets Wai Keong's girl, Li, whom he sees as not reciprocating Wai Keong's feelings for her, rationalises his victory as a moral act:

> He told himself he was doing Wai Keong a favour: a relationship where the feeling ran all in one direction would collapse under its own unequal weight. He was relieving them of future misery.
>
> (p. 200)

But as Tham shrewdly shows, David's envy of Wai Keong makes his winning of Li a product of his own covetousness.

Away and at home, the past and the present, the freedom of lovers and the domestic constraints of being a mother: these frictions underlie Angeline Yap's love poem, 'For Tze, July 1993.'

The poet, who is preparing to say goodbye to her husband before he goes abroad alone, recalls their free and idyllic first year of marriage, spent in the Cambridge and Boston areas of Massachusetts, as she frantically completes a shopping list of their three children's things for him to bring home. Not only in poetry, but also in drama and fiction, the demands made by children, and the relationships between parents and their children, young or grown, are abundantly demonstrated. In 'Memo,' a tongue-in-cheek futuristic poem (written in 2011) by Yap, a poor little rich girl faxes her predicament—a suspected pregnancy—to her parents. Her appeal for help to absentee parents suggests parental neglect, and a consumer-based material relationship as a substitute for the time and attention that her parents might have given her instead.

> At twenty-one
> I got a Jag
> about whose size
> I should not brag.
>
> But Daddy, Mummy,
> What to do?
> My menses is now overdue.
> We've never talked of certain facts.
>
> Please *reply* by urgent fax.

(p. 124)

Not all parents are worthy of respect; not all children are born angelic. As Lee Tzu Pheng observes, 'Not All Babies Have Endearing Faces.' Although some are indisputably offputting in their unappealing features and blemished faces, they bask in the centre of their families' attention. For Lee, the human heart yet 'holds dear a gift, however plain the wrapping.' Parental pride and love confer beauty, no matter how unattractive in others' eyes. Perhaps babies are more readily loveable and cuddly than grandmothers can ever be. In 'Gareth's Room,' by Elizabeth Su, Gareth's initial reaction when told that his seventy-year-old grandmother is visiting, is one of chagrin: she is 'too old to play his games with him or take him shopping.' But his impatience with her turns into engagement as she tells her young grandson about her life and his grandfather's. Her experience disarms him to the extent that he invites his *Po-po* to paint the eyes of the giant squid in the underwater kingdom on his wall, in a replication of the 'dotting the eye' ceremony which marks the launching of a new boat.

Closing Gaps

More than Half the Sky reveals several characteristics of the English language literary scene in Singapore. Literary women are well placed. A perusal of the biodata of the thirty writers furnishes a formidable number of literary awards, national and regional, already won by a good number of them. Secondly, their rootedness in this part of the world is indubitable; their range of interests readily diverse.

Although English was originally a foreign language, the language of British colonialism, and subsequently the language of a privileged elite, it now enjoys a comfortable status not only as a working language but one that can be indigenised and turned into a creative medium of Singaporean expression, as shown in the works of thirty women here and the works of Singaporeans elsewhere. As a language native to none of the major ethnic groups, English is, paradoxically, the language that belongs to us all.

At the time of writing, the English language literary scene shows a dearth of contributions from non-Chinese communities. Much of literature tends to be culture-bound, stories, and plays (and to a lesser extent, poetry) consciously and unconsciously revealing the cultural values and underpinnings of the group or community to which the writer belongs. Several references have already been made to characteristics of Chinese culture, e.g., the potentially and actually problematic relationships between mothers-in-law and daughters-in-law; the distant authoritarian father and the approachable mother; the preferential treatment of sons, to be seen in Gareth's illiterate grandmother's remark that in her family, education was the preserve of her brothers.

A writer may of course choose to write in a relatively culture-free mode, which is more likely to occur in poetry than in fiction or drama, the two genrés which require social landscapes and social interaction. That the majority of contributors to this anthology is of Chinese descent is probably a reflection of the ethnic distribution of population in Singapore. Nevertheless, there is room for other voices to be heard, for other stories, plays and poems to be written and read. I am optimistic that in time to come, more Singaporean women (and men) from the other communities—Malays, Indians, Eurasians and others—will contribute towards the literature in English of a multiracial and multiethnic nation and will help to give it imaginative shape; will tap the potential of its creative diversity and give the Singaporean literary experience in English the richness of texture, the fullness of perspective and expression that its people together possess, and deserve to have represented and recreated in narrative and text.

Afterword

More than Half the Sky concludes with a glossary of abbreviations, and colloquialisms as well as non-English expressions which are part of the Singapore context, and a selected bibliography of writings about women in Singapore; and writings about women in the Asia-Pacific region (an area liberally defined as including the countries of Southeast Asia, Australia, New Zealand, India, Pakistan and Sri Lanka, China, Japan and Korea). Several are feminist in approach or intent; several literary in style and content; the majority addresses the sociological, political, cultural, economic, religious, historical and sexual dimensions of gender, and of being woman.

Biographical notes on the thirty writers follow the bibliogaphy and conclude the anthology. Of significance is the calculated fact that between them, they total at the end of 1997, approximately 1285 years of post-natal life and experience! Between them, they share the multiple roles that women are invariably committed to in one brief lifetime; prove the energy and vitality, courage and spirit with which they work and think; and demonstrate the passion with which they would integrate segmented lives.

This book has taken a good long while to emerge. In the period between conception and birth, several women changed jobs; others had babies; still others moved house; and several who went abroad for further study or research had to be electronically pursued to the North Atlantic coast. Through it all, they demonstrated a remarkable threshold of tolerance for receding deadlines, editorial oversights and unforeseen delays. Through it all, they enquired, but did not press. I wish to thank the twenty-nine women for their good—and great—faith in this collective enterprise; and Christine Chua, then senior editor at Times Editions, for planting the idea in my head and for her unstinting support—through it all.

Leong Liew Geok

Endnotes

1. Total resident population of Singapore at the end of June, 1996: 3044.3 (thousand), No. of males: 1531.1 (thousand) and No. of females: 1513.2 (thousand). Source: *Monthly Digest of Statistics*. Singapore (March 1997); Dept. of Statistics, Ministry of Trade and Industry, p. 3.

2. Labour Minister, Lee Boon Yang, referring to the government's Back to Work programme for housewives and retirees, said in Parliament on October 28, 1996: 'Over the longer term, we hope to attract more and more married women back to the workforce with jobs which allow them to supplement their family income and at the same time, attend to their homemakers' responsibilities.' Reported in *The Straits Times*, October 29,1996.

3. Stella Quah writes: 'It appears that women are increasingly determined to handle both duties—home and job—concurrently [where previously, they worked while they were single, and gave up their jobs to look after their families and homes after marriage] .... The proportion of single women who are economically active has increased from a mere 24.8% of all single women in 1957, to 69% of all single women in 1990. There is a lower proportion of economically active women among wives, but still this proportion increased significantly, from only 14.0% in 1957 to 43.2% in 1990.' See 'Marriage and Family,' *Singapore Women: Three Decades of Change*, ed. Aline K Wong and Leong Wai Kum (Singapore: Times Academic Press, 1993), p. 37.

I have not been able to obtain figures for 1996 or 1997, but they are likely to show further increases in the percentage of economically active married women.

4. The SDU survey covered 815 undergrads and 1000 working adults comprising 204 graduates and 796 non-graduates. Results reported in *The Straits Times*, April 21, 1997, p. 21.

5. At the time of writing, the beginning of the week brought news that three Singaporean women, Mrs Elizabeth Sam (Deputy President, OCBC; Mrs Theresa Foo, Chief Executive of Stanchart in Singapore; and Ms Maggie Lee, Management Director of Shroder Investment) have appeared in the London-based *Euromoney's* top fifty women in finance, traditionally, a male preserve (*The Straits Times*, April 22, 1997), while the weekend saw the breaking of new ground as the Singapore Civil Defence Force announced that in response to interested enquiries from women 'eager for frontline postings with the emergency service,' it would, for the first time in its history, employ and train women as firefighters (*The Sunday Times*, April 27, 1997).

6. Eng Wee Ling, Act 1, 'Wing Tips & Shoulder Pads'; Heng Siok Tian, 'The lady to her scholar'; Lin Hsin Hsin, 'A Woman's Place'; Leong Liew Geok, 'China Girl Not Picture Bride'; Mary Loh Chieu Kwuan, 'Rice'; Amy Sobrielo, 'War Poems'; Nalla Tan, 'Pink Kisses'; Claire Tham, 'David's Story.'

7. The father-*son* relationship, as well as the grandfather-*grandson* relationship is conspicuous for its absence, although men as fathers (of daughters), or as lovers, boyfriends, husbands, colleagues or rivals, and bosses are not. One explanation for this may be that women writers may be more attracted and can relate more intimately, to other women in shared experience.

Doors

Rasiah Halil

Will you close your doors on me
& fail to see
the rays of light
or colour of my skin
or will it be easier
to act unknowing
when rooms are locked
& doors made too big?

I have no tears
or bitterness
as I leave your mansion
for your doors are too confining
& I love the sea
I like to tease the moon
catch dewdrops & stars
watch the bloom of gul bakawali*
& nature awaits
as your doors close on me.

No anger, regrets,
I'm a gypsy
who loves windows
desert, oasis,
& the limitless sea.

* gul bakawali (Epiphyllum oxypetalum): night-blooming cactus with fragrant pale
pink flowers; a mystical flower in classical Malay literature.

Bandong

from Bit of Earth

Suchen Christine Lim

I, Wong Tuck Heng, was born on the 15th of the 7th moon in the 7th year of Ham Fung, in my native village of Sum Hor (Three Streams) in the Canton Prefecture of Kwantung Province … he went over once again what he had composed inside his head when he was still tossing in the middle of the South China Sea, in the *tongkang* which had brought him to this part of the world.

When I was thirteen years of age, my father, Doctor Wong Tin Keng, the village physician, was imprisoned and tortured upon the orders of a corrupt magistrate in our district. This vile slave of the Qing devils had accused my father of being a member of the Heaven and Earth League, a noble society founded by the loyal sons of the Chinese earth to overthrow the Manchu invaders, to destroy the Qing and restore the glory of Ming. Because my father was a loyal son of the Chinese earth, loyal to the Ming Dynasty, he was tortured and sentenced to death by the Manchu dogs who had raped our land. They sent soldiers to torch our family home and I was the only one who escaped death.

He shut his weary eyes against the splinters of sunlight bouncing off the waters of the Sungei Bandong. Once again, he heard his mother yelling at him: Run! Tuck Heng, run! Ai-eee! His mother pushed him out of the door just as a fiery beam crashed upon her. Instantly, she was engulfed in flames.

Screams and the smell of burning flesh had pursued him for the next two years, turning his sleep into nightmares. The Qing devils had hounded him by day and the memory ghosts had engulfed him by night. He had had to watch his mother, his brothers and his sisters burn to death before his horrified eyes, night after night. The screams that rose from his throat were stifled by rough hands. They clamped upon his mouth like a vice, the hands of his parents' friends and relatives, who had risked their lives to hide him from the Qing devils. If they had been caught shielding him, these brave souls and their entire families would have been killed, for the Qing devils were determined to eliminate those who opposed Qing rule. Pull out the weeds and destroy their roots! That was the edict issued by the Qing Emperor. And to avoid the destruction of their families, many Chinese scholars had had to serve the Manchu invaders since the sixteenth century, his father had told him. But not the scholars in our family. Not your great-great-grandfather. He left the capital and returned to our village and we, his descendants, became village doctors instead of scholar-mandarins, his father had said. And he had stored this piece of knowledge like a gold nugget in his chest ever since. Even as he had scuttled about like a gutter rat, hiding in dark lonely places while making his way to the sea coast. After the fire, his sole duty to his parents was to stay alive and this was what had sustained him and given him the tenacity to endure danger, hunger and squalor.

His dark eyes searched the Sungei Bandong for the harbingers of death—the silent lords of the river. A large black log was floating perilously close to their *sampan*. Chan Ah Fook had warned him to look out for those evil beady eyes. It's the eyes; they're the only signs which give them away, he had whispered before they had boarded the sampan. If not for their eyes, ah, you won't know they're crocodiles! *Buaya*, that's what the Malays call them. And only a Malay boatman can bring us up the river safely in a sampan like this, you know or not? Hoi-ya, they've got special prayers and charms, ah! We don't. But remember this; once we're on the river, don't ever say the word, crocodile. You'll offend the beast. You want to say his name? Then, say lord of the river. Don't forget you're in Malaya now. And this peninsula is full of jinns and spirits. Just like back in Sum Hor. Hill, rock, valley and river—all have guardian spirits. A newcomer like you has to be extra careful not to offend them. Understand or not? And he had nodded as he listened to the old coolie in silence.

Their lone sampan with its Malay boatman at the oars was inching its way up the Sungei Bandong, pushing against the current as the boatman's oar sliced through the muddy waters, in stroke after stroke. He kept his eyes on the riverbank, ever watchful for the slightest movement in the thick foliage which fringed the river. The jungle and its vegetation lined the water's edge. For miles, there was nothing but an impenetrable wall of green, broken occasionally by a few brown huts built on stilts at the water's edge.

He wiped the sweat from his face with the sleeve of his coolie tunic. The heat was oppressive, and the silence of the jungle at noon weighed heavily upon him. Nothing was in view but river, sky and jungle for mile after monotonous mile. He had come to the peninsula of foreign devils. White-skinned devils and brown-skinned devils had crowded the pier when he landed on Penang island where Chan Ah Fook had met him. What a babble of tongues and noise then! And now—this unbearable silence—as though they were in a cavern never traversed by man before. He muttered a prayer. Hidden eyes were watching them and he wished the brown-skinned devil would row a little faster. He undid his pigtail, mopped his brow and rewound the length of hair round his head once again. Clutching his cloth bundle, he pressed it hard against his chest. His face was much older than his fifteen years. His brows were creased in a dark frown against the shafts of light bouncing off the river. The afternoon sun seemed to hang in the sky above, still and implacable like a god in this strange silent land.

He fixed his eyes on the back of the Malay boatman. By the power of my ancestors, Malay devil, row faster, faster, he kept thinking and wished that the acute pain in his chest would stop. He would live through whatever ordeal Fate had in store for him in this land of the brown-skinned devils, he promised his father's spirit. He pressed his cloth bundle against his chest. Harder. Harder. He would cut off an arm or a leg if that could ease his pain. Curse this oppressive silence which was making him remember things. There was nothing to do but sit in this rickety sampan and stare at the boatman's back. Curse the Manchu dogs! Curse the bastards! May they die without coffins! Without descendants to mourn them! Without a place to lay their bones!

His hand groped for the metal box in his cloth bundle. His father's box of medical notes was the only thing he had managed to salvage from the fire when the Manchu dogs had torched his home. Not because his father was a traitor but because his father was a true Chinese patriot! A man of Han, Tang and Ming. Never a Qing. Never. His family of Wongs had never served the Manchu invaders. How many families in Kwangtung Province could claim this? His pride eased the pain of his loss a little, and he reminded himself not to forget to mention this to the Lodge Master of the White Cranes when he reached Bandong settlement.

'Psst!' Chan Ah Fook's weather-beaten face came up close to Tuck Heng's ears, his square jaws jutting as he strained to keep his naturally loud voice low.

'This is the spot. Nah, throw this red packet into the water. The sugar will sweeten their mouths and the river spirits will protect you. Pay your respects and tell them you're a new arrival.'

Tuck Heng flung the red packet into the river and watched it sink into the murky depths. In silence. His eyes growing drowsy in the heat. A sudden rustle of leaves startled him. He darted a glance at the riverbank. His eyes searched the shadows. A monkey screeched. A flock of birds rose into the air.

The air was cool at this stretch of the river which was shaded by the jungle trees. The sun had dipped behind the dense wall of green by now. Chan Ah Fook's eyes were also searching the deepening shadows along the riverbank. An uneasy silence seemed to have settled upon the river with the onset of the brief tropical twilight.

'Look sharp!' Ah Fook hissed. 'Those Hakka dogs might ambush us here.'

Tuck Heng's shoulders stiffened at this hint of danger. His nose sniffed the air like a dog on the alert. When a bright blue kingfisher dived into the waters, his hand reached for the knife in his belt. But he relaxed when he saw it was only a bird.

'Hoi, *chepat lah*! Quickly,' Ah Fook hissed at the boatman in a tongue which sounded like gibberish to Tuck Heng's ears.

But the boatman understood Ah Fook's heavily-accented Malay, and the sampan moved faster upriver.

'Nearly there, nearly there; keep your eyes on the riverbank to your left,' Ah Fook leaned forward and switched back to the familiar Cantonese dialect of their native Sum Hor village. 'Hoi! *Baik, baik*! *Sini*! *Sini*! *Telima kasih*!' he called out again in the foreign tongue and thanked the Malay boatman.

27

Tuck Heng was impressed with his companion's facility for speaking the Malay tongue and said so.

'Ha! In these parts you've got to speak the Malay devil's tongue! Don't fear death! Don't fear the scorn of men. Just open your mouth more and soon you'll be speaking like me, *lor*!'

Their sampan slid to a halt. Night had fallen by this time and the riverbank was a mass of shadows. Tuck Heng thanked his gods and ancestors for his safe arrival in Bandong. He stood up eagerly, clutching his cloth bundle and jumped off the sampan, only to sink knee-deep into the soft mud. Cursing his own stupidity and foolish eagerness, he clambered up the riverbank, slipped and climbed again while Chan Ah Fook and the Malay boatman roared and guffawed.

'Aye, you've hit shit, ah! Mud and shit! Symbols of wealth! But let this be a lesson to you, young dog! Learn patience. Always wait for an old hand like your uncle here to lead the way. To show you where the dung holes are! Ha, ha, ha!'

Tuck Heng felt the sting of the boatman's laugh and the cut of Chan Ah Fook's teasing keenly. He loathed mistakes and errors, seeing them as signs of weakness in his own judgement and character. How could he have been such a fool to mess up his first step on the new land! Choy! And he had fallen upon it. Not a good omen at all, he thought, and vowed never again to be so eager and foolish.

'Ha! Humbled by the guardian spirit of this place, heh? Be patient, boy. Those who are too hasty, like your own father, get killed. I speak bluntly but I speak the truth. Follow me, young dog. I know this place. Every hole and corner of it.'

Chan Ah Fook hurried down the path leading to the settlement. The moon had risen and Tuck Heng could make out the dark shapes of the huts and the patches of yellow light beyond the bushes. There were many questions inside his head as they plunged into the wilderness. But before he could ask them, the night was shattered by the clanging of gongs and tin pans.

'The gods, ah! You're in luck, young dog! They're going to drown the bitch tonight! Come, come! You can watch it with me!'

Chan Ah Fook raced ahead and Tuck Heng ran behind him, his heart beating faster as the clamour of the gongs grew louder. When they reached the village square, he found it swarming with hundreds of miners and a sprinkling of women. Everyone had gathered in front of a temple, and the air was thick with Cantonese curses, foul words and obscenities.

'Cut off her cunt! Drown the bitch!'

'Let the whore die!'

'Without coffin or mourners!'

'Hoi! More light! More light over here!'

The men were pushing and jostling to get to the centre of the square. A miner next to Tuck Heng yelled at the top of his voice as he swung his lantern above the heads of the crowd.

'Drown the bitch, I say! Throw her into the river!'

'Not so fast!' another miner hollered. 'Strip and whip her first! Death is too sweet for traitors like her!'

'Right! Right!' the men on the other side of the square roared. 'The bitch must die a slow and painful death!'

'Whip her! Whip her!' the crowd chanted.

Tuck Heng shoved and elbowed his way to the front. Kneeling before the temple was the object of the crowd's wrath—a woman splattered with mud and dung, and bleeding from several lacerations on her face and arms. It was obvious that she had been whipped and the lashes had cut deep into her flesh. A purple gash on her temple had left a trail of blood on one side of her face. Her matted locks stank of pigs' swill and excrement, but still the mob jostled and pushed to get near her. Miners, bare to the waist and sweating like workhorses, were pelting her with lumps of pigs' dung.

'Slut! Slattern! Whore!'

But the woman who was bound hand and foot showed no sign that she had heard. Her eyes were glazed and fixed at a point above the heads of the mob. Her impassive face was oblivious of her tormentors. A miner went forward and gave her a violent kick. She fell on to her side but no sound escaped her lips. No cry. None. She lay where she had fallen. An inert figure which drove the men and women into a frenzy.

'No name! No shame! Phui!' A woman spat at her. Others hissed like angry snakes round her.

'Traitor!' A miner's wife doused the fallen woman with a spittoon of urine. 'Curse the mother who gave birth to you!'

The mob jeered.

Several lumps of pig's dung flew through the air and one of them hit the woman's eye. The mob roared louder and pelted her with more dung.

'The gods in heaven, ah! Look at her! Just look at her! Our ancestors, open your eyes and your ears! See for yourselves the shame she has brought upon us! Upon our village and our name! We women of Sum Hor have a good name! But this vixen has befouled it! Let me gouge out her eyes! Her heart!'

A big-boned woman rushed forward and seized the bound victim by the throat. If the men had not pulled her away, she would have strangled her.

'Right, ah! Good! Good! Ah Lai's mother, kill her with your own hands! Kill your no good daughter-in-law!'

'Phui! She's no daughter-in-law of mine! I curse the day she crossed my threshold!' the big-boned woman screeched.

'Hoi! Ah Lai's mother! Didn't you yourself buy her for your idiot boy? Didn't you? Didn't you?' a voice in the crowd taunted her.

'Curse the dog who asked me! I was blind at the time! By the gods I swear I was blind!' the big-boned woman shrieked, her eyes blazing with rage.

Throughout this exchange, the victim maintained a stoic oblivion, and Tuck Heng wondered whether her silence was that of strength or indifference. He had never witnessed the punishment of an adulteress before, but he had heard stories of how unfaithful women were drowned in rivers and lakes. He peered at the woman as he would a trapped rat. Even a rat would shriek when tortured, he thought. But this one neither cringed nor whimpered as lump after lump of excrement landed on her face and body. Her eyes were closed and her mouth was shut. Her silence was maddening. It incensed the mob. They stoned her when she struggled to get up. Then when she had succeeded in getting up, she knelt before the temple again with her back straight and her eyes unseeing. The mob interpreted this as a sign of her unrepentance and intransigence.

The enraged miners and several of their women started to flail her with bamboo poles.

'Yah! Yah! Whip the bitch! Whip the lust out of her!'

And the louder the men urged, the harder the women hit their sister as if they had to prove to their menfolk that their own fidelity to moral law was above reproach.

'Yah! Beat her to death! Kill her!' the men ordered.

Their women obeyed.

'Stop!' a stocky muscular man finally bellowed. 'Don't kill her! By our ancestral laws, she must die by drowning.'

'Who's that?' Tuck Heng asked.

'Our *Tai-kor* Wong Fatt Choy, Lodge Master of the White Cranes in Bandong. The man you must obey. You heard me?' Chan Ah Fook had emerged suddenly at his elbow. 'I will bring you to him when these troubles are over.'

Tuck Heng studied the broad unsmiling face. The Lodge Master of the White Cranes had a high forehead, and he had let his queue hang down his back like an emblem of his authority while the rest of the miners had wound theirs round their heads as was the fashion among labourers.

'Brothers of the White Crane!' Tai-kor Wong Fatt Choy raised his hands and asked for silence. 'We the White Cranes of Bandong are faithful to the laws of our clan and village in Kwangtung. The laws as laid down by our forefathers in Sum Hor! Hundreds of generations have obeyed our laws! An adulteress shall die by drowning in a pig basket!'

His foghorn Cantonese voice rose above the crowd's, the voice of ancestral authority and continuity in the new land. The miners and their women, uprooted by dire poverty, famine, drought and banditry in their Chinese homeland, clung to that voice and obeyed it.

'Ho-ah! Drown her in a pig basket!' they roared.

'Let me scratch out her eyes first!' Ah Lai's mother lunged forward.

But members of the White Crane yanked her away. One of the men brought out a large rattan basket, cylindrical in shape, loosely woven with thick strong rattan and used for ferrying pigs to the market. Two miners held the basket firmly while another two trussed the bound woman into it as the mob jeered and pelted her with more stones. The basket offered her scant protection since it was constructed in such a way that there were large gaps between the rattan through which one could see the pig or, in this instance, the bound woman.

'Big Dog! Big Tree! Take her down to the river!' Tai-kor Wong Fatt Choy ordered.

Two burly miners, stout and taller than most of the men, stepped forward. Using thick twine, they secured the pig basket to a bamboo pole and hoisted the pole on to their broad shoulders, with the basket swinging between them.

'To the river!' Tai-kor Wong barked.

'To the river! Drown the adulteress!' the mob started to chant.

Tuck Heng trotted beside Chan Ah Fook, his heart torn between pity and excitement. There was a carnival air in the procession. Some men carried paper lanterns to light the way; some were beating gongs and tin pans, and the rest were cursing and swearing at the top of their voices.

'She's going to die, right?' he asked.

'Right! The shameless sow deserves her fate! Slept with a Hakka dog! So we drown her in the river! If she'd slept with one of our own men, we'd drown her in the mining pool!'

'Eh? I don't understand you!' Tuck Heng yelled to make himself heard.

'Hoi-ya! You're a stupid one! If we drown her in our mining pool, we still got to fish out her corpse and bury her, mah!' Chan Ah Fook yelled into his ear. The din was deafening. 'But if we throw her into the river, she'll be eaten by the crocs. Die without a burial! Be a hungry nameless ghost in the next world! What fate can be worse?'

Tuck Heng could think of no other fate worse than this. What could be worse than to be dead and nameless, belonging to no clan?

'Drown the slut!' miners at the back of the procession called out to the men in front. 'Let her be the no-name ghost!'

'Hoi! More lights! Don't push, you stinking son of a bitch!'

'Fuck your mother's arse! That's my head you're burning with your lamp!'

'Out of the way then! Who wants to singe your nut head? I want to burn the sow, not you, son of a bitch!'

A scuffle broke out among the brown sweaty bodies swarming like maggots upon the woman who had transgressed their law. Mirroring brutal nature herself like the mother cat devouring its own young because it was tainted by the odour of an enemy, the wretched miners of Bandong did the same when they smelt the stench of Hakka flesh upon her. Her fate was sealed. She had to die for sleeping with the enemy.

Several miners poked and jabbed the woman in the basket with the sharp ends of their bamboo poles, hooting with wicked glee as she writhed in pain. The pig basket swung wildly between the carriers.

'Prick the shameless sow!' the men called out to one another.

'Prick where it hurts! Down under!'

'Here take this! Stick it into her!' A miner gave Tuck Heng a toothy grin as encouragement.

'Hoi! Do it, young dog! We Sum Hor men have Sum Hor laws! When we catch these sows who disobey our laws, we got to teach them a lesson, right or not?'

'Yah! Yah! Punish her! Give her a hard one!'

The woman in the basket let out a piercing squeal like a pig being led to slaughter. Ho-ah! Ho-ah! Good! They had broken her at last! They whooped and hooted like a bunch of fiends from Hell. A grizzly old miner thrust his hand into the basket and ripped off a piece of the woman's clothing. He flung it into the air, and his mates roared and guffawed.

'Wah! Look at her *char-siew-pao*! See those buns which she'd offered that Hakka dog! What about us, eh? What about us?'

At this, the sex-starved miners surged towards the pig basket. Eager calloused hands, starved for the touch of a woman's breast, thrust themselves through the gaps in the rattan. They squeezed and pinched and groped. Their fingers jabbed into her flesh. The woman screeched and the basket swung wildly about. One of the hands plunged the sharp end of a bamboo stick into her breast. Shrieks pierced the night's foul air. The mob was whipped into a frenzy of cursing and swearing. They banged their tin pans and gongs. Their eyes glittered with malice in the light of the blazing torches.

'Give her a hard one, hoi!' Tuck Heng heard Chan Ah Fook's voice boom next to him.

'Harder! More! More!' he heard himself yelling as loudly as the rest of them.

A devilish fever swept through him. He was a man of Sum Hor. Like the mob, he was gripped by the urge to punish the bitch who had betrayed the Sum Hor clan and settlement.

'Death to the traitor and adulteress!' he yelled as the men plunged into the murky waters of the Sungei Bandong with the pig basket.

More men waded into the dark river after them. They beat the water with their bamboo poles to keep the crocodiles at bay. Those on shore beat their gongs and tin pans. They called on their ancestral gods and spirits to witness their righteous punishment of the adulteress.

The pig basket was dropped into the river. A wild cheer rose from those on the riverbank. The clamour of their gongs grew louder and louder. Tuck Heng stopped. He could have sworn that above the din, he had heard a thin shrill cry. It was uncanny. Its high-pitched note seemed to have sliced through his heart like a blade, and bleeding, he staggered back to shore, pushing his way through the mob.

He made his way back to the village square. It was empty. Only the temple was aglow with the oil lamps and candles. The thatched wooden hut which served as an ancestral temple was painted red. He peeped through the doorway. Inside, some women were laying out bowls of food on the altar. He caught a whiff of boiled sweet potatoes. Ahhh, heaven was a piece of boiled sweet potato now, he thought.

'Hoi! You! What are you doing here?'

The sharpness of the woman's voice startled him. But he

stood his ground, standing in the dimly lit doorway, legs apart and shoulders braced, his eyes alert, ready for fight or flight.

The gaunt woman who confronted him had a face as wrinkled as a bitter gourd left to dry in the sun. Her coarse brown skin and deep furrows spoke of long hours of labour in the harsh tropical sunlight. Looking at her, he was suddenly reminded of home in China. Peasant women, dressed in shapeless garb like her, had given him food and shelter when he was on the run.

'Aunty,' he murmured.

'Ha! Never set eyes on you before. Who are you? What're you doing here?' the gaunt woman asked, her voice hard as nails.

'I, er, I! My name is Wong Tuck Heng,' he stammered.

'Who brought you here?' another woman demanded.

'Yah! Answer! Are you one of the Hakka dogs sent to spy on us? Ha? Tell me!' A stout woman advanced menacingly towards him with a meat cleaver in her hand.

He backed away. '*Aiyah*, aunties, wait! Please listen! Look! Look at me. I'm Cantonese to the bone! Not Hakka. Certainly not! I'm a Wong. Wong Tuck Heng from the village of Sum Hor!'

The words came pouring out of him in quick succession as his eyes darted from one woman to the other. There were six or seven of them inside the hut. One was clutching a meat cleaver and two had sticks in their hands. Swiftly, he assessed the danger he was in even as his tongue was rolling fluently. There was little chance of him escaping unhurt if there was a fight. He was in a new land. These women had to be placated somehow and he had to convince them that he was not an enemy. This wasn't the time to fight. Pride and arrogance counted for little if one were to die before one's time. That was the one thing he had learnt during his two years on the run, eluding arrest by the Manchus.

'Auntie, auntie! I beg you! Please listen to me. I'm new. I'm an orphan. Uncle Chan Ah Fook brought me here. It's true. Ask him! Ask him! Don't do anything rash. If you kill me before finding out the truth, you will regret it for the rest of your life.'

To his amazement, the women burst out laughing. They dropped their weapons and laughed till tears rolled down some of their faces. They shook their heads and wagged their fingers at him.

'Aiyah, what a talker! A dead man listening to him will come back to life!' the stout woman with the meat cleaver exclaimed.

'Stupid boy! Don't you know? Once you open your big mouth, we could tell you're our clansman from Sum Hor!'

'Right, ah! It's your accent. You can't run away from that. And your thick black brows and those eyes, aiyah, just like your father's,' the gaunt woman added. 'But ha!' she scoffed, 'He was fair as a scholar. Look at you. Brown as a coolie.'

The twinkle in her eyes and the smile on her face made him feel welcome. His own stony face broke into a broad sheepish grin. The mob and the drowning had put everyone on edge, he thought. He had been thoroughly fooled by the woman with the meat cleaver.

'It's alright,' she grinned at him. 'It's just your anxiety, this being your first night in the new land. And what a night!'

'Nah! Since we've had a good laugh at your expense, here's a sweet potato. Your belly must be aching.' The gaunt woman handed him a bowl with a steaming hot potato. 'I've been expecting you all day. Sit over there.' She pointed to a bench in the corner.

'Thank you, auntie.'

'Aiyah, just call me Wong-*soh* like everyone else.'

'D'you know who she is or not?' a woman, big with child, asked him. When he shook his head, she said, 'You'd better respect her. She's the wife of Tai-kor Wong, the Lodge Master of the White Cranes here.'

'Wong-soh, please forgive my ignorance. I, Wong Tuck Heng, pay my deepest respect to you.' He knelt and kowtowed.

'Aiyah, get up, get up. No need, no need!' Wong-soh laughed, her deep furrows bunching up at the corners of her eyes which were half closed like curtains hiding the great pleasure she took in the boy's kowtow.

'Aye, good, ah! Our village doctor, the gods bless his spirit, has a respectful son,' the woman with the meat cleaver said. 'Your father cured my father once. You can call me Aunt Loh.'

'My respects to you, Aunt Loh.'

'Aiyah, no need! No need to be so polite, lor!'

Nevertheless the wife of Loh Pang, an elder in the White Cranes, was pleased with Tuck Heng's respectful ways. Boys his age, miners in the settlement, had never greeted her so respectfully.

'Aye, it shows what book learning can do for a boy. So different from the hooligans we have seen tonight,' she sighed.

'Hoi, Tuck Heng, eat your potato. Eat first, talk later. We've got work to do.' Wong-soh turned to the women.

She was obviously in charge. Tuck Heng sat down on the only bench in the hut. On the bench was Ah Lai's mother, the big-boned woman who had wanted to strangle her daughter-in-law. She was sobbing quietly and took no notice of him. The rest of the women, working under the direction of Wong-soh, were trimming the oil lamps on the altar, and wiping the incense urns. They set out the plates of pork, sweet potatoes, yams and chicken as offerings to the gods and ancestral spirits. The altar, painted a bright red like the hut, held a statue of Lord Kwan Goong, the patron saint of the White Cranes, and several tiers of memorial tablets. Written on these wooden tablets were the names of the members of the White Crane Kongsi who had died in the new land, far away from home and family. These memorial tablets ensured that they would be remembered by the living and that no member of the White Crane need ever be a hungry nameless ghost lost in the new land.

'Aye, Kwan Goong Tai Yeh, hear my prayers!' Ah Lai's mother cried out. 'My heart is broken to bits! Broken, aiyah, broken! Have mercy on me! Forgive me, Ah Lai's father! Your name is sitting on the altar. Aye, I'll be joining you soon! Your good-for-nothing wife has no eyes! My fault! My fault!'

She rose from that bench and fell upon her knees before the altar.

'Ah Lai's mother! Not your fault! Who says it's your fault? It's fate,' Wong-soh consoled her. 'You might be the mother-in-law, but you can't be everywhere. How could you have known what she did behind your back?'

She tried to pull Ah Lai's mother to her feet but the latter refused to budge.

'Let me be, I beg you! Spirit of Ah Lai's father, listen to me, your stupid wife! Your *rice-bin*! Your good-for-nothing! Open your ears! Hear my words! See my actions! I kowtow before your tablet.

My fault! My fault! My fault, ah!'

She banged her head upon the leg of the altar with each shout of 'My fault!' The other women tried to restrain her.

'Ah Lai's mother! Not your fault! It's the sow's fault! She brought shame upon our settlement, not you!' the butcher's wife said.

'Our Lee-soh is right. Not your fault. Besides, such things are fated. It's your poor son's fate,' Wong-soh added.

'Right, ah! So many chickens in the coop and you chose this one for him. So it's fate, right or not?'

'Right, Lee-soh! You're so right! I chose the chicken so I brought the shame! I suffer the blame! I, I, I!' Ah Lai's mother went on thumping her breast. 'Whose shame is it? Nobody's but mine! But who knows my pain? What hopes I've had are gone! Slipped away like water through my fingers! My son's marriage was to be my reward. Reward for a lifetime of labour! I've worked hard all my life! So did Ah Lai's father. Right till the day he joined his ancestors. But what for? Tell me, what for? Aye, just so we could save up enough money to buy our son a wife. Our only son. Our only hope for someone who will sweep our graves after we're gone. All of you have hopes. So have I, even though I'm the mother of an idiot boy! Aye, I've eaten bitterness all my life! Let me die! Let me join Ah Lai's father!'

'Aiyah! Choy! How can you say that?' Aunt Loh quickly brushed aside her ill-omened sayings. 'Who's going to look after Ah Lai if you're gone?'

'Right, ah! What's to become of your idiot boy?' another woman joined in.

'Ah Lai's mother, d'you have the heart to leave your son alone in this world?' Wong-soh asked. 'Are mothers free to die? Just think. We women aren't free to die, right or not? Men can up and go like the wind. But we women must remain to look after our flesh and blood, right or not?'

'Aye, my accursed life! The bitter gourd is never so bitter as my life! I was born into grief, and I shall die in grief or else sit like sorrow with a smile on my face, lor! And laugh at my poor fate. How many children have I lost? The gods have punished me! Ah Lai's the only child alive today. Before Ah Lai's father passed away, he said to me, aye, he even held my hand. All our years together, never, not once, had he held my hand before. So I knew his time had come. But before he closed his eyes forever, he said to me, Ah Lai's mother, buy our son a good wife. A wife to look after him after we're gone from this world, he said. We must do our duty by our ancestors, he said. He's our only bit of flesh left. Aye, his very words to me. Our only bit of flesh left. Aiyah, our Ah Lai's father! If your spirit is still on this earth, hear me. My heart is broken! My voice is choked. That miserable sow has failed us. Cheated on our boy. Cuckolded him, ah! He's a laughing stock in Bandong today! Curse the bitch! Curse her! I will curse her to my dying day! Curse her with my dying breath! The shameless whore! Phui!' she spat. 'May she wander about this earth a hungry ghost forever!'

'How much money did you pay for her?' one of the women asked.

It sounded like an innocent question to Tuck Heng. So he was taken aback when Ah Lai's mother lashed out at her neighbours as if she had been hit.

'What? D'you think I've been lying when I said I paid good money for her? It was my hard earned money! And d'you know what that shameless daughter of a whore said to me after one month? She told me that Ah Lai didn't know what to do in bed! He's dumb, she said to me. What d'you expect? I asked her straight. I know my son is dumb. That's why I bought you. Straight from the brothel keeper. A woman like you ought to know how to teach my son. He's your husband now, I said. So you've got to do your duty as his wife. Right or not? I don't expect gratitude from you, I told her. But I do expect to hold a grandson in my arms. And if you think of the money I've spent on you, I told her, I've a right to expect some return, right or not? So much money I've paid for her.'

'How much?' the young woman persisted.

'How much? Half of my life savings, that's how much! Fifteen silver dollars! Fifteen! That's how much!'

'Aiyah! Aren't we like small frogs who've never been out of the well?' Lee-soh exclaimed. 'Fifteen dollars! It's big as a cart wheel to small frogs like us. But to the traders from Penang, it's peanuts, ah! *Sup-sup-swee!*'

'Hoi! Butcher's wife! Upon my dead husband's soul, I swear I paid good money for that sow!' Ah Lai's mother screeched. 'Other women have been sold for less! And fifteen dollars is more than enough for used goods!'

'Right, ah! Buy and sell us! That's our fate,' the woman, big with child, replied. She was a bondmaid who was sold to her tin miner husband, after an accident had left her with a bad limp and she could no longer work in the rice fields.

'Laugh! I know your hearts! Laugh at me! But I know my place! I know we're poor people. I know fifteen dollars is big as a bullock cart wheel to the poor like us! I know I could never buy a nice girl at this price. Besides, my boy's an idiot. No girl from a good family will want to marry him, right or not? But I'd thought to myself, don't despair. A girl from a good family might not want him but a girl from a brothel might thank the gods if I offer her a good home and accept her as my daughter-in-law. And that was why I bought a used hen. Already twenty-five years old. At her age, we would have had six or seven children already. Now tell me, all of you, would you have paid more for her? You people who think I'm a skinflint and a liar! Would you pay more? More? How much more? Hypocrites all of you!'

'Now, now, calm down, Ah Lai's mother,' Wong-soh tried to keep peace among the women.

But Ah Lai's mother adamantly refused to calm down, and she continued to berate the younger women who were poorer than she. She owned a bit of land on the east side of Bandong where she cultivated vegetables for sale, and she was used to being heard even by the men.

'Wong-soh, I will not calm down! The butcher's wife insults me and you ask me to calm down? I don't have enough insults to bear already, is it? You'd let these young ones crush me, is it? You're taking their side, is it?'

'Aye, Ah Lai's mother, I'm on nobody's side. But you'll agree that used goods is soiled goods, right or not? Whatever the price. As the saying goes, once a whore, always a whore. Now since she's from the whorehouse, what good can you expect from her? If we buy trash, we will get trash, right or not?'

'Right! Right! You're all right and I'm wrong! I'm wrong because I am poor!' Ah Lai's mother sobbed copiously. 'If I have had more money, I would've bought him a good bondmaid, lor! A good girl from China! Then no one will blame me! But China is a thousand miles away and my old man is in the next world! What can I do? What d'you want me to do? I am a poor widow with an idiot son. What money I have, I've got to put aside some of it for the years to come, right or not? Aiyah, gods in heaven, listen to me, ah! I curse that bitch! Let her be a hungry nameless ghost forever, ah!'

'Ah Lai's mother, let the dead rest! She's gone. Fate has been just as unkind to her as to you,' Lee-soh muttered, and shook her head. She looked as if she had more to say, but she changed her mind and went back to trimming the lamps.

'What are you saying, eh? Say what you want to say, Lee-soh! Don't swallow your words! I know you! Give me your bitter words! Say them to my face now! Not behind my back later!'

'Ah Lai's mother, we know a person's face but not a person's heart in this settlement. Do you know your daughter-in-law? Did you know that your daughter-in-law used to sob her heart out? Each time we went to the river to wash clothes, she wept. Every day she cried her heart out to me. I'll go mad soon, she said to me one day. My mother-in-law is turning me into a mad woman. Her very words. I'm not trying to insult you, Ah Lai's mother.'

Lee-soh was grim. She was determined to say her piece now that she had started, and she pushed aside the other women who tried to quieten her.

'No, no, I'm just telling Ah Lai's mother what I know! Ah Lai is twenty-eight this year, right or not? But inside his head, he's just six years old. Now you're a wife and I'm a wife. We're all wives and we know how wives are made to suffer in the bedroom. Ah Fah, your daughter-in-law, cried every day because Ah Lai hated her. Wouldn't go near her. Didn't want her to go near him. Shoved her away. Punched her if she tried to get into bed. Every night he wanted to sleep with you, his mother. Every night he screamed for you, his mother. When you locked him in the bedroom with Ah Fah, he kicked Ah Fah and bit her. Yah, bit her. She showed me the teeth marks all over her body. Bit her like a dog. We heard her cries. Our whole village heard her cries. How to bear you a grandson? You blamed her and you caned her. Every night you caned her, she told me. We washed clothes with her every day, so we knew. She showed us the lashes. But, aye, a mother-in-law is the sky and we daughters-in-law are the earth. You can do anything to her as long as she's under your roof. So, I think, rightly or wrongly, she was looking for another roof.'

Ah Lai's mother was strangely quiet after that, and the women resumed their task of cleaning the altar.

Tuck Heng had finished eating. He handed the bowl back to Wong-soh.

'What? Are you still here? Listening to women's talk? Get out of here!' she screamed at him.

He stumbled out.

'And where the hell have you been?' It was Chan Ah Fook's turn to bawl at him now. 'Just look at this mob! How d'you expect me to find you in this sea of mad men, eh?'

'I'm sorry, Uncle Fook. I was hungry so I went into the temple.'

'Chieh! To be smothered by women! Stay close to me from now on!' he snorted, and turning to his men, yelled, 'Potato heads! Look sharp! Look out for the Hakka dogs! Some mother-fuckers might be here among us tonight!'

Ah Fook's dark brows were drawn forward over his eyes as he scanned the crowd filling the village square rapidly.

'The White Cranes are thirsting for vengeance. Just like back home in Sum Hor! Some things never change,' he said bitterly. 'Thousands of *li* away from home and here we are! At war with the Hakka dogs again! Curse this valley! Curse these dogs! Curse these sons of fucking mothers!' He spat in disgust. 'These blood-sucking parasites shouldn't even be here. We had been granted the right to mine in Bandong Valley! You know that?' He turned to Tuck Heng who shook his head.

'Then open your ears and listen. We Cantonese had been the first to mine in this valley! Not the Hakka dogs! The Menteri of Bandong himself had begged us to come here! This valley was nothing but jungle and wilderness then. The Menteri's father had owed the merchants large sums of money. To pay off his debts, he had granted them mining rights in Bandong. Then two years ago, things changed. Those wily Hakka dogs must have bribed the Menteri with a large sum of money. As they say back in Sum Hor, gifts can move mountains. And money can make the devil push your cart.'

Tuck Heng cast a worried eye over the sea of faces before him. Hundreds of miners, thirsting for vengeance, could lead only to one thing—one huge god almighty brawl before the night was over, and people could be killed. And he had thought that he had escaped killing and burning when he left China's shores, he sighed. What an ill omen for him on the night of his arrival! He felt lost. And let down. After three years of scuttling about like a gutter rat to avoid capture by the Manchu dogs, he had hoped to find peace and safety among his clansmen in the new land.

'Hoi! Chan Ah Fook! Hoi! When do we begin?' a man yelled from the back of the crowd.

'Soon!' he bellowed.

'How soon? My beard is turning white!'

'Look here, you swine! As soon as Tai-kor Wong says so!'

Ah Fook searched the crowd for hecklers. The oil lamps and paper lanterns around the square threw an ominous yellow light upon the faces of the swarthy miners. He could not tell friend from foe in this light.

'Look sharp!' he hissed at Tuck Heng. 'Look out for the shit-stirrers! Some Hakka dogs among us.'

Tuck Heng reached for the dagger hidden in the folds of his waistband.

'Got a knife?' Ah Fook asked him.

He nodded.

'Good, ah! A dagger is better than a wife in this jungle. A wife you can buy anytime. Now make sure you deserve the rice Wong-soh has fed you. If you see any of the Hakka vermin move against Tai-kor Wong tonight, use your dagger! You understand?'

Tuck Heng nodded, numb with fear. He prayed to the gods. Let there be no fighting, he pleaded. No killing. No burning.

'Down on your knees and kowtow!' a White Crane guard yelled.

Chan Ah Fook pulled him down beside him. 'Kneel and do as I do!' he hissed.

Two White Crane elders, Big Dog and Big Tree, stood on either side of the temple's door like sentinels at Heaven's Gates. Tuck Heng kept his eyes on the sea of kneeling men, his nostrils flaring as he sniffed out the miners' blood-thirst. Drowning the adulteress had not appeased them.

'Vengeance!' A multitude of voices rose from the village square.

'Kill the Hakka dogs! Kill them!' The rabble roared. 'Kill those mother-fuckers who defile our women!'

The temple's drums boomed. The Master of the White Cranes of Bandong emerged from the temple, accompanied by several men carrying blue flags with the white crane symbol. He was a stocky muscular man. His square bronze-coloured face, with the wide heavy jaws, was unsmiling. His thick queue hung down his back as was the custom when appearing before an authority. In his hands, he held three lighted joss sticks, their incense rising in white whirls above his head. He strode over to the large stone urn in front of the temple, and raised his joss sticks high above his head. At this signal, the whole crowd in the square kowtowed three times and paid obeisance to their patron saint, Lord Kwan Goong, the legendary folk hero in *Romance of the Three Kingdoms*. Revered and canonised by Chinese peasants thousands of years ago, he was their God of War and patron saint of the poor and oppressed, honoured for his loyalty, integrity and justice.

'Kowtow once! Twice! Thrice! Rise and stand!' Big Dog and Big Tree barked, their orders coming in rapid succession in the time-honoured ritual of the White Cranes.

Tai-kor Wong stuck the joss sticks into the urn of ash, kowtowed three times and stood up with hands clasped above his head.

'Your Honour, Lord Kwan Goong, we kowtow before Your Lordship! We bow before you and offer Your Lordship our humble greetings! Please accept your humble followers' kowtows! Lord Kwan Goong!' he bellowed.

His great voice resounded through the square of three thousand miners. The multitudes quietened down. Then he intoned in formal Cantonese:

'Your Honour, Lord Kwan Goong, please hear us! We are your humble supplicants. Spirits of our revered ancestors! The Earth God of Bandong! We beg Your Lordship. Please bend your ears and listen to our report on the drowning of that shameless sow who has defiled our settlement! We stand before you, your unworthy descendants! We beg of you to accept our deepest regrets and our abject apologies for this blight upon the good name of the White Crane Kongsi! We vow before Your Eminence that we will never rest until the honour of the White Crane is restored!'

'Until the honour of the White Crane is restored!' the crowd roared like a sudden thunderclap.

Roosting jungle birds shrieked from the nearby trees in a rush of wings.

'Revenge! Kill the dog!'

'Kill those Hakka sons of whores!'

The miners around Tuck Heng stamped their feet and punched the air with their fists. Vengeance fever was running high.

Tai-kor Wong raised his hands for silence.

'My brothers! I know your hearts! Only an attack upon the Hakka settlement upstream can erase our sense of shame! The White Cranes have lost face! Not to avenge this loss is to invite others to laugh at us! Like dung invites dungflies. We, the White Cranes of Bandong, will fight back! But not tonight!'

'Hoi! Tai-kor! What are you waiting for?'

'Kill those sons of mother-fuckers!'

'Are we, White Cranes, scared of dogs?'

The voices had come from the far end of the square, away from the lanterns. Tuck Heng's eyes searched the faces of the crowd.

'Pipe down all of you!' Tai-kor Wong bellowed. 'Those sons of whores will not escape death! Might is on our side! Right is on our side! We White Cranes are honourable men! If I, Tai-kor Wong Fatt Choy, fail to restore our honour, chop off my head! I swear before the gods that you can have my head!'

'Yah! Fight now or we'll have your head! What are you

waiting for?'

The hecklers were at it again. Ah Fook leapt on to a crate to get a better view of the multitudes, and Tuck Heng's hand was clapped over his dagger.

'Listen to me, White Cranes! Have I ever lied to you? Has your Tai-kor ever led you astray? My brothers! Stop and think for a few moments,' Tai-kor Wong went on, and the tone of reason crept into his voice. 'Have we not more than a pig's wit about us? Do we White Cranes rush into battle like hogs? Ha! The Hakka dogs upstream are waiting for us to do just that! Rush into battle unprepared tonight so that they can kill us! Like squealing pigs! Whoever is egging us on tonight is not our friend! He is our foe! He wants to send us to the next world! But we White Cranes are no fools, right or not? If those Hakka foxes think they can slip into our village and excite us like chickens in a coop, let them return to their dens disappointed! You, my brothers, return to your quarters! Go to bed but be vigilant! Show the Hakka dogs that we White Cranes have the patience of a python! We strike at the right moment! The right moment, I say! Then we will swallow our enemy! Guts, bones and all! Go, my brothers! Return to your sheds! Let the elders of your *kongsi* plan the next move! Good night to you all!'

Pearls on Swine
Wee Kiat

Prologue: The Pig's Story

My name is Oon Oon. I am a pig born on the first day of the Year of the Pig. My mother said that is auspicious and I would be destined for great things. For pigs that meant I could look forward to being roasted to a crimson brown before reaching puberty. Then a waiter in white gloves would carry me on a large silver platter into the ballroom of some five-star hotel. If my luck holds he would set me down on the table with the red tablecloth.

Mothers, however, are not always right. Mine ate and slept her whole life away, so what does she know about greatness? Not even in her wildest food-gorged dream could she imagine what life has in store for me.

The Godown Keeper's Story

You can say I was the one who started it all. It began on the day Ah Hock, my supervisor, called me to his desk.

'Lim,' he grunted, '*Towkay* wants to see you.'

'What for?' I asked, incredulous.

'How do I know? Ask yourself.' He barked back.

I told myself sure must be something serious. For thirty years I have worked for Tan Tai Tee, out of his sight in Jurong, and suddenly he asked for me. Either I was going to strike lottery or become *deep-fried cuttlefish*.

Before I got on the bus to Shenton Way, I telephoned the old lady and ordered her to put two extra joss sticks in front of the ancestral tablets. For once the stupid woman obeyed me. I know because the first face I saw on entering the twentieth floor of Tan Tai Tee Building was so beautiful, can make you die dreaming about it one. Normally her type takes one look at me and turns her nose up in the air but this one smiled like so happy to see me and brought me to Towkay's office. Then the Ah Soh served me with her own two hands a cup of coffee, thick with condensed milk.

Towkay even knew my name. 'Lim,' he said, 'You must know a lot of farmers looking after the godowns at my feedmills. Go and buy my son a nice little piglet from one of them.'

'A small pig, Towkay?'

'Yes, Lim, a pig. The kind your wife puts into your *bak kut teh*. Only my son wants a small one. Why are you frowning, Lim? You are not trying to tell me it is difficult to buy a pig, are you? If you can't do the job I will get someone else.'

'No, no, Towkay, it's easy. You just leave it to me. I sure to make you satisfied. You ask Ah Hock. When Ah Lim does something always *got head and got tail*. Towkay no need to worry.'

I walked out of the Towkay's office like ready to go and get pig already. But my head spinning. If I have the Towkay's kind of money, my good-for-nothing son would want a Mercedes from me. The *Towkay Kiah*, whose father is a billionaire developer, financier and industrialist, only wanted a pig from his father? Even a big pig I can understand but a small one? I asked myself the world turning upside down or what?

My cousin Lam also thought the same when I asked him to sell me the remaining piglet from his sow's latest litter. This cousin of mine, he one-kind type. Very touchy, thinks everyone looks down on him.

'Why rich man want to buy pig to shit in his house?' He asked, like want to pick a fight with people kind. 'Trying to be funny with me, is it?'

'No lah,' I protested. 'Why you always think so bad of people? The rich they just different from us, can or not? Everyday they eat sharksfin and bird's nest until they get so sick they want to eat porridge and salt fish. Anyway, what do you and I know about being rich? Towkay told me nowadays in America very fashionable to have pigs for pets. Towkay Kiah wants to be the first in Singapore to have one, for face lah.'

Just my luck that of all my thirty-eight cousins this one's neck stiff like an ox, just like his father's. My Third Uncle, his heart so captured by this Cantonese woman, he must marry her or die. Never mind his mother, my Grandmother, said she will die if he disobeys her. Even worse, after marrying, his ear so light he listened to the vixen and changed his surname to the Cantonese Lam from the Hokkien Lim.

This kind of father sure got this kind of son like my Cousin Lam. When he is in a foul mood, Cousin Lam don't talk sense you know, he argues just to hear himself talk.

'Ha, *ang mohs*, don't talk to me about them.' He jabbed the air with his hand like a kung fu fighter. 'They different from us, so their pigs are also not the same as our kind. Our pigs have always been bred by farmers on farms. Tan Tai Tee only knows how to make money, what he knows about looking after pigs.'

'Cousin Lam,' I cussed him, 'Why are you so simple one? When you have the kind of money like Towkay Tan you don't have to worry about looking after pigs yourself. His chief gardener was a former pig farmer who went bankrupt buying animal feed from him on credit. The Towkay, he very smart, he makes the man pay his debts by working for him. But he already has two gardeners. So every day the chief gardener shakes leg and tries to look busy. Now the Towkay buys a pig he won't have to pretend anymore.'

Cousin Lam continued to look doubtful. But I am not called Lim The Snake for nothing. I turned the table on him.

'What about you?' I challenged him. 'Soon you will know just as little about farming as Towkay. Aren't you supposed to be resettled into a five-room flat? Your farming days will soon be over. So what you want the pig for?'

Once his head is cleared, Cousin Lam becomes very practical. 'Okay, okay,' he pretended like I forced him to agree. 'But only on terms cash and carry.'

Towkay gave me a big fat *ang pow* for my trouble and Cousin Lam gave me four chickens and four ducks, leftovers from his stock, when he moved to Yishun. The old lady she placed two extra joss sticks before the ancestral tablets to say thank you for small blessings.

The Driver's Story

When they first gave me the job, they made me feel like I was some big shot. The uniform they gave me got class kind. Like army officer with red trimmings. Also a badge that reads, 'Rashid, Chairman's personal driver.'

The car I drive, not like the kind you see everywhere in Singapore okay, like Mercedes or BMW. Mine one Daimler and I got special space to park outside the Tan Tai Tee Building. Like President's car. When the Jaga sees me coming he quickly takes out the ropes to let me in. Wah, real *lawah*. People stare and stare. Sometimes so embarrassing. The other drivers there they pretend not to look, but I not blind. I can see they look at me from the corner of their eyes.

Work longer a bit and I know I not big shot. Same like the washing machine the lazy Ah Chim use to make her job easier. Everybody in the Towkay's family call me to make their life easier. Every little bit must call me to do this and that. Whole day, non-stop kind, until they all sound like broken-down record.

'Rashid, drive Ah Chim to market', 'Rashid, pick up Towkay Kiah from school', 'Rashid, send Towkay Kiah's girlfriend home', 'Rashid, bring the cat to the vet', 'Rashid, go fetch the tuition teacher'. Sometimes it becomes so bad, I even hear them shouting for me in my sleep.

My wife pleaded with me. '*Abang*, resign lah, before you go mad.' But I shook my head. What with the prices of everything going up no choice but be *money face* and take all their nonsense lah. 'The Towkay,' I explained to my wife, 'has many dinners to attend, where else can I earn so much overtime?'

But when the *Towkay Neoh* told me one morning as I drove her to the hairdresser, 'Rashid this afternoon you go to Chua Chu Kang to fetch a pig,' I jammed the brake at the junction of Orchard and Scotts Road.

'Towkay Neoh, so sorry, I resign now.' I turned to tell her politely and got the fright of my life.

Alamak. No wonder the Chinese think we Malays can cast spell over them. I only said the word resign and this rich woman, just a minute ago sitting in the back of a car like a queen, turned into a *pontianak*. Like a cat, her long fingernails flashed out like ready to attack. Lucky for me she sank them into the head rest of the front passenger seat. The eyes, so horrible. Run round and round their sockets, like loose already, looking here and there.

'Resign?' She gasped like cannot breathe. 'No need. No

need. Everything can be discussed.' She giggled nervously. 'Now you quickly start the car before we get kidnapped.' Ah, when she shouted at me she sounded like herself again, a real Towkay Neoh. When it comes to giving orders the Towkay-class never forget they are the ones who pay the salaries.

All the rest of the way to the Promenade the Towkay Neoh kept grinding her teeth and muttering to herself. I pretended to be deaf.

That afternoon, a stranger, a mechanic-looking type, came and took the Daimler away. When I asked the Towkay Neoh how I am to do my work, she didn't answer me just pointed to her BMW. I told myself can relax now, someone has gone to fetch the pig. Then thought what so special about the pig that it must be fetched in a Daimler instead of a BMW?

A week later pig still not yet come and the Daimler arrived back with a glass panel in-between, separating the front of the car from the back seats. I so surprised I looked at it again and again, scratching my head. The Towkay Neoh looked out from a window in the mahjong room. 'Rashid,' she shouted, 'No need to resign. Now no more problem.'

When her head disappeared I could hear her yak yak yakking to her *kakis* as she went back to the game. Soon I heard four women laughing like they have gone mad. The Towkay Neoh thought she was very clever, never mind I let her think like that. I made sure my face looked normal. Towkay Neoh can laugh at me but I cannot stand to see Ah Chim sniggering. Inside my heart, I wished the Towkay Neoh would lose money, lots of it, so that she and Towkay can have another one of their quarrels.

What a stupid woman the Towkay married. My wife knows how to help me get more for my money, his wife knows only how to spend his. The glass panel no good. No point blocking one another out if can still smell the pig, right? Lucky Ah Chong, the head gardener was so busy fussing over the smelly creature he did not notice I have switched off the air-conditioner and wound down all the windows.

I think the pig knew I did not like it. It tried to be funny with me and shit in the car. This time I told the Towkay Neoh, with a

51

grim face, if I have to clean it up I sure resign.

I waited to see her like last time. But this time she laughed in my face. 'No need, no need.' She waved her hand real cockily. 'Ah Chong, he wants to clean it up.' When she walked away she was still laughing.

I heard from the *kaypoh* Ah Chim the Towkay Neoh gave Ah Chong a bottle of perfume costing several hundreds of dollars to sprinkle all over the car, after he finished cleaning it, because she did not want the Towkay to know about the shit.

So, the first chance I had to drive the Towkay, I complained to him about the shit in his precious car. You think he gets angry right? But no, the Towkay smiled as if everyday got pig shits in his car and pushed a crisp five hundred dollar into my astonished hand.

'Treat, treat,' Ah Chim insisted when I showed her the bill.

'What's so special about this pig, Ah Chim?' I raised the dollar note up high as she tried to snatch it away.

'*Aiyah*, how can you work here and not know? Ah Chong won five thousand dollars betting in the 4-D with a number he made up from the date the pig shitted in the car and the last two numbers of the Daimler's registration plate. That very day the Towkay also made a lot of money in the stock exchange. Towkay believes the pig's shit brought good luck.'

Lowering her voice, Ah Chim whispered like telling some state secret, 'Now Towkay Neoh cursing. She thought she very clever don't want pig to ride in her BMW.' Ah Chim chortled and nearly choked. 'Now she the only one to lose money on the pig. Pay for glass window and waste her favourite bottle of perfume.'

Wiping away her tears, the insolent maid said, 'I tell you, Rashid, these animals got some special sense. You good to them they bring you luck. Be bad to them they punish you. Sometimes I think they almost like spirits, you know.'

I ran away not wanting to hear such blasphemy. Got spirit or not I don't know. Only know I had my revenge on the Towkay Neoh.

Ah Chim's Story

When Towkay Neoh told me we were going to have one more extra mouth to feed, I cursed quietly to myself. *Aiyoh*, again more work.

Real *sien*. So back-breaking work. Then she told me it was going to be a pig and I continued to stand there and stare at her sullenly.

Only my hands twitched, calculating how one more mouth, especially one with such a large appetite, can give me more chance to top up the market money and provision shop bill. I let out a burp.

'The wind in your stomach still bad, *Ah Chim*?' She asked solicitously.

I replied with a curt snort letting her know she had outstayed her welcome in my kitchen. What for she always come to my kitchen, to spy on me or what. She dared not make me angry so quickly she got out of my way.

I went to the fridge to take out all the leftovers which I had deliberately over-cooked. I started humming. The best thing about making more money this time is the pig can eat up all the leftovers. I patted my stomach gingerly. No need to suffer from wind anymore.

One thing I forgot was the spoilt Towkay Kiah. Even when he was young, aiyoh, that child always makes trouble for me. Every time I wanted the weekend off he would have to attend a birthday party or something or other. Then the Towkay Neoh would say, 'Ah Chim you have to go with him. Maybe next week.'

Now he is telling me no leftovers for the pig. 'Give my pet only the best and freshest food, Ah Chim. I want him to look healthy with shining skin and sparkling eyes.'

'Okay, if you say so.' I said what he wanted to hear. But I have fiddled with enough household accounts to know you can only take so many chances. So before the Towkay Kiah thinks he can walk all over me, I settled the score with him right there and then.

'But listen, hah, Ah Chim cannot guarantee the way the pig looks okay. Look at you, aiyoh, all bones and no fat. Yet when you were young the Towkay Neoh always buys the best ginseng and freshest chicken for me to make chicken essence for you. You remember or not? I would fan the charcoal flames for five hours to brew those concoctions and you see for yourself how you look. You carry weight also useless.

'Don't say Ah Chim too big mouth ah. But pigs no matter what you do they look stupid. How not to? They sleep all the time.'

The Towkay Kiah gave me a dirty look that said he thought I was the stupid one. 'It's how you do it, Ah Chim,' he replied like he knows everything. 'That s why I want you to serve the pig in courses, the way ang mohs eat. First, serve him special feed from my father's mill, then give him a plate of fresh vegetables followed last by a bowl of fresh fruits.'

'Must cut the fruit into thin slices like the kind I serve you or not?' I asked sarcastically. If he was still young I would surely have brought out the feather duster by now. Even the Towkay I do not go on hands and knees to serve him and the son wants me to do that for a pig.

In Batu Pahat where I come from, we throw all the leftovers together in a rusty old can and feed them to the pigs. No trouble and the pigs look fine to me. I feel like saying to the Towkay Kiah if you want to be so fussy, so *niaow*, you might as well keep a cat. But I kept my mouth shut. Although I looked after that boy for eighteen years, now he has grown up he forgot he used to cry for Ah Chim and would not go to sleep unless I sang to him.

But, I, Ah Chim, remembered and to give him face, for old time's sake, I did what he instructed me to do for four whole months. Can die or not.

Two weeks ago, the Towkah Kiah walked into the kitchen with the pig under his arms.

'Get that creature out of my kitchen, out, out,' I screeched. Aiyoh, the noise. The more I screamed, the more the pig snorted.

'For goodness sake, Ah Chim, what's the big deal?' The Towkay Kiah scolded me like I am the one who gave trouble.

'You no respect for Ah Chim, is it? This is serious. So *suay*, so bad luck. May my ancestors and the gods protect me. To bring a live pig to the kitchen where it can see who chops up its relatives. I am finished. Doomed. It will know who to point the flnger at to the God of the Next World. Aiyoh.'

I was preparing to faint when I saw the look on the Towkay Kiah's face. From that moment onwards he stopped being my *ah boy*. I can never forgive him for looking at me like that. My fears turned into offence. How dare he looked down at the Ah Chim who had wiped his nose and his bum.

Ah Chong came running in, not to see whether I was alright but to check up on the pig. What is this world coming to when a pig is more important than a human being? The Towkay Kiah handed the pig over to the crazy head gardener and waved him away.

Turning back to me he stood upright, all five feet seven inches of him, and tried to look like his father, so stern. But when he spoke he sounded just like his mother when she complained, full of pained resentment.

'Ah Chim, you owe my pig and me an apology. You can make up for the shameful business this afternoon by cooking up a feast. My friends and I are having a "My Pig and I" party. The guests-of-honour will be our pigs. So make the *kueh* and *agar-agar* pig-shaped. No pork in the satay and cook your famous birthday mee. Make sure you dye the omelette the same shade of pink as Oon Oon.'

When I heard what I have to do I know I have lived long enough. All my life I worked hard and sacrificed for my good-for-nothing children and they never even throw a party for me. This pig so grand, do nothing and got people treat it as if it is their grandfather.

Some people really too free. No trouble must look for trouble. Think I also have nothing better to do. Must make my life difficult. So itchified they are. Care less. Spirits or not, that night I made that fat pig suffer. I fed it with cold leftovers so that its shit will stink the whole house down.

The Personal Secretary's Story

I never met the pig, thank goodness. I heard a lot about it though from Rashid, the chauffeur. I gathered there was no love lost between him and the animal.

I was soon to get my own taste of pig mania. It began right after the Chairman and his wife went on their world cruise. I was looking forward to long lunches and shopping sprees on company time when Ralph Tan saw to it they never materialised.

It is not unusual for the dear boy to turn to me to help out with household errands when his mother is away, but what he wanted this time was an unusual request to say the least.

'You want me to buy you some silk ribbons?' I was sure I didn't hear right.

'Yes, Aunt Nancy, the best kind. Jenny, that's my girlfriend, said an all-pink pig doesn't go too well with my hunk image. She suggested a light blue bow on the pig's tail for a macho touch. Could you get it for me today? I need it in a hurry.'

How cute, I thought. I envied the boss and his wife for having such a sensitive son, such a rare gem in today's 'me' generation. Fancy caring for a pig so much to want to buy it some silk. I swore to myself when I have a son I want him to grow up like the young master.

Rashid wasn't too pleased when I paged for him to deliver the ribbons to the Tans' house. The normally cheerful chauffeur scowled at me and growled, 'Who are we working for I want to know, animals or humans?' Tut, Tut, I clucked at his bad temper and put it down to a tiff with his wife the night before. I myself was soon to ask the same question.

Not long afterwards, Ralph called at the office and offered to take me out to lunch. He is really so sweet. The fresh school leaver at the reception desk nearly popped her eyes out with envy when I walked past with him. I asked myself, when did 'A'-level boys grow up to be so charming? The ones who were at school with me were gawky, gauche and pimply.

Ralph waited until coffee was served before he complimented me. 'Aunt Nancy, Dad always said you had such a fine eye for decor. He is fond of pointing out how the art collections at our branches are even more impressive than those in some other companies' head offices.' Even as the coffee warmed me, I knew such accolades came with a stiff price.

'I am thinking of redecorating my room. Mum gave her okay before she left. Wouldn't it be a cinch to do it all up in my latest passion? Have you heard? I am big on pigs. No, Auntie, don't tell me your plans. Surprise me. I have great faith in your resourcefulness.'

My husband reminded me how I often said I could shop until I drop and now he teased me I had to eat my words. Even with no budget limit, creating a decor with a pig theme was not the easiest of tasks. I can count on my fingers the number of pig posters I have seen in my entire life.

Rashid didn't make things easier as he ferried me around. He kept muttering about his letter of employment not saying anything about pigs. Come to think about it, neither did mine.

Before my feet could recover from their blisters, Ralph was on to me about his 'My Pig and I' party. His demands, I noticed, were getting longer. I could hardly keep up with my shorthand.

'Call the lady whose cakes Mummy likes so much and order a Porky and Petunia cake. I also want you to fax the Los Angeles office and ask one of the staff there to scour the shopping malls and buy up any party props with a pig theme. Ask them to get the whole lot, napkins, paper cups and plates.

'Instruct them, in particular, to look out for large inflatable pig balloons. Of course, they have such things, Aunt Nancy. Pigs are very faddish in the States nowadays. It's all a matter of whether you can pay to have them. If need be, we can have them custom-made. And yes, I want them to courier the whole lot to Singapore.

'The party is two weeks from today. Drop by if you and Uncle have the time. It's going to be a real pig-out. Ah Chim is cooking up a storm. But you have to bring a pig, I'm afraid. Invitation is with pig only. Ha, Ha.'

His laughter started to grate on me. I was surprised to find myself being irritated with Ralph Tan. That realisation upset me even more. I hate losing my cool as I consider that very unprofessional. When I found myself quarrelling with my husband at Swee Kee, insisting that we order pork chops instead of chicken rice, I thought it was about time I telexed the Chairman to tell him urgent matters needed his immediate attention back home.

The Chief Gardener's Story

The pig it brought me luck. Three years I have betted on the number plate of Towkay's big car and never won. After the pig rode in it I struck five thousand dollars. I tell you that pig and I share the same joss.

After it came I also got my first raise in three years. Towkay gave it to me as extra for bathing the pig. This Towkay very stingy, increased my pay by only thirty dollars and the pig gets bigger day by day. But even if he did not give me more I would still bathe the pig.

Before Oon Oon came, I was not happy here. My job so boring. My two assistants only want money but don't want to work. They don't know anything about gardening. I teach them but they don't want to know. Rashid, he is always too busy to talk and the Ah Chim, like a real woman, has wind in the head. When she is happy talk to you until cannot stop. When she is in a bad mood see you also cannot be bothered.

The pig, it too very poor thing. Ah Chim looks down on him, Rashid does not want to have anything to do with him and my two good-for-nothing assistants think it is a big joke. So the pig and I become one gang.

We both came from the *kampong* so our hearts the same. We no need to stand on ceremony with each other. The pig so very clever, you know, comes to me when I call 'Oon Oon.' When I get angry with him, it knows—pushes my elbow with its nose as if to say, 'don't be like that lah.' It understands many things, like a human being. That is why I don't like to hear the others calling it stupid pig. It has pride also.

When the Towkay Kiah told me he had invited many pigs to meet Oon Oon I very happy for the pig because it is good for the animal to see its own kind.

'Oon Oon,' I said to my friend, 'on the day your relatives come, you cannot lose face. Remember you are Tan family pig so must behave like one.'

It understood what I said because the day of the party it stood very still for me to bathe it, first time, you know, no running or squealing. When I tied a red ribbon on its tail it swished its tail as if it knows it looks very handsome. After we finished, I took it to see Towkay Kiah feeling sure the young master would be proud of Oon Oon.

The Towkay Kiah took one look and turned back to his own reflection in the mirror. 'Take the red ribbon away,' he said to me, not too happy.

'Red for good luck, young Towkay. First time pig sees its relatives must be auspicious.' I tried to explain.

'I have enough of that rubbish, Chong. First I get it from Ah Chim, now you. Dress Oon Oon with a blue bow instead.' The more Towkay Kiah cannot stand me, the more he splashed himself with water from a green bottle. Why man want to smell like a woman, hah?

How can be blue? My heart still not satisfied. Where got nice and not a good colour for a happy occasion. But what to do? The Towkay Kiah, he doesn't believe in the ways of his ancestors.

The Towkay Kiah entered the living room only when many of the guests have come already. Ah Chim said like that then got style. He walked in with Oon Oon tucked underneath his arms. They looked so good together I no longer worried whether blue or red was better. I asked the Towkay Kiah's girlfriend to take more pictures. Although Oon Oon is my friend I not shy to say the pigs no fight. Oon Oon was best-looking pig.

Some of the other pigs you can laugh one. They wore big collars around their necks made of shining material. Don't know look like clowns or bar girls. The Towkay Kiah so pleased with Oon Oon that he stroke the pig for the first time. Then Johnny walked in with his pig.

Why Towkay Kiah always invite Johnny to his parties, I cannot understand. Ah Chim, who knows everything that goes on in the big house, tells me Towkay Kiah don't like Johnny. Once, I heard the two of them talking and all the time they said to one another I got something better or bigger than you.

This time Johnny's pig much nicer. The skin so pink and soft like a young girl's nipples and it was so small you want to hug it all the time kind. Next to it, poor Oon Oon looked like a country bumpkin, a real *suah ku.* Maybe because his pig so very small, that day, Johnny looked especially tall and his face got this looking down at everybody look. I could not stand, felt like punching him in the face.

The Towkay Kiah took one look at Johnny's pig, never said one word and threw Oon Oon into my arms. I cannot understand these young people. One minute like this next minute like that. Want party for pig then don't care about it. What did he do? Swam in the pool all the time as if he didn't want to be near any pigs.

All those nice food Ah Chim cooked, he didn't touch them. Ah Chim worked so hard okay, not even have overtime. She offered me some leftovers but I have no heart to eat too. So very wasteful. Heaven got eyes, you know.

Just now Mrs Nancy telephoned from the office and said, 'Chong, take the BMW and drive the pig to that place in Jurong. Towkay called from overseas and said okay.'

Epilogue

Chong is my friend and when he leads me to the car I follow happily. The first time I rode in a car, Chong brought me to this nice place here. Maybe this time he will bring me to a nicer place.

Today, however, Chong is not in a talkative mood. He keeps averting his eyes from me all the time.

The car is so nice and comfortable I doze off. I dream of my mother. The stupid woman is shaking her head in great agitation as if telling me there has been a mistake. She keeps trying to tell me something; about what happens when there is too much of a good thing; when too many good forces configure together, the impact can blow the destined good fortune into smithereens. 'Clash,' she keeps shouting at me and holding up two cymbals to clap them together. The noise wakes me up. Awake the sounds are quite different.

Peeping out of the side window, I see the BMW overtaking a lorry which is heading in the same direction as us. It is loaded with the rudest ruffians in cane baskets. They are grunting and snorting in a most unbecoming manner. Can these be pigs? I ask myself. They certainly don't smell or behave like me. I wonder what they can be protesting against to create such a commotion. I suppose I can't really blame them. I will too, if I have to travel in discomfort in those crude contraptions. Not everyone is as lucky as me to be going where I am going in such a grand style.

Satin flowers

Agnes Lam

Some satin flowers given to me
are rusting in their stems—
a faint trace under violet petals.

Will rust spread while dust collects?
When will I throw them away?
Where?

Back in time, I see
the claymaker scooping up clay
the potter turning the vase
the clothmaker dyeing satin
the worker twisting petals
another inserting wires
a third taking telephone orders
a fourth packing foliage
the florist laying out the arrangement
stepping back to assess symmetry
my friends walking to the shop laughing
choosing a ribbon to match ...

And I see myself
remote in time and space
throwing away
bits of several lives
including mine

as sunlight from tall glass windows
flows through conditioned air
making dust invisible and flowers live.

25 July 1995
KK Leung

61

existential
(of those who little complain)

Ho Poh Fun

the gilded life
indispensable to existence
as of air,
borne by breath and lifespans
of bird, beast, insect, fish ...

human will and care;

known moments of engagement
tactically wrought,
less on principle than on truth;
society stratified and aglitter
with mercury, steel and
celebration of youth.

participate, bear, be carried along
by ingenuities disseminated
in flow discreet or indiscreet;
all the gifts of the nation
duly delivered at our feet.

comes time to breathe our last:

note that the progeny will
carry the situation through,
re-define worn theories,
appraise what's still pertinent to the new;
fuse strategies at angles
familiar only to a few.

and as of a bough
that breaks a vein to sprout,
unfurl a blush of colour
that momentarily gleams ...

even so for those who know
no fertilised moment steeped in blood,
such presences, existentials ...
fidelities overwhelmed, betrayals surging,
life lived as through a flood ...

still, with resilience and tenacity true—
by disposition disciplined to a fault,

how like us to be persuaded,
shouldering the contingencies
of every cause propagated—
convinced, won over, rolled under,
even to our dismay;

succumb to life's unbridgeable silences
and, to the elements in flux,
disperse fresh calcium from our clay.

June 1995

from Dragon's Teeth Gate

Stella Kon

A workshopped version of 'Dragon's Teeth Gate' was first performed at the 1986 Festival of Arts.

Playwright's Notes

The harbour of Singapore was known to early Chinese travellers as Dragon's Teeth Gate owing to certain fang-like rocks which have since been removed.

Wang Jinghung (王景弘) was the chief companion of the great Chinese Admiral Cheng Ho, on his seven voyages of exploration in the early fifteenth century. Little is known about him. In Java and Malacca, there are temples dedicated to the deity 'Ong Sam Poh,' patron of travellers. Cheng Ho received the honorary title of 'Sam Poh' from the Emperor, but his family name was Cheng, not Ong. Wang is of course Ong in the Hokkien dialect. It seems that the name of 'Ong Sam Poh' preserves a faint, distant trace of memory still surviving in the Nanyang, of Cheng Ho's constant companion, Wang Jinghung.

I have invented a deity with the religious name, Kuang Ho. 'Kung' means Lord or Master. The Department Store in the play is called Jingqi (景气) meaning Prosperity.

Characters

KUANG HO
FREDDIE TAN, Singapore businessman
MRS TAN, Freddie's mother
LEONG, Jingqi's Personnel Manager
WORKERS of Jingqi
GOON, Singapore businessman
HEE, Singapore businessman

Set

There are only two sets. The first scene shows Kuang Ho's temple, with big gilded statues, altar, red candle-type light bulbs.

Some scenes are described as 'in front of curtain.' This is not the proscenium curtain but a traverse curtain about two-thirds way down the stage.

The other scenes are dominated by the big Jingqi department store, a large walk-in structure at the back of the stage. In daylight we see its exterior view, with its 'glass' opaque, presenting a featureless facade dominated by the big logo, 'Jingqi.'

At night the lights come on, the big gauze windows glow, and inside we can see eager crowds of shoppers milling around.

The steel scaffolding of this structure is painted a bright red which is garish in some lightings, black in others. It might have an upper-level gallery or mezzanine, doubling as a 'god-walk' for divine appearances.

Production and Acting Notes

KUANG HO: His costume black and glittering, his voice flexible, his movements like a dancer, like a treacherous cat; the actor experienced in taichi. Sinister, menacing, sardonically mocking—wracked by inner torment. His long speeches taken pretty fast, with variations of pace and pitch, and full exploitation of their rhythm.

FREDDIE: A modern financocrat, quite well-educated; speaks good businessman's English without much accent. To be played straight, not hammed up. What is funny about him is his complete lack of imagination, his prosaic normal behaviour while cosmic mysteries pass right over his head. He thinks and speaks in commonplaces: he can say 'oh god' and 'oh you devil' without attaching special meaning to them; in his mouth they are just banal exclamations.

MRS TAN: To be played straight and sympathetic. Need not have strong accent—she's probably speaking in Chinese, not in English. The name of JINGQI is pronounced by Kuang Ho with correct tones; Singaporeans just say 'Jingshee' in the same way as they say 'Yaohan.'

Act One
Scene One
Invocation
(Darkness: clanging of cymbals, slow beating of drums: a voice chanting.)

FREDDIE: Kuang Ho! Kuang Ho! Kuang Ho!

> *(Lights rise slowly: dimly revealing a shadowy temple: with altar, incense, red candle-type lights, a huge gilded statue of a god. FREDDIE stands, stripped to the waist, in front of an altar; his arms raised, chanting.)*

FREDDIE: Kuang Ho Kung! Kuang Ho!

> God of winds and storms—protector of travellers in the
>   southern seas.
> Once Admiral of Cheng Ho's fleet—
> voyager, explorer, who conquered rebels and subjugated
>   pirates—
> now throughout the Nanyang worshipped,
> as God of Dragon's Teeth Gate.
> Spirit of the past, hear me!
> Across the years and centuries I summon you!
> I call you by the name you bore in life,
> Imperial Eunuch, Envoy and Admiral, Wang Jinghung!
> Imperial Envoy, Wang Jinghung!
> Kuang Ho Kung! Kuang Ho!

> *(Spotlight: KUANG HO approaches, glittering, dressed in black.)*

KUANG HO: Who calls? Who summons my unrestful spirit from its long wandering between heaven and hell?

FREDDIE: Spirit of Kuang Ho … I am Freddie Tan, businessman. I have summoned you here to Singapore.

KUANG HO: Prepare to die, small insolent mortal, who dares to vex my sullen eternity.

FREDDIE: No! No! You have to help me! I called you down to earth.

KUANG HO: Regret your folly, then. I am Kuang Ho, God of Dragon's Teeth Gate, not for the commanding of any mortal. Better you'd left me undisturbed, than trouble my bitter brooding on my ancient wrongs. Now on you falls my long-held wrath, for your destruction.

FREDDIE: Wait, wait! I want to make a deal—I want to worship you!

KUANG HO: You worship me? My temple has been empty many years, visited only by chirping sparrows, darkened by dust, not incense smoke.

FREDDIE: I'll clean it up for you, I'll renovate the whole temple. I'll bring worshippers.

KUANG HO: Fool, you should know your own materialistic people reject whatever can't be seen or touched or sold. They demand things only of this age, deny old gods, old goods, and do not realise that there is nothing really new. That nothing really changes. This town of yours, this Singapore, is little different from what it was five hundred years ago.

FREDDIE: How can it not be different?

KUANG HO: Not changed at all, from Dragon' Teeth Gate, that deep harbour, the protected shore, the haunt of pirates, merchants, traders: shrewd men all ever ready—to cut each other's throat for a quick profit. Your people are the same today. The same as those who prayed to me, who worshipped prosperity and success, whose God I was. And if they are ... it may be, that here I have a thing to do. Come, Freddie Tan, and let me know you better.

(FREDDIE *approaches*. KUANG HO *gestures, extracting information.*)

Ah, Freddie Tan, what a tiny little mind you have! Your horizons are narrow, your ambitions petty, you are blind to life's real meaning. Being inside your mind is like being locked into a squalid one-room flat, with every fitting broken, windows cracked, no way to get down from the twentieth floor. (*Turns away, laughing softly.*) If all the Singaporeans are like you, they will be easy to shape to my design.

FREDDIE: You mean, you're going to help me?

KUANG HO: Tell me your problem.

FREDDIE: You see, I own a big chain of supermarkets, all over the island. Huge variety of goods, lowest prices! But right now, I'm losing money. I'm being squeezed out by competition from other shops. The top two in the area, their owners are magnates Goon and Hee. They hold my credit notes. They have made an offer to buy me out, for next to nothing. I can't refuse them. I'll have nothing left.

KUANG HO: This can be easily solved.

FREDDIE: Two million dollars minimum would cover all my debts. If you could make the bank extend my loan … two years more, I'd be out of trouble …

KUANG HO: I will arrange a way out of your difficulties. And in return, you'll do as I command. First I will give you great success.

FREDDIE: You'll save my business.

KUANG HO: I will multiply it a hundred times. You will build a new great store called … the Jingqi Centre. Soon it will be the biggest in the country; in ten years you'll own others like it, from India to Japan. And in each place you go, recruit men and women to staff the shops, the servants of Jingqi. They'll live in special houses, train in special schools. At night they'll gather in secret meeting halls, and there I will establish my new worship, with these my servants.

FREDDIE: You mean … these employees, these supermarket staff? What work do you want them to do for you?

KUANG HO: By day they'll work for you, like wage-slaves everywhere. Make what use you like, of their hands and labour. Their souls shall belong to me.

FREDDIE: So—uh—I'm to open a new big shop, Jingqi Centre. And build a temple attached to it. I'll get the best craftsmen from Taiwan, to do carvings and sculptures.

KUANG HO: No need of that. For not with stone and wood I mean to build my new and more enduring temples, but with greed and fear, those twin lusts, forever tearing at men's souls. I know, I who was Imperial Envoy and Admiral, these two drive men to all achievement: deep insecurity and discontent that no success can pacify, and ravenous greed, striving to fill that desperate want: these are the dragon's teeth, between whose clashing men sail out for gain or glory. On these I'll build a new dominion, here in Singapore: and you will help me, as I help you.

FREDDIE: You said—I'll expand to India and Japan.

KUANG HO: I promise you a great commercial empire. This modern Singapore suits our purpose well. From here your trade shall spread island to island, following the old trade routes; from sea to sea, to further continents, a bright advance of glittering prosperity. Your stores will multiply, filled with glossy goods and ingenious contrivances; they'll make friends, become part of the community. A million lives will know my influence, some distantly, some I'll touch more closely. (*Gesturing*) And you, Freddie Tan, you'll be the greatest merchant Asia has ever known. Who'll dominate the Stock Exchange? Whose name will be respected, where tycoons gather?

FREDDIE: Jack Chia, washed up. Shaw brothers, show over. Freddie Tan, the man to watch. Fred Tan Holdings, the one to buy!

KUANG HO: So fix your mind on that. Go in confidence, prepare to open your new enterprise; while I take care of your old troubles. They will trouble you no more.

(*Exit* FREDDIE *and* KUANG HO.)

Scene Two
Mum

(In front of curtain. Day. Enter FREDDIE *and his mother,* MRS TAN, *the typical tai-tai with diamonds and jade.)*

FREDDIE: Don't worry, Mum. Everything's going to be all right.

MRS TAN: Really, Freddie, are you sure it's all right? I tell you, you should take my diamonds and sell them, use the money to help your business. I don't want you to be bankrupt and lose everything.

FREDDIE: No need to sell your diamonds, Mum. You know you told me to go and see that medium in Geylang.

MRS TAN: Yes, very good, my mahjong friend Mrs Loo she always goes to him. You saw him?

FREDDIE: At first I thought it's all nonsense. But I had nowhere else to turn. Sometimes a man is so desperate, he will try anything that maybe could help him … So I went to him. And he sent me to that old temple in Kallang Road, you know, the famous one, very historical.

MRS TAN: Oh yes, everybody knows, the travellers used to pray to Kuang Ho Kung for safe journey, against storms and so on. Did you pray to Kuang Ho Kung?

FREDDIE: What I did—I am not allowed to tell you. But you don't have to worry. I am going to be all right now.

MRS TAN: I will be very relieved. I really was so worried, could not sleep at night.

FREDDIE: Thanks to you, Mummy, who advised me to go to that medium. All problems solved. You know what … I'm going to open up a new department store, much much bigger than the one before. I have interviewed one chap called Leong to be the Personnel Manager to help me recruit new staff. And I tell you, I'm negotiating to take over a big multi-storey building up Macpherson Road, you know, Kallang Pudding area.

MRS TAN: My goodness, so you're really sure you can start your business again!

FREDDIE: Yes, now I've got confidence. Mummy, come I take you down to People's Park Centre, we have lunch there, then we go across to your favourite goldsmith's shop. You choose a nice pair of new earrings.

MRS TAN: *Aiyoh*, never mind about earrings lah. The important thing is your business will be all right.

FREDDIE: Everything will be fine. Kuang Ho Kung will take care of all my problems.

(*Exit* FREDDIE *and* MRS TAN.)

Scene Three.
Murder
(*In front of curtain: dimly lit. Two businessmen,* GOON *and* HEE, *conversing.*)

GOON: Come, Mr Hee. Tan's arranged this meeting at my house.

HEE: He'll send his representative, he said. To negotiate some more.

GOON: To yell and shout, presumably, even make threats. Tan hasn't got the cash to save his company; he's getting desperate.

HEE: Goon, do you think he might try something violent?

GOON: This place is quite secure. My house, my servants watching every entrance; all the doors are locked.

(*Suddenly a white light behind them:* KUANG HO *materialises out of the darkness.*)

KUANG HO: Good evening, gentlemen.

HEE: Who's that?

GOON: How did you get in?

KUANG HO: No one prevented me. My name is Wang. I come with Tan's authority to deal with you, prepared to take your terms. We'll settle, we'll capitulate.

GOON: (*Incredulous*) He'll take our price?

KUANG HO: Yes, we'll accept your offer as it stands. Tan will hand over everything he owns, shares and share holders, control and company.

GOON: Well, this is very reasonable!

HEE: Quite unexpected, but I'm very pleased.

(*They come on either side of* KUANG HO. *He walks them downstage, confidentially.*)

KUANG HO: Come, let's negotiate most amiably, all the minutia of when and how; in cordial atmosphere, with goodwill on both sides.

HEE: I'm sure we'll be happy to deal with you.

GOON: I hadn't hoped you'd yield, but just in case you did, I brought along an instrument of transfer.

KUANG HO: Oh, well prepared to meet the chance! Eventuality— is upon you now. (*Turning with dancing grace, he draws a long knife and stabs* HEE. *As* HEE *falls,* KUANG HO *turns on the horrified* GOON, *flourishing the bloody knife and stuns him with a left-hand blow.* GOON *falls.* KUANG HO *plants the bloody knife on him.*)

KUANG HO: One cut loose from mortal bonds! The other, captured blood-drenched in a tight-sealed room, will soon be sent to follow him. My task is well begun, my plans proceed. (*He disappears, leaving two bodies on the stage.*)

Scene Four

[This transitional scene involves subsidiary members of the cast, including Beng, the mentally retarded twelve-year-old son of Lee, a smalltime trader turned agent for Jingqi Centre, Freddie Tan's new department store. In this scene, several members of the Kallang

Pudding Sports Club are practising a lion dance, in anticipation of the forthcoming National Day celebrations. They invite the inept Beng to join in, with the promise that he may appear on television if the dance is filmed. Lee comes upon them and asks his son to distribute promotional gift coupons from Jingqi Centre to those present. However, to his chagrin, Beng, with the aid of a rubber band, arranges the coupons on his own head, somewhat like a crown. Infuriated, Lee grabs the tokens and storms off. Ed.]

Scene Five
Servants of Jingqi

(*Night. We see the huge Jingqi department store, brilliant with exterior and interior lights. Through screens of gauze we see the bright interior, with crowds moving inside.* FREDDIE *and his mother come out of the building.*)

FREDDIE: So how do you like Jingqi, Mum?

MRS TAN: Aiyoh, Freddie, it is marvellous. It is excellent.

FREDDIE: Good, eh?

MRS TAN: I brought Mrs Loo along. You know she is so fussy one, she tried on forty pairs of shoes. The salesgirl helped her all the time, still smiling, still so pleasant and helpful. We were so impressed.

FREDDIE: Ah, you know all our staff have special training from us every day.

MRS TAN: With such good staff, I'm sure you will be very successful.

FREDDIE: Yes, Mum. We will be successful. In a few years' time, we will have big shops like this all over Singapore. And then, Centre Jingqi Bangkok! Jingqi Manila! Jingqi Jakarta! We are going to expand and expand.

MRS TAN: You are a great businessman just like your father was. He would have been so proud of you.

(*The interior lights of Jingqi go out: it is closing time; some customers leave.*)

FREDDIE: So we're closing the shop now, Mum; you'd better be getting back.

MRS TAN: Aren't you coming home, Freddie?

FREDDIE: I'm sorry, Mum, I have to stay back for this ... training session. I told you, we have special training for all the staff, every evening.

MRS TAN: So late, ah? Oh yes, Mrs Loo told me, her sister lives opposite. She says every night they hear prayers and chanting going on till late. Is this staff training or is it a Chinese temple?

FREDDIE: Anyway, Mother, it is for the staff only. Now they're all going to the meeting hall.

(*A large number of the sales staff emerge from the shop;* LEONG *greets* FREDDIE *in passing.*)

LEONG: Good evening, Mr Tan ... Mrs Tan.

FREDDIE: Good evening, Leong ... I'll see you later. That's Leong, our Personnel Manager. Very hardworking fellow ... but a bit snaky. I heard he lost his last job because he tried to cheat the boss.

MRS TAN: So why you want to employ him, so unreliable?

FREDDIE: Here he won't dare to cheat ... Mum, I have to attend the meeting. I'm sorry I can't send you back; I will call a taxi for you.

MRS TAN: When will you be back?

FREDDIE: Probably we'll finish late ... (FREDDIE *ushers his mother out, and returns.*)

LEONG: Mr Tan, why not invite your mother to attend our meeting?

FREDDIE: No, it's for workers only.

LEONG: Your mother can come. She would be interested.

FREDDIE: No it's not suitable for her. You hear me, Leong, I don't want my mother to get involved.

LEONG: Sure, sure, sure. I understand you, Mr Tan.

(*The workers of Jingqi assemble in semi-darkness in front of the dimly-lit store. They include sales staff, manual workers, executives—all in black. A great drum starts booming slowly.* LEONG *comes forward.*)

LEONG: Do you believe in Kuang Ho?

WORKERS: We do!

LEONG: Will you do whatever he commands you?

WORKERS: We will!

LEONG: Kuang Ho is a powerful god. Kuang Ho rewards those who pray to him.
When the factory worker thinks of a raise, let him call on Kuang Ho.
When the office clerk hopes for his increment, ask for Kuang Ho's help.
Civil servant seeking promotion, say Kuang Ho's name.
Managers chasing high targets, officers seeking new contracts, with Kuang Ho's help you'll succeed.

WORKERS: Kuang Ho! Kuang Ho! Kuang Ho Kung!

LEONG: Keep his faith! Do not reveal these secrets to any enemy. Some people are against us. Some people want to make you fail, block you, frustrate you. But Kuang Ho, God of Dragon's Teeth Gate, will defeat his foes. Worship Kuang Ho! Worship him, god of prosperity and success! Call on his name!

WORKERS: Kuang Ho! Kuang Ho! Kuang Kuang Kuang Kuang … Kuang Ho! Kuang Ho! Kuang Kuang Kuang Kuang …

(KUANG HO *appears.*)

KUANG HO: Across the dark pit of time and beyond the gates of death, I hear the cry of those who call on me. Worship me, and I will aid you. In my name, you shall have success in all you do.

LEONG: Master, command me to do anything. I will walk over burning coals. I will slash myself with knives.

KUANG HO: All this and more you shall do, unharmed, in the power that I will give you. In all struggle you shall triumph and succeed. Come. Swear to serve me only, all your life.

LEONG: I swear.

KUANG HO: Swear always to obey me.

LEONG: I swear.

KUANG HO: Swear that your mind and heart and soul are mine, now and forever.

LEONG: Mind and heart and soul, given to you, Kuang Ho Kung, for all eternity!

WORKERS: Kuang Kuang Kuang Kuang … Kuang Kuang Kuang Kuang …

(KUANG HO *disappears*. FREDDIE *comes forward*.)

FREDDIE: Workers of Jingqi: here are some facts and figures about our company's performance within the past month. Kuang Ho Kung has made us do very well. The profits in the department store were up by three percent over profits in the preceding month; in the supermarket section up by two point six percent, and in the outdoor sales section profits rose by a magnificent four and a half percent. Net overall profit for the month is up by three point two percent and the projected profit for the whole quarter shows an increase of four point six percent on the previous quarter. This splendid result reflects the devotion shown by each and every one of you.

The Master Kuang Ho Kung is very pleased with you. He tells you all to keep up the good work, and continue to work diligently for future success.

(*The workers leave, followed by* LEONG *and* FREDDIE. KUANG HO *appears; soliloquy.*)

KUANG HO: So again men call on me for convoy through their

peril ... as once they sought protection against wave and storm. Sailors still remembered me, when other men forgot, I, Wang Jinghung, Admiral of Cheng Ho's ships: they remembered our mighty fleet, that tamed these Southern Seas.

Bright were these waters when I sailed them long ago, cleaving the waves of Dragon's Teeth Gate. With brassy gongs, and thundering drums, and arrows falling thick as monsoon rain, we subjugated all these islands, exterminated pirates, made vassals of the sultans; then turned west towards Arabia, and Africa, where China's ships had never been.

We sailed across jade oceans to far shores of pearl and coral, then turned south on coasts unknown. We saw black men, strange beasts. Giraffes, zebras and ostriches we sent back for our Emperor's delight. Days and months we voyaged on, each new dawn showing a new coast, still southward tending; and the land full of marvels, the sky full of strange stars ... and the world bigger than anyone ever knew it to be, more wonderful.

No more for me, those far horizons, those boundless seas. I command these darker oceans now, whose tides of trade control men's fates; where winds of commerce blow ruin or riches to the nations. I'll rule the markets of the world; the ebb and flow of wealth I will control, as once the seas and storms. Prosperity and poverty I'll deal out as I please, my blessings to those who call on me ... who worship me, Kuang Ho, now God indeed of those who dare the Dragon's Teeth.

(*Exit.*)

[*end of extract*]

Prosperity

(for my parents)

Verena Tay

Characters

MR TAN, or HUAT, a man in his late fifties or early sixties

MRS TAN, or MEI, his wife, also in her late fifties or early sixties

Setting

The present. It is Chinese New Year's Eve, just before midnight, some time after the Tans' New Year's Eve dinner, in the living room of the Tans' corner flat in Toa Payoh. The flat is immaculate and simply decorated for the festive season; there is a Chinese altar to one side. The only odd thing about the flat is that there seems to be too many tangerines, or kum, on display.

MRS TAN is agitatedly putting the finishing touches to her New Year preparations. She surveys her handiwork. Her eyes zero in on a pile of kum; the longer she looks at the kum, the angrier she gets. She picks up a fruit, as if to crush it; but she cannot, because it would be a waste. As she puts down the kum, MR TAN enters through the front door. He is carrying two bulging plastic bags. At first, she does not see what he has brought in.

MRS TAN: Gek and James gone or not?

MR TAN: Everything's OK. All gone home. Mei, that was a good dinner. That little girl can eat!

MRS TAN: Our granddaughter's just greedy. Wartime, we had nothing, always hungry, nothing wasted.

MR TAN: Yah. Late already. You're tired—go to bed.

MRS TAN: Where got time to rest? Tomorrow's New Year—so many things to do. What's that? Gek forgot to give us something?

MR TAN: In case we run out. Ah Soon downstairs' clearing stock last minute. So cheap. Really desperate—business this year is quite bad …

MRS TAN: What did you buy?

MR TAN: *Kum.* The best Swatow type.

MRS TAN: What?

MR TAN: Kum, Swatow kind. Very sweet, very juicy. Try some?

MRS TAN: Why did you buy them?

MR TAN: Special offer …

MRS TAN: Are you mad? Why're you always like that …

MR TAN: What are you talking about?

MRS TAN: Look around the house. Look carefully.

MR TAN: (*Hesitatingly*) Very neat. Nice …

MRS TAN: Some more?

MR TAN: So?

MRS TAN: SO MUCH KUM, and you CAN'T see?

MR TAN: This is Chinese New Year, Mei—you never know when you might need more kum. You must have enough for everyone to eat, enough to give away …

MRS TAN: But we don't get many visitors. Only Gek and her family, your sister, my brother, your colleagues. That's all.

MR TAN: During Chinese New Year, everyone's greedy. Look at the little girl; you know how much she likes to eat kum.

MRS TAN: People can only eat so much, Huat. Gek already told you to give Sally only two oranges; you don't listen; then she throws up …

MR TAN: You never know, if someone suddenly visits …

MRS TAN: Stop being silly; nobody visits us. I just don't understand you. You keep saying: we must have enough this, enough that. But you never know when enough is enough.

MR TAN: You're the one who's scared we never have enough. When there's enough, you complain. When there's not enough, you complain and like magic, expect everything to fall from heaven. Remember last year—we didn't have enough kum to give away; you made so much noise.

MRS TAN: You never think properly. Look at this room. All kum. Come here. Look in the closet—kum. And then, come here, look in the bedrooms. More kum. All this not enough? Why must you go and buy some more?

MR TAN: Like I always say, you never know when you need extra. Nowadays, we can afford to be generous. Everyone can bring home eight.

MRS TAN: Don't be so stupid. Who wants to carry eight kum? And you think we can afford to be so generous? Huat, we work our whole lives and you want to waste our precious CPF on kum?

MR TAN: We're not wasting money. This is good Swatow kum bought at the cheapest price possible. Here, try some. (*He reaches for one and starts peeling.*) Ah Soon said this kind is the sweetest, the best type.

MRS TAN: Why should I try?

MR TAN: (*He passes her a segment.*) Just try. (*She eats the segment.*)

MRS TAN: (*Rushing for a tissue and gagging into it*) Huat, you idiot! This is not sweet. This is overripe! (*She hurriedly checks the rest of the kum in the bags.*) The rest're just as bad. Tomorrow, they will all go bad. No wonder lelong. So like you—anything on special offer, never think, just buy and buy …

MR TAN: I chose them myself. And Ah Soon guaranteed …

MRS TAN: Ah Soon this, Ah Soon that. You should know by now not to trust this man. See the kum you bought yesterday? (*She picks up the kum she almost crushed earlier.*) Feel. (*She gives the tangerine to him.*) See? Squashy already. He's a cheat and a liar and you believe his every word.

MR TAN: Ah Soon is a good man. He always gives good bargains.

MRS TAN: Really? What about last year? Instead of buying kum, you spent a fortune in that man's shop buying what? Fifty kumquat trees. Why? Because he gave 'a good price.' What to do with fifty plants, I ask you? Even Gek said, 'Mum, we have enough kumquat trees at home; ask Dad not to give us anymore.' So the whole house was full of plants—no place for visitors to sit! When the kumquat died, no, we can't get rid of the dragon urns because you said they were 'an investment'. So for one whole year, there's nothing but dragon pots all over the place …

MR TAN: But I got rid of them last week, didn't I? And they were a good investment. This year, everyone wants to decorate their houses with dragon urns, so Ah Soon bought them back for a good price. And I spent the money to buy kum for this year.

MRS TAN: Yah, rotten kum from the same idiot who sold you the dragon pots in the first place. Huat, why are you always so foolish? If you want to spend money, spend money on something really useful, something worthwhile, not all this junk. Why can't you even see that man is taking advantage of you? Why are you always so … mad until you buy so much kum? What are we going to DO with all this kum?

MR TAN: Mei, look. It's late. You're tired. I'm tired. I don't want to quarrel with you again. If we start now, we will never stop. Tomorrow …

MRS TAN: I quarrel? You're the one who started all this …

MR TAN: I said let's discuss this tomorrow …

MRS TAN: No. We discuss it now. You're the one always telling Gek when she was young to finish what you've started. You always say one thing, and then do something else.

MR TAN: Don't start all over again …

MRS TAN: You don't understand, Huat. We have dozens and dozens of overripe kum. If we don't decide what to do with them now, they will rot. Tomorrow, we'll have to throw everything away. Then, all the money will really be wasted.

MR TAN: (*Half-angry, yet half-realising the import of her meaning*) Mei ...

MRS TAN: What?

MR TAN: (*Giving up*) Never mind ...

(*They stand in silence for a few moments. Slowly, a thought dawns on him. Reluctantly, he chooses some kum from his plastic bags, walks over to the altar and makes an offering to the gods. His set of kum joins a pile of kum that already exists on the altar shelf.*)

MRS TAN: What are you doing? Why are you praying now?

MR TAN: Shhh ... (*He completes his obeisance.*) If we're going to quarrel into the New Year, we might as well make offerings now and ask heaven to forgive us. Then, some kum got use.

MRS TAN: Good. But the rest?

MR TAN: Put some in the fridge.

MRS TAN: Cannot. The fridge is full.

MR TAN: Take some food out.

MRS TAN: You dare take out the food I spent the whole week cooking, I'll throw every kum down the rubbish chute!

MR TAN: Are you mad?

MRS TAN: No.

MR TAN: What now?

(*She refuses to respond.*)

MR TAN: (*Slowly*) I suppose we better start eating ...

MRS TAN: What?

MR TAN: Eat. Start eating.

MRS TAN: You mad?

MR TAN: No. If I put them in the fridge, you'll throw them away. If we don't put the kum in the fridge, we still have to throw everything away. So, start eating. At least, we won't waste some …

MRS TAN: You're not mad, are you? You expect me to eat all this kum?

MR TAN: YOU WANT TO THROW AWAY OUR PROSPERITY, IS IT? No, Mei, I'm not crazy. Don't worry, I'm also eating. Come, let's eat. (*He chooses a fruit and starts to peel it. She stares in disbelief. Reluctantly and slowly, she reaches for a kum and peels it. The door bell rings.*)

MRS TAN: Who's that so late? Must be Gek—probably forgot Sally's coat.

MR TAN: I'll answer.

MRS TAN: You stay. I'm nearer the door.

MR TAN: No, I'll do it. I know who …

MRS TAN: How you know?

MR TAN: It's Ah Soon …

MRS TAN: Why is he here now?

MR TAN: Delivering more kum. I bought his entire stock.

(*They stare at each other. The door bell rings intermittently.*)

end

A Woman's Place

Lin Hsin Hsin

in our society
man is better placed
& a woman's place
is being misplaced

in the first place
man is always brought into play
& a woman can be used for play
or display

quite often, in the office
man plays upon
& woman gets played against
or played on

when man achieves
man gets played up
and woman gets played down
however, woman plays along

when a '*playman*' jokes
he can make a woman
feel out of place,
she walks away, leaves her place

in our society
when man & woman are face to face
woman must always keep a straight face
else she might get defaced

when a man looks into a woman's face
she must face up to the man
& face down
for man cannot lose face

if a woman looks into a man's face
man will return a gaze
put her in her place
& make her feel out of place

in our society
no place for woman
is better placed
than being misplaced!

1993

from Wing Tips & Shoulder Pads

Eng Wee Ling

'Wing Tips and Shoulder Pads' was first staged by ACTION! Theatre as a lunchtime performance at The Shell Theatrette in March 1991.

Characters

LOH KEEN YIN, in her twenties. Attractive in an unconventional way, but not a raving beauty. Not one to be overly concerned with her looks. Has an arty air about her. Dresses in long skirts, soft, slouchy clothes and flat shoes. Wears glasses.

BOB LEE, also in his twenties. An average-looking sort of guy. Precise, neat and careful in his manners and dressing, the kind who looks like he would fit nicely into a corporate structure.

ANNE, secretary. Not necessarily very beautiful, but she thinks she is and her body language and dressing show it.

CLEANER, male or female

LAM (unseen), male or female

BOSS (unseen), electronic voice

The scenes in the play should flow smoothly with no breaks in between. Various areas of the stage are lit at different times to denote different times and places.

Two desks at centrestage. One is KEEN YIN's, *heaped with books, magazines, art layouts, reports, a box of tissues, posters, letters, a leather portfolio, lots of multi-coloured paper, a telephone which is practically buried and a desktop computer. The other desk is where* BOB *will sit. Some of* KEEN YIN's *things have spilled over onto it.*

Upstage left is a small sitting/waiting area, consisting of an uncomfortable-looking chair and a small coffee table heaped with trade magazines.

Downstage left and downstage right are the two dressing areas for BOB *and* KEEN YIN. *Each area has a rack of clothes, a mirror and a chair to sit on.*

Act One
Scene One

BOB: (*Enters DSL to his dressing area wearing a pair of boxer shorts, a pair of grey-dotted socks, maybe [socks] suspenders, a watch, spectacles, perhaps but not much else*) Today, I start on my first job as a deputy junior trainee assistant manager and first impressions are so important. (*Looking through the rack*) Yes, something young, but serious, practical but smart, a matching tie that also adds a dash of colour (*As he talks, he picks out a white cotton shirt, charcoal grey pants and a grey and red striped tie.*) And for a bit of fun and finesse, wing-tips! (*Holds up shoes, starts to dress.*) My first attachment is to the Marketing Department. Wonder what the Marketing Manager is like. I'll call him Mr Whatever and if he asks me to call him by name, it'd be a good start. Then, I'll find out what sports he plays and arrange a game or two. Maybe tomorrow or what I'll casually ask him to go for drinks, then tell a few dirty jokes to break the ice. You know, be one of the boys sort of thing. (*Finishes dressing, picks up his laptop computer.*) There! All set. What can possibly go wrong? (*Leaves.*)

Scene Two

T*he office is a hive of activity and a cacophony of phones ringing, voices of people, computers and other business machines. Once in a while, someone will leave memos, letters, reports, etc on* KEEN YIN's *already cluttered desk. A cleaner comes in, takes one look at the mess, throws his/her hands up in despair and leaves the mess untouched.* ANNE *comes in with stationery for the other desk. She moves* KEEN YIN's *mess that has spilled over onto it back to her desk. She leaves.*

KEEN YIN *enters looking hassled, with breakfast and coffee in a paper cup. She tries to find a place to eat breakfast and rearranges the mess on her table but without much success. Dumps some things back on the other desk and manages to clear a tiny spot to eat. Coffee is placed right on top of a stack of memos, files and papers.* ANNE *comes in with yet another memo for her.*)

KEEN YIN: (*Taking memo from her*) What's this 'bout?

ANNE: Chinese New Year promotion. Bad news. Boss wants plans this afternoon.

KEEN YIN: But I thought he said next week?

ANNE: Yah, but MD flew in this morning and Boss wants to show off some of the new stuff.

KEEN YIN: Cannot! I'm already up to here and my secretary's on maternity leave! And where's that assistant he keeps promising me? (ANNE *shrugs.* KEEN YIN *rifles through the papers on her desk.*) Look at all this. I haven't even read half of it! And this … (*Knocks over the coffee, papers and some other things onto the floor in the process.* ANNE *leaves.*) Oh, shit!

(KEEN YIN *disappears under the table to rescue some things.* BOB *enters, looking cool, crisp and immaculate. He sits in the waiting area.* KEEN YIN *emerges from under the table. For want of something better to do, he studies* KEEN YIN *casually and flips through the magazines, licking his finger as he turns the pages. She doesn't notice initially as she tries to save the papers and mops up the coffee with tissues, etc … Eventually, the sound of* BOB *turning the pages gets to her.*)

KEEN YIN: Excuse me, are you waiting for someone?

BOB: Er, yes. Sort of. I'm the new deputy junior trainee assistant manager, Bob Lee. I was told to report to the Marketing Manager, Mr Loh Keen Yin.

KEEN YIN: Loh Keen Yin?

BOB: Is Mr Loh in yet? Are you his secretary?

KEEN YIN: Um … yes.

BOB: How long have you been working for him?

KEEN YIN: Oh, a long time. For as long as he has worked here.

BOB: Then you must know his character very well.

KEEN YIN: You could say that.

BOB: Oh, good. What's he like, ah?

KEEN YIN: What do you want to know about him?

BOB: Well, how old is he? Is he married? What games does he play? Tennis, squash, golf ... Uh, favourite drink? Temperament, personality, that sort of thing, lah!

KEEN YIN: Is this your first day?

BOB: Yes, and ...

KEEN YIN: And you're asking a lot of questions.

BOB: It always pays to know your boss. You know the old saying— 'Forewarned is forearmed.'

KEEN YIN: True. So why have you been sent here?

BOB: Attachment. To learn about the business, I suppose.

KEEN YIN: And how long are you going to be here?

BOB: I don't know. Maybe Mr Loh can tell me.

KEEN YIN: I doubt it.

BOB: So, what time does he normally come in?

KEEN YIN: Oh, about ... 8:55, maybe.

BOB: (*Checking watch*) Oh, it's already 9:20. Where is he?

KEEN YIN: I am he.

BOB: But you're a she! I mean, I thought you're a man. I mean, you're kidding, right? (*He laughs but she doesn't.*) Uh-oh.

(*Lights go down on office and come up on dressing areas.* KEEN YIN *crosses to* DSR *and* BOB *to* DSL *and they start to strip.*)

KEEN YIN: Mr Loh indeed! I hate the way he assumed the manager would be a man. So typical, isn't it?

BOB: A woman boss! And she's only about my age! Can you imagine reporting to her?

KEEN YIN: I bet you he's one of those who think women can only type, make coffee or answer the phone. Male Chauvinist Pig! Neanderthal! It's written all over his face.

BOB: They're ball-breakers, every last one of them. Why couldn't she just say she was Loh Keen Yin instead of making me feel like a fool? What was she trying to prove?

KEEN YIN: He sure looked stupid, sucking up like that. I'm glad I made a fool out of him. Show up his true colours. That'll teach him some respect.

BOB: She must think I'm damn *kiasu*, the way I was going on. But did you see her desk? And the coffee? What a slob! How can someone like that be manager? I bet you I'm better than her!

KEEN YIN: God, that thing with the coffee! (*Covers her face in shame.*) Didn't do anything for my credibility, did it? But you saw the way he licked his fingers to turn the pages? And the way he sat? Civil servant type.

BOB: She's sure to see me as a threat and she'll try to get rid of me. But you know something? I'm going to get her before she gets me.

KEEN YIN: I wanted an assistant. Not some stupid trainee. And why didn't anyone tell me he was coming? (*A thought strikes her.*) Is he after my job?

BOB: (*Starts to dress*) First of all, this IBM-type image is all wrong for this job. Must look a bit arty; like her.

KEEN YIN: (*Wears a pair of detachable shoulder pads*) White shirt, grey pants, ha! Want to play power dressing, right? These should do the trick.

BOB: Striped socks?

KEEN YIN: (*Adds on another set of shoulder pads*) One more. Just in case.

BOB: No, too tame. Floral better!

KEEN YIN: (*Wears a jacket blouse*) This will show him who's boss.

BOB: (*Holds up a pair of plaid pants, wears them*) Good, ah?

KEEN YIN: (*Slides into a tight black skirt*) Yes!

BOB: (*Wears an exceptionally gaudy patchwork shirt*) Cool!

KEEN YIN: (*Slips on a pair of dangerous-looking black high heels*) No way he can look down on me now.

BOB: (*Campy*) So drama!

> (*Lights go down on dressing areas and come up on office.* BOB *and* KEEN YIN *enter at the same time. Each is startled at the way the other person looks. They go to their respective desks.*)

KEEN YIN: (*Reading his resume*) It says here you are a Biology graduate.

BOB: Yup. Direct honours. Fish physiology. Guppies.

KEEN YIN: So why management?

BOB: Why not management? (KEEN *is stumped.* BOB *makes a mark in the air to show he has scored.*)

KEEN YIN: You'll have to ask Office Admin. to install a terminal for you.

BOB: Not necessary. I have my laptop.

KEEN YIN: I know that model. It's not compatible with our mainframe.

BOB: (*Miffed*) I've done my best work on it.

KEEN YIN: Well, we'll see if your best work is good enough. Here. (*Tosses him a stack of files.*) Read these and tell me your ideas.

ANNE: (*Entering*) Keen, MD is here. He wants to ask you a few questions about the New Year promotion.

KEEN YIN: Now?

ANNE: Now. (KEEN YIN *leaves.* BOB *flips through the files, looking lost*) Hi, Bob. How're things?

BOB: OK, lah. Can do.

ANNE: Is Keen killing you with work?

BOB: (*Lying, macho-like*) Of course not. Why do you ask?

ANNE: Well, you look swamped. Actually, I know I shouldn't be saying this, but I don't like working for women. They can be so petty, especially when you're prettier than them. I prefer men— they always treat me better.

BOB: I'm sure they do. Is Keen like that? You know, petty?

ANNE: She's OK. She's one of those—don't care about her looks type. Sometimes when I look at her, I think she doesn't even own a mirror. You know she's the only woman manager here, right?

BOB: Is it?

ANNE: Oh, yes. All the rest are men. Married men. Happily married men.

BOB: That's nice.

ANNE: (*Sighing*) Yeah … How about you?

BOB: Oh, I'm not married. Not even attached.

ANNE: Oh? Well, you might end up meeting the love of your life here.

BOB: I doubt.

ANNE: You never can tell, Bob. Things happen in offices. (*She checks her watch.*) You can have lunch with me, if you like.

BOB: Well, I, er … I'm busy.

ANNE: How about tomorrow? I could squeeze you in.

BOB: Oh, I don't—I mean, let me check my diary. (*While trying to look like he's checking it.*) So, tell me all about Keen.

ANNE: So are you free for lunch tomorrow?

BOB: Yes.

ANNE: I thought so. Well, Keen has something of a reputation for being very tough and demanding. But she is where she is because she's good.

BOB: (*A little too quick and eager to know*) How good?

ANNE: Having ideas?

BOB: W … What do you mean?

ANNE: It's more like, what do *you* mean? (*She turns to leave, laughing.*) Oh, and don't forget, we have a lunch date tomorrow. (*Exits.*)

(*BOB's afraid his intentions have been discovered. KEEN YIN's computer beeps suddenly. Bob jumps but ignores it. It beeps again and again, irritating him. He goes over to check and reads the screen out loud.*)

BOB: 'Keen, great news and some ideas on the American Express deal. Call me and we'll talk. Lam.' (*Starts to walk away, then stops.*) American Express, eh? (*An idea strikes him. Looks about and finds the internal office directory.*) L … L … Lai … Lam! Sales 248. (*Sits at KEEN YIN's desk, hesitates, looks around nervously, then he types on her terminal.*) 'Hi, Lam, sorry can't talk today. Lost my voice. Please e-mail ideas. Thanks, Keen.' (*Keen's intercom buzzes.*)

LAM: Keen? Keen?

BOB: (*Puts on a hoarse voice*) Yah? Who is it?

LAM: Lam here. What happened to your voice?

BOB: Um … ate too many durians, lah. No voice.

LAM: I thought you didn't like durians?

BOB: Oh, I … er … er … suddenly acquired a taste for it!

LAM: You sound terrible! Almost like a man. Hey, how about lunch?

BOB: Oh, cannot. I've got to go and see the doctor. Can you just send the stuff now?

LAM: OK. (*Hangs up. Then as the message comes in, BOB takes notes, all the while looking around guiltily. He finishes, returns to his desk and is looking for his pencil when KEEN returns.*)

KEEN YIN: (*Finds his pencil on her desk*) Yours?

BOB: Oh, er, yes. Ah, what's it doing on your desk?

KEEN YIN: I should ask you the same question. Did anyone call for me?

BOB: Um ... no. (KEEN YIN *picks up her handbag and goes off. BOB types out a memo.*) 'Memo to Boss. Could I see you at your convenience on some ideas I have on the American Express deal ...'

(*Lights go down and* BOB *leaves.* KEEN YIN *enters; spotlight falls on her.*)

KEEN YIN: What was he up to? He looked so guilty and the pencil ... What was he doing at my desk? (*Checks through her things, then goes over to his desk. Finds nothing on it. His drawers are locked.*) What's he hiding? (*She then opens his laptop and fiddles around with it.*) 'Memo to Boss ...' What the ...! (*Lights go down on office.* KEEN YIN *storms to her dressing area. Removes the jacket blouse.*) How dare he!? The American Express deal is mine! The rat! Swine!

BOB: (*Strolls to his dressing area. Changes into a paisley shirt and bow tie, singing happily*) Oh, what a beautiful morning! Oh, what a beautiful day!

KEEN YIN: (*Wears a severe-looking shirt blouse*) Just you wait, Bob Lee! I'll make you suffer! Hmm ... I need something more. (*Adds on a jacket.*)

BOB: I've got a beautiful feeling, everything's going my way!

(KEEN YIN *crosses to office and clears her desk.* ANNE *enters.*)

ANNE: Hi, Keen, here's the feasibility study you've been waiting for.

KEEN YIN: Finally! I haven't been able to do a thing without it. (*Clips it to a file.*)

ANNE: How come nowadays dress so differently?

KEEN YIN: Nice, right?

ANNE: Very smart, but take it easy on the shoulder pads, lah. Not the fashion now. Also makes you look like a vulture. (*Goes over to Bob's desk and leaves a memo.*) Looks like our friend here is going places, huh. (KEEN YIN *grunts in response.*)

KEEN YIN: (*Writes out a memo*) 'Bob, extremely urgent. To be done by five today. (*Pins memo and report to file, thinks about it, then removes report, chuckling to herself. She's about to put it on* BOB's *desk when she catches sight of memo. Reads it, then rips it up.* BOB *enters, smiling, humming.* KEEN YIN *looks at her watch.*) Five minutes after nine, Bob? Tsk! Tsk! (*That wipes the smirk off his face.* BOB *goes over to his desk. Sees the file and reads the memo.*)

BOB: All this by five o'clock?! Are you serious?

KEEN YIN: What's the matter? Can't do it?

BOB: No... yes, I mean, there's so much to read!

KEEN YIN: No pain, no gain. A bit of hard work never killed anyone. (BOB *defeated. Reads the file. Leaves through the stuff in his IN tray, looking for something.*) Lost something?

BOB: Um ... no. I was expecting a m ... something.

KEEN YIN: A what?

BOB: Nothing.

ANNE: Meeting in ten minutes, Keen.

KEEN YIN: Right. Thanks, Anne. (*Picks up a file and leaves.* BOB *promptly starts to sneak over to her desk. She surprises him by returning.*) Yes, Bob?

BOB: Nothing, nothing. (*She leaves.* BOB, *under his breath.*) Suspicious old hag ... (*When he is sure she is really gone, he tries her drawers but finds them locked. Taps into her terminal but it just beeps back at him.*) 'This terminal is not accessible to unauthorised users. Password?' Shit! (*Finally, he empties the contents of her wastepaper basket on her desk. Finds the torn bits of the memo to him.*) 'have received' (*Takes another torn bit.*) 'when I' 'with Keen Yin' (*And another torn bit.*) 'To Bob Lee' (*He thinks for a moment how to take revenge. Finds the remnants of her MacDonald's breakfast. Empties the packets of ketchup, chilli sauce, salt and pepper into her coffee and stirs it up. Clears up her desk and returns to his own.* KEEN YIN *rushes back in and picks up her cup of coffee. Drinks it on the way out and sputters all over.*) Oh dear, coffee too strong?

(*Lights go down with KEEN YIN giving BOB murderous looks. They cross to dressing areas.*)

KEEN YIN: Mutiny! Insubordination! Treachery!

BOB: (*Takes off bow-tie, wears suspenders*) That look on her face was priceless!

KEEN YIN: (*Throws on a long coat. She bears an uncanny resemblance to Darth Vader in 'Star Wars'.*) This is war! Shoot on sight! Take no prisoners!

BOB: But better be careful or else she'll start to suspect me. (*Unbuttons a few buttons, wears a huge medallion and does a 'Saturday Night Fever' pose, a la John Travolta, and singing, falsetto.*) Stayin' alive, stayin' alive. A-a-a-ah stayin' ali-ve!

(*Black out.*)

Scene Three

(*Back at the office. KEEN YIN is heaping files on BOB, who's looking dishevelled for once.*)

KEEN YIN: I want you to rewrite this.

BOB: What's wrong with it?

KEEN YIN: Everything. No style, no impact, no good.

BOB: I don't get it.

KEEN YIN: That's obvious. Look, I can't be spoon-feeding you all the time, you know. I need it by this afternoon. And this one … (*Throws another file in his face.*) Terrible! Show some originality, can or not? This idea is as old as the hills.

BOB: Anything else, Miss-s (*Hissing.*) Loh?

KEEN YIN: Yes. I'm going to the ad agency now. But I want the slides for tomorrow's presentation by the time I get back at about four.

BOB: Yes, ma'am; certainly, ma'am.

KEEN YIN: By the way, Bob, I think you should know that I'm the one who's going to do your performance evaluation. (*KEEN YIN picks up handbag/briefcase and art portfolio and leaves. BOB makes rude signs behind her back. She doubles back, startling him.*) Any problems, Bob?

BOB: No, no. Of course not. (*Lights dim and Keystone Cops-type music comes on. Movements are jerky, as in the silent movies and in double-time. BOB beavers away. ANNE comes in with sandwiches and coke for him, leaves. Music fades out. Movements go back to normal. BOB looks at his watch and hatches a plan. He picks up the phone.*) Hi, Anne? Bob here. Just called to say thanks for the sandwiches. I was so caught up with work, I forgot about lunch. Yah, busy like anything. Is it always like that around here? Oh, by the way, have you seen Keen? She went out at about 11 and still not back yet. I need to ask her something. Aiyah, this is such a busy time of year and she just goes off like that … No, she didn't say. Big boss where got tell small fry where she goes, one? Oh, is it 3:30 already? So-o late, ah? I had no idea. Long lunch, I suppose. Ah, can you ask Boss if I can see him about the asparagus promotion? Please? Can? Oh, like that, ah? Then no choice, *lor*. I'll have to wait for her. What? OK, I'll tell her. (*Hangs up. KEEN YIN returns, exhausted.*) Oh, Boss says for you to see him as soon as you come in.

KEEN YIN: What about?

BOB: (*Shrugs*) Ours is not to reason why …

(*KEEN YIN leaves, BOB snickers. Lights dim and come up again. KEEN YIN re-enters, fuming.*)

KEEN YIN: All right. What's your game?

BOB: Sorry?

KEEN YIN: What're you up to?

BOB: Me? (*Indicating the mess on his table*) This, what else?

KEEN YIN: Don't play innocent with me. Why didn't you tell Boss I was at the ad agency?

BOB: Were you?

KEEN YIN: Yes! And I told you before I went off.

BOB: I don't remember any such thing.

KEEN YIN: Dirty liar!

BOB: Oi! Watch it, OK? Who you calling liar?

KEEN YIN: You! I'm calling you a stinking liar! You were trying to sabo me, making it look like I was skiving when I wasn't! You're even lower than a worm, you scumbag! Sleazeball! Snake in the grass …

BOB: Sticks and stones may break my bones, but words will never … (KEEN YIN *picks* BOB's *bottle of coke, places her thumb over the mouth, gives it a good shake and lets the foam dribble all over his desk.*) What the hell … My report! My report! (*He pushes her away and tries to clean up. Shifts his precious laptop to the floor, near* KEEN YIN's *desk.* KEEN YIN *then goes to her desk, finds a tube of Superglue and squeezes the contents onto his laptop.*) Oi! What the shit do you think you're doing?!

KEEN YIN: Giving you a taste of your own medicine! (BOB *tries to snatch the glue from her, but she has already put the final touches to her handiwork.*)

BOB: Stop! Stop! (*He tries to open it, but it refuses to budge.*) Noooo!

KEEN YIN: If it's Selley's, it works. (*Laughs while* BOB *hugs his laptop and weeps hysterically. He stops and looks up with a maniacal look in his eyes. He closes in on her menacingly.*) Wha … what you doing? (BOB *merely growls and advances towards her. She removes one shoe to defend herself but he wrenches it from her.*) Back off! Back off! You crazy or what?

BOB: I'm going to teach you a lesson you'll never forget!

KEEN YIN: Y—you think I scared, is it? (*She is.*)

BOB: I'm going to break every bone in your body …

KEEN YIN: Don't come any closer or I'll … I'll do something

drastic! (*Looks round frantically and grabs the letter opener.*) I mean it! (*He is undeterred and she throws letter opener at him. He ducks.*)

BOB: S-l-o-w-l-y … P-a-i-n-f-u-l-l-y …

KEEN YIN: (*Takes her other shoe*) But you started everything. The American Express deal, the coffee …

BOB: You tore up my memos!

KEEN YIN: So what if I did? Tit for tat. Bob is a rat! Tit for tat. Bob is a rat! … (*Pours coffee all over his desk. BOB sweeps her things to the floor and rips out her keyboard. KEEN YIN hammers his laptop with her shoe.*) And this is what I think of your precious laptop! (*He goes berserk and threatens to hit her with the keyboard.*)

BOB: Die!!

(KEEN *screams and defends herself with a chair. Suddenly there is a loud buzz. They both freeze.*)

BOSS: This is an announcement for the Marketing Department. (*Pause, then booming.*) What the hell is going on here? There's been nothing but trouble for the last two weeks. Now, buck up, get some work done or everyone gets fired!

KEEN YIN: YOU are going to get the sack!

BOSS: You're BOTH going to get the sack if I don't see any improvement within the next forty-eight hours!

KEEN YIN: This is all your fault! You started this!

BOB: Me? You're the one who tried …

BOSS: And I don't care who started what. Settle your differences right now or you can pack up and go!

Scene Four

(*In their respective dressing areas.*)

KEEN YIN: I could kick his arse. Trust him to screw up everything I've worked for.

BOB: Shit! Nobody wants to employ someone who specialises in guppies. It took me a whole year to get this job! I don't want to lose it just like that.

KEEN YIN: (*Removing coat, blouse and one set of shoulder pads disgustedly*) This isn't working! That idiot's going to drag me down with him!

BOB: (*Removes medallion*) This is stupid. (*Realises.*) Oh my god, SHE'll be doing my evaluation!

KEEN YIN: (*Wears a soft, simple blouse*) All right, I'll give him ONE chance. If he messes about with me, he's— (*She draws a finger across her throat.*)

BOB: (*Buttons up shirt, wears a jacket over it*) One shot. That's all. If it fails, I'll resign.

(*Lights go down in dressing areas. BOB crosses to office, starts to clear the mess. KEEN YIN enters.*)

KEEN YIN: (*With difficulty*) 'Morning.

BOB: (*Strained*) 'Morning.

(*There is an uneasy silence as they both clean up, then settle down to work. BOB crosses over to KEEN YIN's desk and sticks out his hand.*)

BOB: Um ... Truce? (KEEN YIN *thinks about it, rubs her palms and offers her hand. He shakes it.*) Anything um ... you want done today?

KEEN YIN: (*Scrutinises to see if he's sincere. He is.*) That file I gave you that day? (*Hands him the feasibility study.*) Feasibility study. You'll need it.

BOB: You mean you ... I mean, thanks. Keen Yin?

KEEN YIN: Whaddaya want? (*Remembers, then nicely.*) Yes, Bob?

BOB: I, er, about the Amex thing ... Listen, I didn't really mean to. The temptation was too great and I, well, you know. I guess it was because you hated me and I wanted to prove myself.

KEEN YIN: I still think you had no right to steal—I mean taking the information. As for hating you— Well, you didn't exactly endear yourself from day one. Anyway, you're not crazy about the idea of a woman boss, are you?

BOB: Well, I'm ... not used to it. I've never—you know—Sorry.

KEEN YIN: Most people aren't, I guess. Listen, we don't have to like each other to work together, right? So let's just be professional about it and get the work done because I want to keep my job. (*Returns to her work.*)

BOB: Me, too. And yeah, right. We don't have to like each other.

(*Lights go down on office area. They cross to dressing areas.*)

KEEN YIN: (*Kicks off the high heels gratefully*) So far, so good. Four days already and he's still behaving. Let's see how long this will last.

BOB: She's starting to hate me less. At least, I hope so. (*Reluctantly.*) And she's not too bad, also, I guess.

KEEN YIN: (*Changes into a long skirt and flat shoes*) He's actually not that bad in his work. Not brilliant, but he tries hard. And he's organised and he actually meets deadlines.

BOB: (*Wears a pair of plain pants and a tie*) God, this marketing business isn't as easy as it looks! How does she keep coming up with all these new ideas?

KEEN YIN: Tomorrow is the big presentation. Let's see if he bombs out.

BOB: She said she'll let me do part of the presentation tomorrow. I hope she doesn't go back on her word, but what if I cock it up?

KEEN YIN: I wonder what he thinks of me now. Sometimes, he gives me these funny looks.

BOB: I hope her opinion of me has improved. I could learn a lot from her. If only I can forget she's a woman.

(*Crossing back to office. They enter together.*)

BOB: (*Tentatively*) Well?

KEEN YIN: Mm ... you were a bit shaky at the beginning but after that you were ... (*Pause.*) How shall I put it? (*Pause.*)

BOB: Tell me! Tell me! What upon ten?

KEEN YIN: Seven (*Beat.*) and a half.

BOB: Seven and a half? You mean it? All right, man! (*Dances around.*)

KEEN YIN: (*Laughing*) Look at you, just like a kid. Actually, I should deduct half mark for your intro—'H-h-hello, m-my n-name is B-b-b-Bob'.

BOB: I was so nervous. All those people and the directors; I was scared shitless! But you were so cool and steady. Especially when the MD asked for those statistics ...

KEEN YIN: Nah, no big deal. He likes to do things like that. You get used to it.

BOB: And the way his mouth fell open when you started to rattle off the figures! (*They laugh.*) I think we should celebrate.

KEEN YIN: Fine! Lunch is on me.

BOB: No, no. I never let a woman pay for me.

KEEN YIN: I'm not a woman. I'm your boss.

BOB: Still ...

KEEN YIN: Never argue with your superior. Let's go.

[*end of extract (Act One)*]

War Poems

Amy Sobrielo

The bell had just rung for recess at Dover West Secondary School. It was a typical government school, four blocks of classrooms arranged to form a square, built some time in the seventies; if you'd seen one you'd have seen them all. The only outstanding feature was the garden right in the middle of the school, its cactii and rock section being the pride of the school. Pushing up his spectacles to sit more firmly on his nose, diminutive Mr Lim gathered up the already grubby and dog-eared science workbooks of Sec. 4B, and then made his way to the Common Room, dodging the excited, chattering children going in the opposite direction to the canteen.

Arriving at his neat and orderly desk, he carefully stacked the books on the top left corner of the desk, being extra careful as he did so, not to infringe the space where Miss Jacqui Koh's desk met his to form a continuous surface-top. Casting a jaundiced eye over the veritable clutter of books, pens and pencils and other articles on her desk and then looking at his own, he smiled ruefully as he recalled a poster he had once seen in a department store which read, 'A Clean Desk is a Sign of a Sick Mind.' He then noticed that her class register was carelessly lying half on her desk and half on his. With an audible sigh, Mr Lim placed it firmly on her side. He always made sure he kept to his own desk in the forlorn hope that she would keep to hers. So far, it wasn't working out. Yesterday, he'd found a whole pile of exercise books on his desk and had had to shift it to the top of the low cabinet behind their chairs. She'd come in later demanding to know who had done that, what right anyone had to touch her belongings.

'Hey! What's wrong with Ali. He rang the bell five minutes late. I checked with my watch.' Jacqui Koh had arrived, eyes flashing dangerously, multi-coloured, plastic bangles jangling, earrings swinging wildly. Had Mr Lim been deaf and blind, he would still have known that she had come in. The strong scent of her perfume heralded her appearance. 'What's that smell?' he had once, unwisely, asked. 'I'll have you know that the correct word is "scent." It's a perfume … it's called "Poison" and it's by Christian Dior! Philistine!' she had snapped in annoyance.

Literature teacher, Jacqui Koh, didn't suffer fools, especially fools of English, gladly. Her way of dealing with them was to serve them sharp lashings of her tongue spiced with thick slabs of sarcasm. She was especially stinging when it came to mispronounced words and Singlish, that odd combination of English with local languages. And the worst miscreants, in her eyes, were the science teachers. They were at the receiving end of her most barbed remarks. She had apparently decided that her role in life was to be Professor Higgins to their Doolittle. With her it was not so much a case of 'they do little' as 'they know little.' Today, no one reacted to this comment about the bell. Miss Tan was peering apprehensively into her lunch box, as though she half expected the contents to bite her; young Siva was talking to one of his pupils and Mr Lim was being very careful not to be drawn into another argument with the 'dragon lady.'

'Ah! So that's where my register is! I was looking everywhere for it!' she said loudly to all at large. 'Why is everyone so quiet? Miss Tan, have you begun teaching that scene with Sir Toby and Sir Andrew yet? You know, the funny interpretations I've been getting for that line, "She's a beagle, true bred, and one that adores me …" unbelievable! They all keep mentioning Snoopy.' She screamed with laughter. Miss Tan, a very recent graduate teacher from the National Institute of Education, smiled weakly. She was rather scared of this loud, outspoken and often argumentative woman.

Young Siva, having dismissed his student, was now seated opposite Lim, drinking coffee from the cap of his blue plastic flask. He looked up and jokingly said to Lim in Malay, '*Apa lah dia cakap?* So erudite like what, I can't understand lah!'

Lim grinned; he liked Siva, always cheerful, always joking. Jacqui was not amused. She glared at Siva and snapped just one word, 'Philistine!'

Siva, unrepentant, whispered in mock contrition, 'Sorry, I not understanding lah!'

'One day, Siva, a student will come in and catch you speaking like that, then where will you be?'

'Right here, of course!'

'Oh, you! It's no joke. We should be role models of speech for them at all times. Here are we, English teachers trying to get them to speak grammatically and you, science people, speaking so badly!'

'Hey! Come on, it was only a joke, OK? I can speak as well as anybody and don't you forget it. OK?' Siva was beginning to get riled.

Later, after recess, when she had gone off to teach and both Lim and Siva were still in the Common Room (they both happened to have a free period), the two of them got to talking about her.

'What really annoys me is the way she puts us down. Just because we don't spout poetry and whatnots like she does!' Siva said. 'And calling us "philistine" every time.'

Lim grinned. 'I had to look that word up in the dictionary,' he admitted.

Siva grinned too. He never stayed grumpy for long. 'But I'd sure like to get my own back on her. Pay her in her own coin.'

Lim smiled softly. 'You know … I've been thinking along the same lines. I've been thinking about something … can't tell you right now because I haven't worked it all out yet. Fight fire with fire! That's the way to go in this case.' (If Jacqui had heard them, besides being furious, she would also have been very surprised … for science teachers, Lim and Siva were handling idioms pretty well!) And for tiny Mr Lim, who was considered a rather quiet, unassuming man, this was very strong language indeed.

'Miss Koh, what's the meaning of "nobble"?' asked Mr Lim the next day when they were having their break. Siva, who was marking some science homework, looked up in surprise and was about to say something but thought better of it. Miss Koh also, was somewhat taken aback … fancy Lim asking her for the meaning of a word.

'"Nobble"? … How is it used? I mean, give me the sentence you found it in,' she said slowly with a frown.

'I was reading this novel … ('Reading a novel!' thought Siva in disbelief) … and there was this line, "He nobbled him after the conference and asked him about it" … something like that.'

'Oh, it means to get that person's attention.'

'Thanks. I thought it had something to do with preventing horses from winning … so I was puzzled. I just didn't know what was meant in this case.'

Jacqui, delighted at this chance to educate Lim, generously went on to discuss the different meanings of the word and even went so far as to look it up in the dictionary to prove her interpretation correct. Siva sat there, almost shocked out of his socks!

The next day, Lim casually remarked that he had just finished re-reading *Pride and Prejudice* ten years after having studied it in school. Jacqui Koh positively beamed with approval and the two of them launched into a discussion of the main characters in the book while Siva looked on, with great interest and a dawning suspicion in his sparkling eyes. It was a highly entertaining and lively discourse. Even timorous Miss Tan paused from marking her pupils' compositions (they were of the 'It was a dark and stormy night' variety), and joined in the discussion.

Apparently, Mr Lim had suffered a sea change. In his quiet way, he remarked that he had gradually begun to feel that his view of life was too restricted. He felt that he needed to broaden his interests. He had decided to educate himself further in the arts. Miss Jacqui Koh was absolutely delighted! In her eyes, no longer was Mr Lim a philistine. Instead he was a willing, eager proselyte at the Altar of the Arts … and it was up to her to help him realise his quest.

So day after day the quest went on. Books were discussed, characters dissected, words bisected and idioms ingested. And Siva got quite tired of hearing Lim ask earnestly, 'Miss Koh, what is the meaning of …? Miss Koh, what do you think this refers to? Miss Koh, where does this line come from?'

Miss Koh revelled in all this. She knew the answers to all the questions, because if she didn't, she made it her business to find out, assiduously researching in guide books and critiques.

One day, Lim showed her a poem and asked if she could explain it to him. It was vaguely familiar, but she couldn't quite place it. Frowning, she read it again and then again:

'I hear an army charging upon the land,
The mud that cracks on cheeks when wretches smile,

Arrogant, in black armour, behind them stand,
And give their laughs more glee than shakes a child.

They cry unto the night their battle-name:
Where death becomes absurd and life absurder.
They cleave the gloom of dreams, a blinding flame,
Not to feel sickness or remorse of murder.'

'Whom is it by? I can't quite place it ... although bits of it seem to ring a bell,' she said.

'It's by W. James, you know, the up-and-coming war-correspondent turned poet.'

'Oh!' There was a rather long pause. 'Yes ... I think I've read about him, but I'm afraid I haven't read any of his poems. Let me see now. I guess he's talking about the futility of war ... its horrors .. he's using an *abab* rhyme scheme by the way ... You know, I can't do it justice until I study it more. Leave it with me! I've a class right now.' Hurriedly, she took the poem with her.

Lim looked at Siva and grinned happily, his glasses positively glittering as he gazed at Jacqui's retreating figure.

'The bait is set, the trap is sprung,' he announced gleefully.

'I thought you were up to something! Tell me, come on, tell me!'

When Miss Tan chanced to come into the Common Room a second later, she noticed Siva and Lim whispering together, every now and then breaking into laughter, especially Siva who at one point got so excited that he smote the table-top and laughed so much, that he ended up in a coughing fit and had to wipe his watering eyes. She wondered what they were talking about but was too shy to ask.

'Whom did you say the poem was by?' asked Jacqui Koh the next day. (She made it a point to say 'whom' instead of 'who,' but had carelessly ended her sentence with a preposition!)

'W. James,' said Lim.

'Are you sure? What does "W" stand for?'

'You don't know? I thought you said you had read about him?'

'Oh yes, but you know ... we ... we always refer to some poets by their initials till we forget what the initials stand for. Like T.S. Eliot for example. Isn't that so, Miss Tan?'

Miss Tan smiled timidly.

'Anyway I tried to look the poem up but I can't seem to be able to locate it in any of the poetry books in the school library. It's so annoying when poetry anthologies don't have first-line indexes,' she complained, wondering, fleetingly, whether she should have said 'indices' instead.

Indexes! Couldn't find ... that was a lucky break! thought Lim.

'I thought maybe, Miss Koh, you could just explain it ... you know, what is he saying; nothing detailed, just the main ideas .... I know it's about war ... at least I think so ... he being a war-correspondent ...'

'Let's have a look at it,' said Siva, joining in the conversation. He took the poem, which had been typed on a loose sheet of paper, and read it quietly. Miss Tan, her interest roused, also took the opportunity to look at it. 'Can't make head or tail of it,' Siva said finally. 'Sounds like nonsense, all rubbish!' he declared firmly.

'Trust you! Philistine!' said Miss Koh scornfully, 'You don't know good literature when you see it. It's obvious, what it means. Lim was right ...' She beamed at him as at a favourite, clever pupil and Siva half expected her to pat Lim on the head in approval. '... It's all about the ravages of war ... there they are, the soldiers, charging to battle ... splashing in the mud which dries on their faces, the poor wretches, but ... they are proud, proud to be fighting for their country and bravely they laugh aloud at danger and at death.'

'Wow!' said Siva, 'That's some poem. Here, let me read it again.' Both Lim and Siva bent their heads over the poem and read it again. Even Miss Tan looked at it again.

> 'I hear an army charging upon the land,
> The mud that cracks on cheeks when wretches smile,
> Arrogant, in black armour, behind them stand,
> And give their laughs more glee than shakes a child.'

'Who's the "them" in the third line?' asked Lim.

'The soldiers, of course,' said Jacqui with a confident smile.

'But then who's standing behind them arrogant in black armour?' asked Siva.

'The sol … let me look at that again.' She grabbed it back and read it hastily. 'Oh … of course! It's simple!' She gave a somewhat shaky laugh, paused for a while, then took a deep breath and said 'You know how in battle there are different divisions. Come on, you guys. You should know more about this than I do … you've done your national service … well it's obvious that the narrator, the "I" of the poem, is an infantryman and … they, the infantry, get the worse of it because they are on foot and have to tramp through the mud, the poor wretches; meanwhile … the armoured section, maybe in their tanks, well … the armoured tanks arrive behind them … probably to lend support,' she ended up triumphantly, rather pleased with her own explanation.

'What about the second verse?' asked Lim and read it aloud:

> 'They cry unto the night their battle-name:
> Where death becomes absurd and life absurder.
> They cleave the gloom of dreams, a blinding flame,
> Not to feel sickness or remorse of murder.'

'Let me read it again.' She took it back, brow furrowed as she strove to make sense of the verse. She felt something wasn't quite right but then … there was, after all, such a thing as poetic licence … In a less confident tone she ventured an interpretation. 'I think, I'm not sure, mind you, … he, the poet, … says … the soldiers shout out their battle cry, probably to give themselves courage … and remarks that, the poet I mean, says that death, and … and even life, for that matter, are absurd, and … and … the soldiers … all they have are their dreams … which … which they use to blind themselves from feeling sick at having to kill other people, "murder" he uses that word … murder other people. Well, … something like that.' She wasn't too comfortable with her own interpretation.

Miss Tan, looking somewhat dubious, was quietly rereading the verse.

But apparently Lim and Siva were satisfied. In fact, Siva was very impressed. 'Wow!' he said, 'Pretty strong stuff!'

She was pleased. There was hope yet for these philistines!

The next day, after a double period of literature with Sec. 4B, Miss Jacqui Koh returned to her desk in the Common Room. She found a sheet of paper on her desk, placed strategically where she couldn't fail to see it. Picking it up, she sat down to read it. Miss Tan, the only person in the room at the time, heard a sudden intake of breath and on looking up, noted an alarming change of expression on Jacqui Koh's face. All colour seemed to drain from her, making the rouge on her cheeks stand out in contrast to the pallor, like two lurid almost clown-like blotches. Miss Koh looked up, noted Miss Tan's eyes on her, jumped up from her chair, looked wildly around the room as if in search of someone, crushed the paper and threw it into the wastepaper basket. Then, covering her mouth with her hand as though to suppress a scream, she ran out of the room.

Miss Tan couldn't help wondering what had upset her so intensely. She debated with herself for a while, then unable to curb her curiosity any longer she got up and went to the basket. She picked up the crumpled sheet and read it. It contained two poems, clearly typed out, with certain lines underlined … and a note, in what she recognised to be Lim's neat handwriting below:

<u>I hear an army charging upon the land,</u>
    And the thunder of horses plunging, foam about their knees:
<u>Arrogant, in black armour, behind them stand,</u>
    Disdaining the reins, with fluttering whips, the charioteers.

<u>They cry unto the night their battle-name:</u>
    I moan in sleep when I hear afar their whirling laughter.
<u>They cleave the gloom of dreams, a blinding flame,</u>
    Clanging, clanging upon the heart as upon an anvil.
                (From 'I Hear An Army,' by James Joyce)

I, too, saw God through mud—
<u>The mud that cracked on cheeks when wretches smiled.</u>
War brought more glory to their eyes than blood,
<u>And gave their laughs more glee than shakes a child.</u>

Merry it was to laugh there—
<u>Where death becomes absurd and life absurder.</u>
For power was on us as we slashed bones bare
<u>Not to feel sickness or remorse of murder.</u>
(From 'Apologia Pro Poemate Meo,' by <u>W</u>ilfred Owen)

The note read, 'I'm afraid you've been had. Siva was right. It was all nonsense—rubbish.' It was signed 'Philistine Lim.'

For a moment, timid Miss Tan was horrified; but slowly, as she thought about it, she began to giggle, softly at first and then, uncharacteristically, she laughed so loudly in the empty staff room that the Chinese teacher who walked in at that moment, mug of Chinese tea in hand, looked at her in amazement.

'These English-educated people! So peculiar!' he thought.

Women at Odds

Lesley Yeow

Walking past the last of the lanes that led to her mother's house, she felt the all-too-familiar throb start up somewhere above her stomach, and shivered involuntarily. When you cut yourself (by accident or design), the first sharp incision has a clean, fiery pain that lasts mere seconds. Thereafter, the dull ache throbs with every pulse of the blood, hurts when you touch it but never quite goes away, lingering on the margins of consciousness, muffling gradually into non-pain.

She had been throbbing for years now, and it seemed as though each time she turned the corner and walked the home stretch she touched the wound again. Faint, now, the pain, but still there.

Piano music trickling through the haze of heat sounded faraway and alone. Painstakingly and repetitively executed, the obviously-exam-piece failed to quicken the butter-thick afternoon languor.

The lightweight outer gate of Number 28 clanged noisily shut. A few steps brought her past the baking front yard of the terrace house, completely cemented over for as long as she could remember, and sprouting red-ribboned cactii in stone circles. Opening and shutting the wrought-iron gates and glass-panelled doors ('Why do they have to keep everything closed?') she found herself in the cool gloom of the house. She was home.

Funny how you could never get away from calling it home, even when you had been married and living in your own place for years. Casting an eye on the everything-in-place living room, she made her way to the kitchen where, from the banging it was emitting, she knew she would find her mother.

'Why don't you call if you are coming? Now I have to fry an omelette. Your father sprained his back yesterday trying to shift the armchair to mop underneath. As if I don't tell him all the time he's too old to do this sort of thing anymore ...'

Sometimes she wondered if it was worth trying to greet her mother, since the latter never did. But there would be hell to pay if she didn't. And was there any use in explaining that she hadn't come for dinner?

'I brought lychees.' She put the plastic bag on the kitchen table.

'Why waste money? We have so much fruit in the fridge. Ah Hock Chye, Number Five's younger son, is getting married. The dinner is next Sunday. We will all go in Han's car—be here at 6.30; don't be late: your father is always so touchy when we're late. We have already given the *ang pow* and put your name. No need for you to give since you're not well off.'

Struggling not to rise to the remark, she tried to convince herself not to waste energy quarrelling about something that was never going to be resolved. Usually she and Des would make their own gift, ignoring the fact that their family had already acted on their behalf. But today, the irritation that her mother assumed she could not afford a wedding *ang pow* persisted.

'You don't have to give for us—we can afford to give our own. We're both earning,' she said, trying to sound pleasant, but knowing the words were ungracious enough.

'Earning?' The sarcasm was edging in. 'Since when is the church paying you to work for them? You're giving them free labour!'

'I think I've told you often enough that we're not working for free and we both get regular salaries,' she said coldly, losing the carefully nurtured pleasantness. It was getting dangerous.

'You are a university grad and so is your husband. You don't have a car, you live in a three-room government flat and you can't even afford to have children.'

'That's *not* true,' she retaliated, 'We're just not ready to have children yet, and I've also told you this before. Mother, will you please stop misunderstanding everything I do.'

'What is there to misunderstand? I can't understand you at all. How can you waste your life like this?' She looked, for a moment, genuinely puzzled. But for her daughter, she had already gone too far.

'I am not wasting my life, you can be sure of that. And I don't

113

want to discuss this with you anymore. Let's change the subject.'

'You are such a strange girl,' she murmured.

She felt that, all in all, she had been a satisfactory mother, even liberal. She had supported Fang's decision to go to the university, even when her husband had had his doubts; even with that niggling fear at the back of her mind that a degree would frighten off the potential suitors, leaving her daughter on the shelf.

She had restrained herself from nagging when, at twenty-five, Fang was still not dating—after all, that had eventually been rewarded. She had even allowed her to be baptised, after long and exhausting years of wrangling. When your child has changed her religion, will it make a difference to forbid her the rites of initiation? Moreover, she had thought at first that they might get away with agreeing that it was the same God they worshipped, only in a different manner. But no.

'How could you suggest that? The gods you claim to worship are spirits which lead you astray and will eventually drag you down.'

She had been deeply hurt by that. How dare she! It was as bad as suggesting that she was worshipping demons. Didn't her daughter credit her with enough sense to observe the difference? The ingratitude had cut her to the core. These gods, that Fang so derisively scorned, these had been her protection all her life. She remembered the time Fang had been desperately ill with pneumonia and the temple medium had given her a square of blessed paper to burn and drink. Not a shadow of the sickness remained today. She remembered the countless offerings she had made each time an exam came round—Fang had graduated with honours in Business Administration. It pained her more deeply than she could feel to realise that her daughter had merrily turned her back on those to whom she owed her continued existence and good fortune.

And then the final straw: becoming a church worker. No, what was it she called it? A full-time Christian worker. She thought it meant working with the church. Fang said it wasn't. Of all the contradictions of her daughter's life, this was the chief foolishness. To give up a promising career to embrace a life of poverty. Well, not exactly poverty, she had to admit, but a life of abstinence and

114

deprivation. What a waste of an education! Let those who did not finish school become priests. Not her daughter with the glowing future. Was this what she had worked and fought for? To see her child struggling to make ends meet when her peers were executives and reaping all the benefits for which their education had primed them? It was betrayal to her who had been the impetus, the force behind that striving, who had worked so this girl could live as she could not.

The vegetables hissed loudly in the wok and she added to the din the vigorous scraping of her fish slice. The soup bubbled satisfactorily in the pot and the fish steamed to perfection on a tray in the steamer. She turned to Fang.

'*Hoi toi.*' She noticed that it was already done.

The wedding dinner was not as much a wreck as she had expected, thankfully. They were kept laughing at cousin Benny's antics and were entertained by Han's little son, who had not yet learned to talk, but was nevertheless producing captivating gurgles. Han's wife, looking plump and sedate, was content to take a back seat in the conversation, demurely acknowledging the compliments about their baby.

Mother spent the better part of six courses 'doing her rounds'—touching base with the various relatives' tables, so peace and amicability reigned, more or less.

Going back in Han's car, he became voluble about work irritations, 'You should see these new grads—my God! You wonder what sort of education the university is giving them. Telephone manners: zero. Simple social skills: minus two! And as to using office equipment, this classic fella last week didn't even know how to send a fax.' Han had joined Asia Assurance directly after gaining his diploma from SIM. His scorn at the so-called better educated but less canny was increasingly becoming an axe to grind, fuelled, perhaps, by his own none-too-secure sense of worth.

'And another thing,' he continued, 'have you seen the way they write memos?' Obviously no one had. Li Ling was a full-time mother and neither Des nor Fang worked in anything approaching a corporate setup.

'They can't even spell. I told this girl off—she's always putting on airs about correct pronunciation and all that—I told her, "What does your degree teach you to do, hah? Put on accent, right? If you want to talk like that, why not go and work at TCS, don't come and join this firm. Here we do real business." Of course she had to break down and cry—always a woman's last resort.' More expressions followed in Cantonese, evidently catering to Mother's benefit. She chuckled appreciatively from the back of the car and added, 'So lousy and can get a job in a good firm. Just shows you that people can do well with little effort. No need to make life unnecessarily difficult for yourself.'

Back home, Fang let forth as soon as the doors closed behind them. 'I'm never going for another of these farcical dinners with them,' she stormed. 'All a load of pretensions and nothing more. Han is insufferable, the way he goes on about grads. Come on! We all know you don't have a degree—there's no need to push the point—who's ever looked down on you for that?' Des, being all too used to these tirades, calmly went on undressing and putting away his things.

'And Mother—this time she's gone too far. Accuse me to my face if you must, and we've had this out before, but to make innuendos in front of Han and Li Ling—that's just too much!'

'Aren't you being overly touchy, dear? That remark may not have been aimed at you.'

'Of course it was! Didn't you see her glance our way when she said it? And you jolly well know how she feels about us being in ministry. Huh! You're involved too, you know.'

'I still think you should give her the benefit of the doubt. But even if that's not so, there's no reason to stay mad. This is a choice we've made and we knew from the very beginning there'd be consequences, some not so pleasant. Mother may not see your point of view—ever. You should consider that possibility. Or would you rather find a "better" job to pacify her?'

'No, there's nothing she'd rather see. I'll do it for myself or not at all.'

They had gone over this before. But tonight she wanted a partner to her agitation, and his reasonableness only aggravated her further. She sat in the study smouldering late into the night.

There was nothing she wanted more than to see Fang give in, resign
and find something more worthwhile to do. And when she finally
did, she would be able to look her friends straight in the eye again.
It was a nuisance having to keep silent about your brilliant daughter
because she was doing something altogether inconceivable.

Not that she was unaware of what it was costing them: the
unreserved communion they shared was a thing of the past. Once
upon a time, Fang had even dared to speak about her newfound
faith, confident that the bond between mother and daughter
could not be severed by religion. But then, she had done the
unforgivable: taken a job with no career prospects and a salary
insultingly beneath her. Her actions defied logic. After that, the
talk had ceased.

Sometimes, she convinced herself that she was almost there.
Fang looked ready to give in. At other times, she appalled herself
realising that their feud had reduced her to being always on the
defensive, resorting to nagging as a weapon, and Fang, the loving,
bubbly daughter to an aloof stranger, dutiful but never warm,
cheerful but never spontaneous. And all the while, the knot of
their contention tightened just below the surface, threatening to
snap into bright red conflict, or would it harden into indifference
after all, as the years wearied them?

Despite the satisfaction of the dinner tonight, she felt deflated.
She took off her reading glasses and folded them up into the case,
then switched off the light and groped her way upstairs.

The telephone rang with irritating persistence. In the middle of
preparing for the evening's talk, she was in no mood to answer
it. Surely there was somebody else in the office besides her? Just
as she became convinced that she would have to be the one, the
ringing stopped. She settled gratefully back to work, murmuring
under her breath, 'Models of reconciliation in O.T. ... in N.T. ...
Jesus' example as expounded by Paul in 2 Corinthians ...' She was
suddenly startled to find someone at her desk.

'Sharon?' See Khiong. He must have come early and been

sitting in the meeting room. She hadn't noticed he was there. 'It's for you and ... I don't wish to alarm you, but it's SGH calling.'

The voice at the other end was crisp, businesslike, dispassionate. It crackled across the distance from another world, one in which sorrow and passion seemed inadmissable.

'Miss Chan? I'm sorry to tell you that your mother, Mrs Chan, has had a stroke and is now here in the ICU. She was admitted an hour ago and we have been trying to contact you ....' The words got fainter and fainter. She couldn't feel the receiver cradled to her ear, or the ground beneath her. The only sensation was a vague and noisy throbbing, that resolved itself into words. Not now, not like this, all of a sudden, with nothing resolved. It was too ironic, too sordid a way to end. As she gave mechanical answers to the person at the other end, the words reverberated within her skull: nothing resolved, nothing resolved.

She never forgot that evening. Leaving See Khiong with a terse message and the office keys, she made for the lift, stumbling in impatience. It took forever to get downstairs and through the entrance. The blast of leftover afternoon heat, entangled with oily fumes and the choking of parched carburettors, dealt her a blow as she emerged. A taxi! Now! Obligingly, four or five whizzed by, all occupied. It was madness trying to hail one now, at the height of rush hour. It would take forever.

Although subdued lighting and heavy carpets went some way to dampening the hilarity, it did not succeed in obscuring the presence of so many women, earnestly having tea and catching up on gossip. Above the earthy clink of crockery and feminine trillings, the strains of a disembodied *erhu* could barely be discerned. Against the hearty flow of conversation, steaming bamboo trays of succulent *tim sum* made little headway.

Something had changed today, shaken the balance of her tenuously achieved security: the slight discomfort of a heartburn that went beyond the merely physical. The conversation of her friends was lost on her as she leaned back in her chair, ears straining to catch the suppressed argument at the next table.

'Why didn't you bring the children? I told you to—you know

how much I wanted to see them,' the older woman was saying with ill-concealed disappointment to someone who must have been the daughter. She seemed to have asked the question many times.

'I told you already. They have music lessons and other activities after school.' A calm, self-assured voice, sounding deliberately nonchalant. 'They have a life of their own, you know.'

If the remark had been aimed to hurt, it found its mark. The older woman seemed to sink into the too-soft chair in defeat. Then, mustering her reserves, she said, 'They should see their grandparents more often. Otherwise, how will we know how they're growing, what's happening with them?'

'Everything is fine, Mother,' she said, with the slight impatience one employs in condescending to the elderly, 'I'm doing well: you know that. I'm due to be promoted again, the children are enjoying school, Ping Seng is fine.'

'Why don't you invite us to your home?'

An uncompromising silence followed.

'You think we're too coarse for you, is it? Are you scared to lose face, scared the neighbours think we are fishmongers or something? Cannot be seen in your nice condominium?'

'Think what you want, Mother, and keep your opinions if you must. I've already said everything's fine. What have you to complain about? I'm not shaming you in public, in fact, I'm doing you proud. If you need more money to run the house, you only have to tell me. Do you want some more tea?'

'Don't want,' the mother shook her head petulantly. Shrugging as if her mother's geriatricisms couldn't be helped, the young woman turned to a passing waiter and asked in crisp, assured English for the bill.

Her own group was paying, and she had to refocus her attention on their antics. After the bill had been fought over with appropriate zeal and at appropriate length, she extricated herself from her friends in some haste and made her way through a soulless shopping mall. The evening crowd had not yet descended and in the quiet cold, the branded leather and designer wear oozed a sophisticated canniness, a sleek self-sufficiency. The young woman had had one of those Lancôme model looks. She had stolen a quick glance as they threaded their way past her table. The cool, powerful scent she exuded still lingered in her head.

She felt a sudden oppressiveness amidst the luxury, and decided to go home.

Passing a phone booth on the way out, it occurred to her to call to confirm that Fang was coming to dinner on Sunday, but she remembered that she was working late today.

In the end she took the train, running all the way from Outram Station to Block 7. She tore past bewildered and gloomy visitors with petulant inmates in tow and even more petulent children down corridors smelling of disinfectant, until she reached the ICU. A staff nurse blocked her path.

'Are you Nurse Kwek? I'm Ms Chan—we talked over the phone. My mother …'

'Your mother is in the operating theatre undergoing bypass surgery. You can wait in the …'

'I can't wait! I need to see my mother.'

'You can't go in, Miss Chan,' her tone became slightly sharp— 'The surgeon is performing an operation right now.'

'But I must see her. What if she doesn't survive the op?'

'I assure you we're doing the best for her …'

She almost cried with frustration and panic. After fruitless minutes hailing full taxis, the heel-tapping wait for the train, the seething delay as yet more people made last-minute dashes for the train doors, why could this obtuse, dispassionate person in front of her not see how crucial it was that she see her mother, talk to her, tell her …. Tell her what? That she was around, as plain as that.

She trembled with the effort to keep cool, to stand before this obstacle and not snarl at her in unwonted impatience, to remain civil and reasonable. Her voice shook as she tried again.

'Nurse, if you don't mind, I really must see my mother. Just to look at her face and speak to her would be enough. Please try to understand, even though I know I sound deranged,' she laughed nervously, 'it would mean a lot to me to be able to look at her. Is there a way I might just don one of the robes and go in?'

'I'm sorry, Miss Chan.' After the aggressive stance awhile ago,

Nurse Kwek was surprisingly gentle. 'This is not the maternity ward, you can't go into the operating theatre. You will just have to wait like the rest of your family. Now, please let me bring you to them. Your sister had to see to your father and was very anxious that we contact you.'

Faintly, above the throb, she caught the words, and catching them like the last wisp of a fleeing dream, she grasped the essential thing; realisation exploding silently inside her head. With an effort she whispered, 'I don't have a sister ....'

'Hah?' The nurse was sharp and alert again, 'Aren't you Chan Soo Chen?'

Soo Chen. Her colleague, Teo Soo Chen—of course! See Khiong wouldn't have known that Soo Chen's maiden name was Chan and had passed the phone to her, whom he had always known as Sharon Chan.

Branches locked arms overhead forming dark trellises against the night sky. It was still hot, and insipid night breezes fanned in wavelets against her chin and face. This was how she remembered it as well, walking back from the bus stop at night after studying late during exam time, with dinner waiting hot but dry in the oven, the rice grains hardened, the juices from the fish overpowering. Or even earlier on, when they had taken their lanterns around the estate as children, the coloured lights bobbing and glowing in harmony with the round moon.

The outer gate was already padlocked, though it was barely nine o'clock. She breathed irritation and dug into the recesses of her bag to see if she carried the house keys with her, the set they insisted she have. ('Why do they have to lock everything?') Finding them, she let herself in but hadn't made the front door when it clicked open and her mother stood before her, fumbling with the iron gate in a ridiculous looking housecoat, her hair grey and unstylish.

'Aiyah! Come so late for what?' She turned on her heel and went in, expecting Fang to follow.

'I was passing by so I thought I'd drop in. I bought you *pau* from that shop you like in Outram Park.'

'No need to spend so much money.' Fang let her grumble,

knowing it gave her pleasure. 'I went out for *tim sum* this afternoon with Auntie Kwan and the others. Now I'm so full. You know her daughter ...' She petered off, but saw on her daughter's face a swift flicker of truculence.

Fang composed herself with an effort and managed to sound non-committal. 'Yah? Her daughter?'

'Oh, nothing, nothing. Sometimes these women, they talk so much nonsense.'

They stood awkwardly, wary as forest animals, each surprised at the other's magnanimity, but alert and ready to bolt at the first sign of danger.

'Pa okay?'

'As usual. Grumble a lot and sleep early. Gone to bed already.' Their conversation struck her as being totally inane, if not extraordinary. The civility unnerved them, but they were reluctant to let go.

'Well, I better go. You're going to sleep already. I'll talk to you on Sunday?' It seemed a plea more than a statement.

'Yah, yah,' she agreed with alacrity. 'Come early, ah? Nowadays Han wants to eat quickly and go home earlier because he goes to work very early on Monday. Huh, his job takes so much time. Interested in money only.'

She walked back up the road, concentrating on getting home, forcing herself not to ponder the significance of that last remark, whether it had been approbation or merely innocent. Despite having heard the gate and doors close behind her, she could not help imagining that her mother was still standing, looking after her as she walked the path. As the tension of the day finally slid off her shoulders into the night, the drops swelling beneath her eyelids like beads of blood from an incision, gathering and quivering, burst soundlessly and spilled downwards, freeing her.

tongues

(*for my mother, sarojini parimala puru shotam*)

Nirmala PuruShotam

when i came
this place was a catalog

   house.
   stone.
   road.
   trees.
   sky.
lettered with their tongue

such singular pronouncements
shamed by my naked use of them
they refuse to be tutored
grow wild thick tall
whirl whorling echoes

silenced my Voice lumbers
amidst this songless tune
opening endless voids
where my language dissipates

in its brooding shadows
i mutate
become hungry
a silver fish
seduced by new terms
i eat my own script.

Memo

Angeline Yap

You babied me in 'baby Guess'
My diapers were the very best.

At eight and 'Reebok'd', I received
Key to the house, braces for teeth.

At twelve, when I began to chafe
Got combination to the safe.

Then at eighteen
to me you gave
Gold Card, L-Plate,
Apologies for being late.

At twenty-one
I got a Jag
about whose size
I should not brag.

But Daddy, Mummy,
What to do?
My menses is now overdue.
We've never talked of certain facts.

Please *reply* by urgent fax.

Fondest Regards

Your daughter,
5 August 2011
Singapore

from Separate Lives

Rebecca Chua

The Marriage

Years later, when it was too late, Lindy would wonder why it was that she hadn't been more resolute. His words would come back to haunt her: 'You shouldn't have to wait for what you want in life.' I should have gone out and grabbed it. But, then, she had been young, and she had believed that everything would fall into her lap as inevitably as it had in her idyllic school days. The head prefectship, the school debating championship, the tennis tournament sweep. The pick of the boys, the adulation of the younger kids, the pride of her parents. It had been a breeze, being the only child in the family, valedictorian par excellence , the top girl in her school, one of the top grade-achievers in the country, and a President's scholar to boot. Patience, her mother had counselled. Patience is its own reward , she had stitched on the twin pillowcases she had arranged on her bed. Patience. But what was it worth now that it was too late? She turned from the plates nestling in the sinkful of suds in the warm kitchen, wiped her hands on her apron and got out a fresh towel from the second drawer of the formica-topped cabinet to her left. Beyond the open kitchen door, the screeching of tyres culminated in the piercing whine of a police siren, and a sudden spurt of frenzied dialogue replaced the up-tempo music emanating from the twenty-six-inch screen before which her husband sat transfixed. It was, after all, his favourite past-time. Every night, he lounged in the same easy chair, slouching over the same pastel silk cushion. Sat in his striped pyjama bottoms and his singlet, watching the celluloid run. Every night after dinner, when he did come home. He didn't always. Especially on Saturday nights when the discotheques swung way past the witching hour. Sometimes he stumbled home at four, not exactly drunk, his breath stealthy with Chivas Regal, his impeccable shirt just a touch dishevelled, the hint of stale perfume and smoke lingering about him. She invariably heard the car engine purr to a stop. Or thought she did, amidst the early morning erratic traffic zipping down the expressway, just a stone's throw away from where they lived on the fourteenth floor of the Laguna Park apartments. He would let himself in, not noisily enough to wake the two children, now teenagers, to whom he normally spoke, perhaps grunting if he bothered at all to address himself to Danny's attachment to his Walkman, or Sharon's incessant yapping on the phone. He would open the bedroom door and, in the light from the pale golden street lamps, would strip off his shirt, climb out of his trousers and pull on his pyjama bottoms, before getting into bed, where he would fall asleep instantly. They no longer shared the same bed, hadn't since Sharon turned four. But, for that matter, he never used to snore. She used to stare soberly at the shadow patterns the street lamps made on the wall, the minute he fell asleep. Now, she squirmed to the rhythm of his snores and kept her eyes shut tight, her mind tired, her body still resentful of the wakefulness imposed, the pleasures denied, until Danny's alarm clock rang in the next room at six o'clock in the morning. Then she would get up; fold the light towelling blanket she used in lieu of the duvet he preferred; brush her teeth in the bathroom; and start preparing breakfast for her son, who was now in junior college himself, and was always out of the house by seven, even on Saturdays, when he could be found working on the college newspaper. Her husband worked a five-day week, and never woke before eleven, as a matter of routine, on the sixth day of the week. She had long since stopped creeping into their bedroom on a Saturday morning, just to look in on the sleeping man, the stubble on his chin, the bags beneath the lids, the lines furrowing his brow as his chest heaved and he still snored, oblivious to the daylight streaming in. Once, when Sharon was, oh, about two, she had tried to wake him, playfully, and had learned to regret it. He had been away for a whole month. Travelling on business, she had told everyone, wondering when he would come back. Or if he would come back at all. Nowadays, he didn't travel so much any more. Or perhaps it was simply that she no longer noticed his absences. Did it matter any more, long after the excuses had worn thin, and reasons were no longer deemed necessary? Of course, she read the newspapers, especially of cases in which hefty alimonies were awarded maligned wives of wayward husbands by a magnanimous court. But a divorce was unthinkable. She had married him, after all, for better or worse. And, really, she knew she was no worse off, certainly no better, than other wives she knew. Women who dressed in designer labels, like Mrs Cheong, whose businessman husband supported a Taiwanese songstress mistress, and plied his associates and clients with liquor and bargirls to lubricate so many business transactions. Even someone like Arabella Teo, who had carved an enviable reputation for herself as one of the top legal brains in the country, and had snared such a prize when she had married the most eligible bachelor in their cohort, the Chief Justice's son. Even Arabella Teo was no better off. Rumour had it that, while she was in court, Anthony was having a field day with each of the oh so delectable, oh so ineluctable secretaries that staffed their lucrative law practice. So much for putting her much vaunted education and training to good use. After all these years, Lindy had gotten used to, if not exactly come to terms with, the pitying looks and the whispered asides of her peers. People who invariably threw up their arms and told her what a WASTE it was that she had given up the best years of her working life to become, in her words, a homemaker. Homebody, she knew they meant. She could hear the accusation in their voices, in the way their eyes swept her from head to toe. She still wore her hair in the same bob she had sported in pre-university. Her clothes were simple, unassuming. And her finger- and toenails were quite bare of varnish. Was that how Ean looked at her, too, she wondered with a sudden stab? For the sake of the children, she told herself. For her own sake, too, she would have to admit, if she were honest, which she was not accustomed to being. It was, after all, a not altogether uncomfortable niche. Certainly one that society accepted: wife, mother, nonentity. It ensured her a place in the general scheme of things. When all was said and done, she knew she was no worse off, certainly no better, than other wives she knew. Women like Fatimah binte Suleiman, who had had to share her husband with two other wives, one a beauty from Cipanas in Indonesia, and the other (actually his brother-in-law's younger sister) from Ipoh in Malaysia. Even if she had not stopped working, it wouldn't necessarily have guaranteed her a faithful husband. After all, everyone knew about the Chief Justice's son's numerous paramours. No, even Arabella Teo was no better off. Not that Ean had a mistress that she knew of. He was no saint. He indulged in the occasional affair. But who didn't, in this day and age? Nancy Shaw, who was fifty-four if a day older, was quite nonchalant about her husband's flings.

'Flighty young things,' she dismissed them. 'They make eyes at him in the office, they tell him how handsome he is, how virile. He's such a fool, he can't resist them.' Trust Nancy not to underestimate the pleasure he took in having pretty young things hanging on his arm. Especially when their eldest son was thirty-two, and the father of two, a five-year-old and an eighteen-month-old. And Nancy realised she had put on some weight over the years. 'The only thing that matters,' she pronounced matter-of-factly, 'is that he treats you well.' Nancy had her own car, a Renault 1300; a liberal allowance which she squandered with her cronies, a bunch of faculty wives all similarly intent on decorating their homes with Persian rugs, Balinese wayang kulit figures or Rococo Peranakan aka Malaccan replicas; and an imposing residence in Queen Astrid Park. 'What more could you want?' demanded Nancy in a voice that rang strangely strident even when she did not raise her voice. In her callow youth, Lindy had been shocked by Nancy's worldly cynicism, and tried to keep to herself. But, now that she had turned forty, these things didn't seem quite so shocking as they had, once upon a time. It was not, after all, happiness that moved her. How foolish she had once been, to think that was the earth and sky. Happiness, she had contemplated as a philosophical abstract while an undergraduate. She remembered that the tenets of logic had eluded her, because she had been so caught up in its celebration. She had been happy then— or (she corrected herself) thought she had been. She had thought, fleetingly, of the gossamer nature of happiness, when she realised that Meng wasn't going to marry her. But, by the time she had married Ean, she had not worried unduly about happiness. She was happy enough on her wedding day, she thought now, idly, though the brief visit to the registry had been prosaic. In fact, the couple who had been married just before Ean and Lindy had been downright *sua-teng*: the young man in a Hawaiian shirt and brown trousers just fronting a pair of rubber flipflops; the girl, not more than eighteen, already frowsy and obviously pregnant in a paisley housecoat. It had been a little disturbing, but not enough to cloud her sense of pride, even of achievement. She had set her heart on a European honeymoon, and Ean had obliged. Sixteen capitals in twenty-eight days, the kind of whirlwind tour to match the romance. In retrospect, it hadn't been much of a honeymoon. Ean had hated being dragged out of bed at 6.30 in the morning, to have communal continental breakfast with six other couples in an equally somnolent state, not to mention an assortment of aunts, two divorcees, grandparents, a gaggle of teenagers and a quartet of bratty kids. Ean chafed at the long hours cooped up in tour buses that dissected the country, and complained that he couldn't understand a word of the heavily-accented speech dispensed by the tour guides. Only Lindy, because it was the first time she had ever been to Europe, bore with the innumerable toilet stops, the tea breaks, the obligatory shopping sprees and the pro forma Chinese dinners. She toted her state-of-the-art instant camera, snapping everything from the Mannikin Pis and the Eiffel Tower to the Coliseum and the Parthenon; and bought up every souvenir in sight, to be distributed among relatives and friends. But, if the truth be told, Europe left her cold, and she was glad to return home, forever to savour, if only in memory, that singular foray abroad.

The Children

She stopped working two months after Danny was born, as much because she wanted him breast-fed, as the fact that he was hyperactive, and would wake five times in the wee hours of the morning. And, since Ean was capable of sleeping through a typhoon, she bore the brunt of the child-minding. Actually, it was Ean who suggested that she quit. But neither remembered that. Ean's mother, a teacher, had stopped teaching when Ean was born. After her pupillage at a distinguished firm of advocates and solicitors, Lindy had been induced, by a promise of partnership, to join a small firm belonging to a business associate of Ean's father. After three years of indifferent toil, the partnership had yet to materialise, and the work had developed into a kind of routine, predictable but uninspiring.

When Danny was six months old, her primary school classmate Fiona had flown in from Paris and spent a week in her home. Fiona, the travelling auditor, had taken a welcome break both from her own punishing pace of life, as well as from her sculptor lover. But she was appalled when Lindy told her she had become a full-time wife and mother.

'You're joking!' Fiona had told her. 'You must be out of your flipping mind!' Lindy had looked at her friend and smiled.

'Do you realise what you're doing? You're going to become a vegetable!'

'Don't be silly,' Lindy had admonished, already embarrassed. 'It's not going to be that bad. I'll keep up.'

'Like real you are!' retorted Fiona. 'How? By watching "Sesame Street"?'

'Oh, come on, Fiona!'

'You come on, Lindy! You're going to become a flipping housewife!'

Lindy had bit her tongue then. Fiona didn't understand, and she couldn't explain, what it meant, and why she was content, to clean house, go to the market, to cook, sweep, and sew. Once, Fiona had been her ally. But Fiona had left both marriage and civil service with little compunction.

'They were both so-so—' and she studied her manicured nails before she spat out the verdict, 'boring.'

But then, what did you expect, married to a man with a name like Herbert, who was some bigwig at the Ministry of Finance? Fiona had started working at the Ministry of Finance after graduation and, after a couple of years, had married her boss. The marriage only lasted nineteen months. When Fiona announced, quite blithely, that she was divorced, Lindy was still conservative enough to be sensitive to the stigma. Fiona only laughed.

'Why do you think I left the Ministry of Finance to join an oil company?' she asked. It was the men, of course. Well-heeled men in rooms with a view of the waterfront and the building construction in progress; a few dishy, many dull, some bald, a couple downright lecherous, and the rest, just beer-bellied. 'The kind you can chat up over cocktails,' smiled Fiona, 'and look forward to some action with after dinner.'

Lindy didn't care for cocktails, or the lurid details. She remembered the old days, when Ean used to take her to those drinks-before-dinner affairs which she had found so excruciating. What did you say to the glittering and glamorous Chinese-educated woman who virtually sat on the managing director's lap, whom you knew couldn't possibly be his wife? It had been a relief when Ean stopped having her accompany him. Not all of a sudden. But gradually, so that she hardly noticed it. Once, when she was pregnant with Sharon, she had actually had this urge to dress up and make a grand entrance to the Singapore Symphony Orchestra's last concert of the season. She could see herself on Ean's arm, engaged in scintillating conversation with, perhaps, the Chairman of the Arts Festival Steering Committee. No such luck: Ean's interest in the arts had plummeted after an initial spate when he was first courting her. Then, they had savoured plays, art films, concerts, art exhibitions, even a visit to the museum. In the intervening years, they had probably been to two concerts, the odd play, and maybe half a dozen movies. Not that she minded, Lindy told herself, having made up for lost time once the children were old enough to be chaperoned to children's theatre and film festivals. At least, the children lapped it all up. The last time she and Ean had been to a movie, he had fallen asleep midway. He had put it down to the strenuous games of tennis he had been playing in preparation for the company championships, and she had said nothing. Once, they had bested each other on the court, trading volley for volley. Once, they had been inseparable as their racquets, always ready for yet another game. The last time they had played together, he had told her she was out of form. That was before Danny was born. He hated the way she pursed her lips. In the old days, her determined silence would have provoked a fight. 'Yah, go ahead, just sit there and pout!' he would taunt her. But, the last time she had pursed her lips like that, he had not said a word. He merely went out and got determinedly drunk. As a matter of fact, Ean got drunk very seldom. He held his liquor well. He had to, he used to tell her in

the beginning. 'It's part of the job to wine and dine your clients.'
She had gone to a couple of those boisterous ten-course banquets
for dealers at the Shangri-la Hotel and had spilled sherry on her
white dress, while Ean had drunk a competitor under the table.
She had never gone again. He hadn't asked her.

Somewhere along the line, he stopped coming home and telling
her about the wheeling and dealing in the office. Somewhere,
somehow, he stopped cracking jokes about his colleagues and
clients. And she didn't ask. Maybe the children were more
important then. She nursed, first, Danny and, then, Sharon through
smallpox, and chicken pox, and then the mumps. And then there
were always their exams, and then the PTA meetings, and the fun
fairs. When the children were growing up, she always found herself
in the thick of some group discussion or other, among the many
anxious parents who pored over school workbooks, or supervised
an environmental awareness project, or banded together to
raise funds for the building annexe or swimming pool. She had
watched the children grow up and away from her, often with pride,
sometimes with exasperation. Knowing that she had helped mould
their temperaments, guide them through the tempestuous years
of childhood, and build a rapport with them that she had never
enjoyed with her own mother. Knowing all these things gave her an
inordinate sense of pride, of accomplishment. Danny was never any
trouble in school. He was an exemplary student, except in Chinese.
She tried to augment this with bedtime stories in Mandarin, and
wholesale prompting when he had to turn in an essay or complete
a comprehension exercise. But she was often stumped by the new
shorthand, *jianbizi*, since she prided herself on the full, meticulous
brushstrokes of traditional calligraphy. That's why she eventually
acquiesced and decided to hire a tutor. He had a whole string of
half-baked, pimply-faced or pock-marked types who hadn't been
initiated into *hanyu pinyin* before she bowed to popular wisdom, in
the shape and form of Norma Fernandez. Norma's son Clive had
a Chinese tutor who was expensive but effective. The tall, ascetic,
pasty-faced young man became Danny's tutor too, and was later
engaged to supervise Sharon as well. Sharon, unlike Danny, liked
languages and did well in Mandarin. She had also begun to pick

up a smattering of Japanese from the neighbours, as well as some Malay from Cik Minah, her dressmaker. But Lindy figured that it didn't hurt to reinforce Sharon's Mandarin. Thanks a lot, Norma,' murmured Lindy. 'No problem,' replied Norma expansively. 'What are friends for?'

The Talk

Norma was not only a good friend, she was an inquisitive and well-intentioned one. She was full of questions, hints and suggestions. Her world was peopled by relatives and friends, all well-meaning, each one providing a timely example of the way matters should be conducted. Norma was also full of the comings and goings in the neighbourhood. She knew the intimate details of Pearl de Souza's brief marriage and traumatic abortion. She was privy to the months of agonising before the Naidus finally migrated to Australia. She learnt that Joseph John had been given the sack just before Christmas, that the Tans' niece, Mabel, had married a German ski instructor, and that Mrs Chew's youngest son, Victor, was on drugs. She even found out that Roberta Aw-yong, that pretty salesgirl-turned-model, was actually a transsexual; and that Gerard Hoffman, the young German lecturer, had seduced his Filipino maid. Perhaps Norma was too friendly with all and sundry. In any case, Lindy had long ago come to accept that Norma was the friendly neighbourhood gossip, and that Norma knew everything there was to know (or to find out) in their little corner of the world. But it was not Norma who brought the bad news. It was Mrs Shigetsu. Mrs Shigetsu, who rented the flat next door, and accompanied her husband to all major company functions because she was beautiful, gracious, and one of the few Japanese women to have mastered fluent English, avoided her for an entire week before she fluttered by in contrition.

'I'm so sorry,' she kept saying. 'So sorry.'

At first, Lindy couldn't fathom what Mrs Shigetsu meant. Yes, Ean had moved out. But he had moved out before. When Sharon was nine, he had spent three months in a rented flat in River Valley Road. Practising Yoga. Meditating. Another time, he decided to take up oil painting and, because the smell of paint drove her and the children crazy, he moved into his brother's flat for a spell, while Shaun was in New York on a year's sabbatical. But it was not that unusual. There were weeks when none of them saw Ean at all, because he would take off on a fishing trip to Malaysia for six weekends in a row. So accustomed had she become to his absences that it was a while before Lindy realised that, this time, Ean had moved out and would stay out. After all, she hadn't seen him for months.

But others did, including her friend, Rachel. 'Who's the bitch?' demanded Rachel.

'I don't know what you mean,' responded Lindy evasively.

'She wears diamond drops in her ears,' said Rachel, 'and little black Chanel numbers.'

'I don't know,' said Lindy nervously. 'Mrs Shigetsu—'

'Who's Mrs Shigetsu?' asked Rachel.

'My neighbour,' replied Lindy, close to tears.

'But my dear,' said Rachel, 'how long has this been going on?' And then, as if it were an afterthought, 'The swine!'

'I don't know,' said Lindy.

'I don't believe you,' said Rachel.

'I really don't know.'

When it became obvious that Lindy really didn't, Kitty called up. Kitty, who had studied Arts and Social Sciences while Lindy had been pursuing Law at university, called up after—what was it?—eleven years, corroborating the evidence. Amazing. Even the washerwomen, hers, and the one who did the family upstairs, were talking about it. Lindy overheard them as she stood on the fourteenth floor corridor while waiting for the lift to come. It was so utterly humiliating.

'I wish you would reconsider,' her mother said. 'There's nothing to reconsider,' said Lindy stiffly. Her mother pursed her lips. 'You know your father and I weren't in favour of this marriage,' she said. Her mother had always had a soft spot for Meng. Because he flattered her, and pandered to her vanity. Because he never stopped telling her mother how beautiful she was, or reminding her how much she looked like her mother, with her high cheekbones and fine teeth and rosebud lips.

'Oh, mother! You never stop reminding me,' said Lindy through bared teeth. 'You never gave us a chance.'

Her mother raised her eyebrows. 'It's not my marriage that's on the rocks, Lindy,' said her mother evenly.

The words tumbled out of her mouth: 'Yes, but it was bound not to work—' then Lindy bit her tongue.

'If your marriage didn't work, Lindy,' admonished her mother, 'it wasn't because we didn't give it a chance. Your father and I are happy enough—'

'If you call that happy.' The words rushed out unbidden. Lindy had always resented her stepfather. For supplanting the father she never knew. For always being there, and, yet, in that cut-and-dried, formal way of his, curiously absent. He never spoke to her, or touched her. He hardly said a word to her mother.

'We've been married thirty years,' sniffed her mother.

'Thirty years,' snorted Lindy, 'of having a doormat.' A pink welt swelled where her mother had slapped her across her left cheek. But the only sound was that of running water in the sink. She had said it, finally and irrevocably, Lindy knew. Her mother would never forgive her, nor try to understand. She felt faint and hollow, standing in the warm kitchen with the water draining into the evaporating suds, not looking at her mother, now it was too late to retreat. But how could I tell you, Mother, that my husband is sleeping with another woman? Or that he wants the divorce, not I? Three years before she had met Ean, they had set their hopes on her marrying Meng. They had liked him. He was young, promising, and, not altogether immaterial, he was rich. They had long been family friends, having lived in the same neighbourhood and been a part of the same social circles, and the match had seemed ideal. Lindy had not questioned the conventional wisdom that she and Meng were an item. He was, after all, her constant companion. She found him witty and warm and amusing. More than amusing, actually. He had such a devilish sense of humour. But there was more to Meng than just his sense of humour. He was bright, no doubt about it.

'It's almost unfair,' her best friend, Mei, had upbraided her.

'What do you mean?' Lindy had laughed.

'Think about it, Lindy: Intelligent. Good-looking. Irresistible.'

Lindy couldn't help laughing. Mei was always panting after one of the boys or another. If it wasn't Gordon, the rugby player with the biceps, it was Perumal the long-distance runner. 'So who's the lucky guy this time?' she queried.

'I'm talking about Meng,' pouted Mei. 'Your Meng,' she added for emphasis. 'Oh, come on, Mei.' 'Think about it. He's almost too good to be true,' Mei pointed out. But, at that age and stage in life, Lindy wasn't much given to introspection. Or analysis. She had only laughed. She hadn't taken him seriously when Meng said he wanted to make the army his career. No one had. They all knew that he had his life mapped out for him. No one else was expected to take over his father's business. And when he decided to read law after national service, she thought it only natural. She had done law, herself. It was the option of the brightest and the best. Then, after serving his pupillage, he told her he intended to see the world. Hitch-hike his way up the Malayan peninsula into Thailand, then make for India via Burma. Then keep going until he had seen Europe, both East and West. He would not come home, he said, until he had traversed the length and breadth of the Americas. She didn't question him. All the undergraduates, especially the boys, made such a vow. Few of them ever carried it through. It didn't occur to her, then, to wonder why he had not asked her to go too. It didn't occur to her to even want to go. No, hitch-hiking wasn't her idea of travel, even if it was punctuated by train and bicycle rides along the way. The day he was packing for his marathon trip round the world, she had dropped in on him.

'You will write, won't you?' she had asked.

'I won't have much time to write you long letters,' he had said. 'Maybe the odd postcard or so.'

She nodded.

'And one other thing,' he had said, as casually as if he were asking her to feed his dog, Deng Xiaoping, who was getting quite old now and had lost most of his teeth.

'Yes?' She had turned expectantly to him.

'I don't want you to wait for me.'

There was a silence in which she felt her throat turn dry. 'What do you mean?'

'I don't want you to wait for me, ' he repeated quietly.

'I don't understand,' she whispered.

'Oh, I might not come back,' he had said airily. 'I might become a car washer or a bell hop in an L.A. strip,' he reminded her jauntily of one of their favourite cartoons, one that had become a private joke.

She had nodded and smiled. 'Yes, I can see you now,' she responded, 'in your bellhop's cap and uniform.'

And he had clapped her on the back and told her, 'That's my girl!' He had not wanted her to see him off: 'You know how I hate goodbyes.'

'Then can I welcome you home?' she had asked.

'Sure,' he had replied, too quickly. 'By and by.'

'Talk to him. He'll listen to you if you talk to him,' his mother pleaded with Lindy. Lindy shrugged, almost helplessly.

'You know I can't do that,' she said. 'I can't make him do something he doesn't want to do.' It wasn't until long after she was married and the mother of two kids that Lindy realised she could never even make Meng do anything she wanted him to.

'He's just selfish to put his own interests before the family's,' complained his mother petulantly. 'He's always been wilful, that boy of mine. I don't know what his father will say!' And she sighed deeply.

'Don't worry, it will be alright,' said Lindy, patting her on the hand. 'You'll see.' But the old lady only shook her head.

She had come home the day Meng told her he did not want to marry her, unsure of how she should feel. For weeks after that, she did not feel numb or hurt or depressed. And months after his absence became obvious, and her mother enquired about his whereabouts, she only admitted, 'He must be somewhere in Europe by now.'

'What on earth do you mean, Lindy?' her mother had asked coldly.

'You know Meng always talked about hitch-hiking to Europe,' Lindy reminded her.

'Don't tell me he actually took off!' Lindy nodded.

'Well, how long is he going to be away?'

'I don't know,' said Lindy. 'As long as it takes, I suppose.'

'And what do his parents have to say about that?' demanded her mother.

'I don't know,' said Lindy. Her mother thought she was being deliberately defiant. Only Lindy knew she was speaking the truth. She hadn't spoken to or visited his parents ever since he had left on his marathon journey. She knew she could not meet his mother's keen gaze. She felt ashamed, somehow, of having failed to have stopped him from embarking on his pilgrimage, as his mother would have wanted. Searching her conscience, she knew she had not consciously avoided them thereafter. But, over the years, though some people would take it upon themselves to tell her how they were doing, or even asking if she had heard from Meng himself, she did not trouble to renew the ties. She never stopped to ask if Meng had taken over his father's business, or whether Meng had ever returned. Not even after her mother became a regular mahjong *kaki* in Meng's third aunt's entourage. It would have been impolite to ask, she told herself, especially now that she was a married woman.

The Other Woman

She had SEIZE THE MOMENT emblazoned in bold red letters on her sweater.

'I've always thought,' she said, playfully nibbling on his ear, 'that it should have been my school motto, instead of something as preposterous as "The Best Is Yet To Be." I mean,' and here she flung her arms out, 'who knows what the future will bring? Can you tell?'

He shook his head in mock horror.

'I mean, you sit around waiting for the future, and just about waste the best years of your life! It's senseless, absolutely senseless!'

He couldn't agree more. In fact, he couldn't think of a time when he wasn't in complete agreement with her. He was intoxicated by the faint animal odour she always exuded, even after a shower; the fragrance of her naturally curly hair, especially when it was newly-washed; and the smooth texture of her skin, scrubbed a little pink, and particularly delectable after a steamy hot bath. She had a kind of feline grace, but there was also something inexorably predatory about her. He was always expecting her to pounce when he least expected it. On an experimental notion he wanted to test. On a throwaway line he tossed. On an idea he found novel, but which he had not bothered to develop. He was always caught unawares. Never anticipating the way she caught and balanced it between her two uneven front teeth, before hurling it back into his lap, a conversational hand grenade. She had this knack of turning everything he said into something suggestive, something dangerous. It excited him. He found her face fascinating: the eyes, large and luminous; the lips, always a little parted, her nostrils flaring; her ears pinned close to her head, like some antennae. There was something at once waif-like and endearing, yet leery and troubling, about her. A quality about her that was frighteningly ephemeral. He could not quite put his finger on it, but he sometimes felt as if he had known her from another life. Which was patently ridiculous, he told himself, because he did not believe in other lifetimes. It was just one of those Egyptian fetishes to which she subscribed. And he refused to be drawn into it. Absolutely. No question about it. He sighed.

'What's the matter?' she asked softly, stroking him gently. At once solicitous.

'Oh, nothing,' he replied. But it seemed to him that she had him so much in thrall that he was beginning to think the way she talked.

'It's our thought patterns,' she pronounced. 'Our auras are beginning to merge.'

His instinct was to dismiss it all as 'Rubbish!' But the initial irritation he always felt, whenever she started on what he chose to call the occult and she preferred to label the spiritual, invariably disappeared when she placed her cool fingers on his throbbing temple. She excited him, delighted him, and aroused in him both passion and protectiveness. He found himself thinking of what they had talked about the previous evening. He found himself looking forward to subsequent evenings together. They were moments of intense debate and incredible ardour. They would spend hours arguing the pros and cons, weighing each conceptualisation, every execution with a precision he had come to admire. She was no intellectual lightweight, this woman who challenged him and galvanised him. And yet, he had to admit, she had an inexplicably soothing effect on him. Somehow, the realisation exhilarated him. Made him feel as if the boundaries he recognised were mere illusions, that the obstacles he acknowledged were just hallucinations.

'Have you actually looked at architectural plans?' she demanded. 'No? Well, take another look. All they are are two-dimensional drawings. Drawings,' she repeated, as if to drive home the point. Drawings. The point at which calculation and creativity converged. From which emerged a new reality. An edifice, all concrete and glass. That you raised from the ground for posterity. To touch and to hold. 'To touch and to hold.' Her voice rang in his mind's ear. There was something concrete that she held out. Something real. Lasting. For all her restlessness, and her impatience. The prospect excited him immeasurably. No, not exactly what he expected from an architect.

'An architect!' Lindy was apoplectic when he finally broke the news to her. Irony of ironies, a Piscean (or, if you prefer, a Cockerel) just like Lindy, a woman only sixteen days her junior, who had been brought up in the capitals of Europe, educated abroad, and practising in Canada and the United States. Who had returned to help design a junior college and a luxury condominium—these were the tiny little details that only someone like Norma had been able to ferret out, God only knew how. Lindy was too civilised to tax Ean with her new-found knowledge. In any case, it wouldn't have made an iota of difference. By all accounts, he had been squiring this woman, off and on, for nearly a year. Nearly a year! She could kick herself for being so blind, so bland, so unaware. For fooling herself into thinking that he meant less than the children did, after all these years of marriage. 'Can't we talk this over?' Her tone was tentative, uncertain. 'Try again?'

'There's no point,' said Ean, almost kindly, 'I intend to marry her.'

'You can't be serious!' she told him witheringly—then could have bitten off her tongue. It was the wrong thing to say.

'Perfectly.' His accent was clipped. She recognised the early warning signal from their early courtship days. Oh, she should have learned from their early disagreements. But here she was again, falling into the same old trap. Ean never fought. He never rose to the bait, even though she would have welcomed the kind of argument that would have cleared the air, and brought a reconciliation. No, once he had made up his mind, he would brook no further discussion. But still she tried.

'You have a wife, Ean, and two teenage children,' she said.

'I'll make sure you get a decent settlement, of course,' he said.

'Of course,' she repeated sardonically. 'And I know you'll want custody of the kids,' he said, as if ticking off each item on a mental list.

'Naturally.'

'You won't have to worry about their university education, or anything. I'll take care of that,' he assured her.

'You've thought of everything, haven't you?' Lindy demanded insultingly. But he deflected the barb effortlessly.

'Probably not,' he admitted. 'I've tried to. But there'll probably be a lot of little details we'll have to work out together.' Little details. Lindy's mind seethed. It seemed so long ago, so utterly impossible, that she had once been charmed, nay, reassured by his very objectivity. His calmness. His cool, methodical approach. His eye for the finer details. Anything that had veered 360 degrees from Meng's headstrong impulses. For a moment, blindingly, his face swam in her vision, and she had this unreal feeling that it was not Ean who stood facing her, but Meng all over again. Meng throwing away everything he had known and owned to embark on this perilous journey from which he might never return. Only this man was her husband of many years, and he was embarking on a different journey, with a different travelling companion.

'She's practising witchcraft on him, I'm sure of it,' his mother pronounced. 'One of these Thai love potions.'

'She's an architect,' said Lindy dully, now that the tears were spent.

'Whatever. She's got a Thai mother, hasn't she?' demanded Ean's mother, as if genetics determined everything. That was just one of the incidental details Norma had unearthed, that and the peripatetic childhood that came with having a father who was a Singapore Airlines station manager. Oh, how glamorous a lifestyle it presupposed, Lindy thought with just a touch of envy. It made the woman sound so worldly wise, so well-travelled. Perhaps, after all, that was what had attracted Ean to her. Lindy stared out of the window into the dark and dreamless night. It was one of those hot, airless evenings when there was no breeze, not a leaf stirred. She had lived so long in a limbo of knowing and dreading, of hoping that it was merely some nightmare, of wishing that it were not happening to her, that it was difficult to force herself to come to grips with the inevitability of the situation.

'I don't know what to say to Danny and Sharon,' she confessed.

Her mother-in-law sighed. She, too, was at a loss. Norma, on the other hand, was more sanguine. 'Whatever they are, your kids aren't stupid,' she said. As it turned out, Norma was right, although Sharon was the one who took it relatively well. But then, as Norma would later point out, Sharon had always been closer to Lindy. Lindy chose to tell the children separately. She was direct. No point beating about the bush. 'Your father and I are getting divorced,' she said.

'Oh, Mum,' Sharon sighed, throwing her arms around her mother's neck, and giving her a big hug. Lindy had to steel herself to talk to Danny, who must have got bad vibes about the news, or maybe he had been warned by his younger sister. It seemed to Lindy that he was deliberately ignoring her presence all day, or maybe she, too, was trying to avoid him. In the event, she went for the jugular: 'I know it's my fault,' she admitted to her son.

Danny growled at her: 'It's both your fault!' Why was it, that with the men, with both Danny and Ean, she found herself putting her foot in her mouth? That was not what she had meant to say. It had come out a lot more easily with Sharon. How much more uncomplicated was her relationship with her daughter, she reflected with a sigh. But the damage was done. Danny was taciturn and moody for a long time after the announcement. Even after both she and Ean agreed that, in the interests of the children, they would remain civil, and Ean would always have access to them, whenever the phone rang and Ean asked to speak to him, Danny refused to comply. The boycott lasted five months. Danny was obdurate. Lindy tried at first to talk to him, then resorted to getting Sharon to persuade him, but all to no avail. He just wouldn't budge. There was a pinched look to his face, and an anger in his eyes which she had never seen. But it reminded her achingly of Ean.

In the end, it was the architect who built bridges. She managed to get him to the phone, and issued an invitation for him and Sharon to visit her in her new apartment. It was apparently sumptuous, like something out of a decor magazine, according to Sharon, who took quite well to her father's new wife-to-be. She was full of what the woman had to say, the desserts she served them, and the view from the thirty-ninth floor. Danny was less loquacious, but evidently he had been appeased. Lindy felt betrayed. She knew she was behaving unreasonably, and it was with a sense of relief that she learnt the wedding was being scheduled for some date during the school holidays, since she could take advantage of the number of package tours available to whisk herself and the children on a long-promised visit to Disney World. There had been a scene at Kissimmee, in a small fish-and-chip shop, where Danny had drawn the line at being dragged half-way across the other hemisphere just so she could avoid the wedding, when he wouldn't have minded attending. Lindy had been hurt beyond belief: 'You never said anything about wanting to go to the wedding!' she had imploded.

'You never asked!' retorted Danny. 'You just run our damned lives just to suit your convenience!'

Sharon had, diplomatically, kept out of the fracas. The rest of the trip had been uneventful. They had been days frenetic with activity, nights spangled with fireworks, the hours interspersed by boisterous queues and fast food pig-outs and souvenir collecting. Later, when they pooled their shutterbug-happy efforts together, they managed an impressive collection of snapshots. There were assorted lopsided grins, thin arms around Mickey Mouse's broad one, miniscule specks in front of Sleeping Beauty's (or was it

Cinderella's) castle, and a few more of special effects and enormous teacups and hazy whizzing objects. No shots had, of course, been taken in that fish-and-chip shop. When they returned, Norma reported that there had been a small but lavish reception at the Hilton Hotel, attended by various dignitaries from the civil service, a sprinkling of local celebrities, and some relatives flown in from such disparate domiciles as Hawaii, Washington, and Arkansas, not to mention central Sumatra, northeastern Thailand, and western Australia. Norma also added the fillip that Ean and his second wife had chosen to honeymoon in some suitably remote resort in the Philippines. Lindy wondered how long it would take before her topsy-turvy world returned to normal, but had no doubt that it would. After all, Ean had promised that he would do the honourable thing, and, in the final reckoning, she had her children. They were the ones who mattered; whose opinion of her counted; and whose lives, in the final analysis, counted for most.

The Daughter

'I don't think my mother ever quite recovered from the divorce,' Sharon said candidly, putting the last-minute touches to an intricate flower arrangement of pink, white and red carnations interspersed with choice ferns and baby's breath.

'What makes you think so?'

'Well, for one thing, she was such a pain about dating,' huffed Sharon.

'What do you mean?'

'Well, you know my mother's still an attractive woman,' explained Sharon patiently. 'So there were plenty of suitors, but she was always so coy about going out with any of them.' She cast a quick eye over the table settings, their burnished mirror images impeccably reflected in the high gloss of the polished mahogany dining table, and satisfied herself that everything was as it should be. After all, Sharon prided herself on being a good hostess. 'My mother was of that generation that didn't think a divorced woman should date,' pronounced Sharon. 'She never gave herself a chance, she was such a fool.'

'Perhaps she didn't think she needed another man in her life.'

'Not need a man? Not my mother. She's no feminist,' snorted Sharon. 'She was of that generation that didn't believe that life was complete without a man. They couldn't do anything without one. No politics, no social causes, perhaps, no enduring interests. But not no man.'

'Oh, Sharon.' Leslie's tone was mildly admonishing.

'It's true,' Sharon maintained with equanimity. 'If you ask me, I think she's still pining over that boyfriend of hers, the one she had in pre-u. She's never quite got over him either.'

'Not, surely, after all these years, Sharon! Don't forget she got married and had two kids.'

Sharon shook her head. 'The trouble with my Mum is that she's always living in her own time-zone. She can't come to grips with her past or her present, and she doesn't realise that there isn't going to be a future without either!'

'Aren't you being a little hard on her?'

'Hard on my Mum? No way!' retorted Sharon. 'After Dad remarried, she confided in me a lot, so I know a lot more about what makes her tick than anybody. I guess she didn't have anyone else to talk to. We used to talk for hours. And we used to do all kinds of things together. We took aerobic and swimming classes together, we signed up for those *dim sum* and flower arrangement classes at the community centre, we even went to see film shows together. When I was in pre-u, I'd come home with a project I'd be working on, or some topic we'd be discussing in tutorial, and it would set her off on this nostalgia kick. She was always going on and on about this guy she was going steady with.'

'Chan Meng. Yes, that's right.' Leslie flinched. It had taken Sharon years to track down the connection.

'Except the way Mum talks about him, he's the sweetest, kindest guy in the world. So sweet and kind he dumps her and goes off on this round-the-world odyssey!'

'Oh, Sharon!'

'Oh, stop Oh, Sharon-ing me!' Sharon mimicked the irksome phrase with annoyance. 'Why do you think Dad divorced her? My Aunt Fiona was right. She'd become just a little doormat. I mean, everyone said she was a brilliant scholar, and they all expected her to be a hotshot lawyer when she graduated. But she just gave up. She settled down into a routine after she got married, and turned into a vegetable!'

'Oh, Sharon,' Leslie sighed. 'You're getting downright vindictive!'

'You bet I am!' Sharon tossed her head. 'All her life, she's just let everything go to waste, every opportunity, every single opportunity! Well, let me tell you, I'm never going to let that happen to me.'

'You're not your mother, Sharon.'

'I've made something of my life,' said Sharon. It was true. She had built a career and a reputation on skills she had assiduously cultivated and honed. She had launched a business so successful at home that it was being replicated abroad. In fact, when the business had first been listed on the stock exchange, it had ignited considerable participation. Now the conglomerate she controlled had become so powerful, it was a force to be reckoned with, not just locally, but regionally. Sharon was not so much disinterested in the minutiae of balance sheets and bottom lines. Her mind, long accustomed to the arcanum and chicanery of commerce, was more comfortable with the intricacies of multi-digit transactions. Nobody knew that better than Leslie, who was a trained accountant. It hadn't taken Leslie long to figure out Sharon, her moods, her predilections, her preferences and peeves; in short, to figure out the many doors which led to a mind that worked like a steel trap. Sharon kept only one picture of her mother in her apartment, on one of the side tables between her favourite armchair and its twin. She looked down on it, with the light cascading onto it from a reading lamp. No doubt about it, it was a flattering portrait of her mother, one that her father had taken many, oh, too many years ago. Sharon shuddered. 'Sometimes she scares me. She's led such a wasted, wasted life.'

Leslie frowned. 'Don't start now. They'll be here soon,' she reminded her.

But Sharon seemed to have forgotten that the table was set for guests. 'You know her problem?' she demanded. 'She's just never been able to figure out her men.' A reflective pause. 'Not even Danny, whom she worshipped. He was her son-god, you know.

Nothing was too good for him. Anything that he wanted, he had to have. But Danny's really ruthless when he's made up his mind. I remember when she told him about the divorce, Danny kind of cold-shouldered her. He wasn't even on speaking terms with Dad for a long time. He took the break up really badly. He was bad-tempered all the time. I remember he used to snap at me for no reason at all. He was always accusing me of taking or hiding his Walkman, or borrowing his tennis racquet, or something silly and unreasonable like that. Then we got invited to Phornsiri's one day, and he really flipped over her. Yah, I must admit I liked her, too. I mean, she just wasn't like any of the grown-ups we knew. She dressed different, she talked different. Not down to you, the way some people would, asking you stupid questions about what school you were in or what your favourite subject in school was. She was on your wave-length, you know, and she made you laugh. Danny had such a crush on her!' Sharon shook her head at the memory. 'After we got back from that holiday in Florida—it was such a disaster! He and Mum were always arguing about everything, it just ruined everything for me. Then, after we got back from that holiday at Disney World, he was always at Phornsiri's place. He'd drop in there at the slightest excuse. I suppose that's how he got interested in architecture. That's also when he started playing golf with Dad. God, those two were fanatics!' There was a long silence. Then, in an expressionless voice, Sharon continued, 'You know, he wasn't even at the funeral when Dad died.'

It had been an ignominious death, one of those countless traffic statistics in which a lorry had rammed into the car Ean had been driving on his way home from work. Lindy had turned up, of course, sombre in black, her lips ash-grey under the pink lipstick, but otherwise composed. Phornsiri had been thin, gaunt, distraught. But all Sharon could think of as they stood gathered together in the crematorium was where Danny was. He never showed up.

'They were that close,' she said, holding up her index and third fingers in a twinning gesture, then lapsed into silence. Leslie sat comfortably in her chair, not having to say a word, not needing to break the silence. After a pause, Sharon resumed her narrative: 'Mum may have been upset when Danny boycotted her about the divorce. But she was heartbroken when he deserted her for Phornsiri after the wedding. It was Phornsiri this, Phornsiri that, all the years he was in university, doing architecture. Come to think of it, Mum never met any of the string of girlfriends he had until he married Irene. And, even then, it wasn't until after Xiong's birth that they were reconciled.' There was a brittle look on Sharon's face. 'There was the sound of a car driving up, and Sharon stopped in mid-reminiscence to look out the window. A long, sleek, British racing green Porsche was reversing into one of the parking lots. She cast a glance at the wall clock. 'Just the neighbour. Don't worry, they're always late,' she said, by way of explanation. Her eyes drifted to a larger picture she had on the wall, one of those formal studio family portraits of Danny and Irene, Xiong and Min.

'It's funny how things work out, isn't it?' Sharon pursed her lips contemplatively. 'Now they're so close. She's always at his place. She dotes on the children, and I hear she gets on really well with Irene.'

'Do you mind?'

It was not a question. A look of annoyance crossed Sharon's face. 'Mind? What's there to mind?' she demanded.

'The way it turned out,' responded Leslie drily.

'I don't really care,' said Sharon, affecting her trademark nonchalance. 'Whatever suits them. As long as they're happy.'

'And you, are you happy?' probed Leslie.

'You're such a bitch, you know that?' Leslie shrugged. 'All the relatives used to think I was her pet,' allowed Sharon. 'I guess even Dad did. He always used to divvy us up: Danny for him and me for Mum.'

'But you were always playing second fiddle to Danny.'

'That's enough!' Sharon snapped. Leslie got up from her chair. 'Oh don't go, Leslie,' cried Sharon quickly.

'I really think I should,' said Leslie softly.

'Don't be absurd! I only have my mother, and Danny and his family over for dinner once a year. It's no big deal. And anyway,' Sharon added lightly, 'it's time you met.'

The Mother

Sharon was surprised to discover how her mother had aged. The mental picture she carried of her mother corresponded so closely to the picture she had on the side table beside her favourite armchair that, for a moment, she couldn't reconcile the image with the reality of flesh and blood. Lindy's hair was almost all white, and the texture of straw, but she wore it in a short bob that was kind to her face. It was a face that had grown soft over the years, almost as soft as those of her two grandsons, who liked to press their noses into the lines of her cheek. Her eyes were gentle, absent, as if lost in some reverie. But it was in the area around her mouth that her age showed, an area that collapsed softly inwards around the gums, and there were little, pursed, vertical lines in her upper lip.

'Mum! Danny! Irene!' Sharon was quick to extend a hand to her mother, usher her brother and sister-in-law, and shoo the two boys into the house. 'Min! Xiong! How they've grown!' The two boys tumbled in, clutching their computer games, laughing and talking. Sharon turned to Leslie. 'This is my friend, Leslie.'

Lindy smiled her absent smile and nodded. Danny and Irene shook hands with Leslie. They had no idea. No idea at all. Sharon led them into the living room. Irene admired the upholstery, the pictures. Danny said, almost as a reminder to himself, that he really ought to get Sharon a more recent picture of the two boys, they were growing so fast.

'Come here, Xiong!' Sharon summoned her nephew. The little boy obliged. 'You've grown really tall, haven't you?' she murmured in admiring tones. Xiong drew himself to his full height, pleased with himself.

'Me, too!' added his brother.

'Me, too!' Sharon grinned at Ming. 'So you are! Do you want to go to the playroom?' The two boys jumped up and clapped their hands. Sharon had a playroom equipped just for them. It was a treasure trove of games and toys, and the boys just loved the water guns and the tent. 'I'll take them,' offered Leslie, glad of the excuse, and, taking one little hand in each of hers, she led them in the direction of the playroom.

'Does she look familiar, Mum?' asked Sharon. Lindy's face

was a blank. She shook her head. Danny frowned, Irene looked askance at her. 'Chan Meng's daughter.' Sharon enunciated each syllable slowly.

'Oh, you mean the electronic kingpin,' said Danny, recognition dawning in his eyes. 'Not the one that's rumoured to have underworld connections?' cried Irene in alarm.

'Really?' queried Sharon. 'I hadn't heard that.'

'The same family who owns the casinos in Genting Highlands, isn't that the one?' asked Irene.

'No, no,' Danny corrected his wife, 'That's Chung Meng. This is Chan Meng.'

'Oh,' said Irene. 'You mean the one with Indonesian and Thai business connections.'

'That's the one,' nodded Danny.

'Meng's daughter,' said Lindy slowly.

'Yes,' replied Sharon.

'I don't understand,' said Danny.

'It's a small world, isn't it, Mother?' said Sharon. 'Such a small world.'

'That's Singapore for you,' said Danny robustly. 'Everybody knows everybody else—or is related to somebody.'

'Let me take a good look at her,' said Lindy after a long pause. 'She's got his eyes and his mouth, and her mother's nose,' said Sharon.

'Ahhh,' replied Lindy, letting the word out in a long breath, and nodding. No one said anything for a while.

'I've often wondered whom Meng married,' Lindy finally admitted softly.

'Elsie Soong,' said Sharon quickly. 'She was at Harvard Law School when he met her. In Boston.' The ghost of a smile touched the fringes of Lindy's eyes. Knowing Meng, it must have been a whirlwind romance. 'Leslie's their only child,' said Sharon soberly. 'Her mother died in childbirth.'

'Oh.' Lindy's voice was small.

'The poor thing,' said Irene.

'And her father? How is he?' asked Danny, giving voice to the thought his mother would not ask.

'I've never met him,' said Sharon. 'He's always travelling. Leslie hardly sees him herself.'

'I see,' said Lindy.

'Perhaps if—' began Irene, putting a gentle hand on her mother-in-law's arm. But Lindy was already shaking her head before the sentence could be completed.

'Thank you, Irene,' she replied. 'But it's been a long time. Too much water has flowed under the bridge.'

'Oh, Mother, surely there's no harm—' But Sharon was interrupted in mid-sentence by Lindy shaking her head once more.

'I'm glad you're friends, Sharon,' said Lindy. 'She seems a nice girl.'

'She's my right-hand person,' acknowledged Sharon.

'Let's just let things be,' said Lindy. Danny remembered, with a sudden pang, that that was exactly what Lindy had said when she had told him about the divorce all those years ago, when he had raged at them both: 'It's both your fault!'

She had bowed her head then, and murmured, 'Let's just let things be.'

But I don't want it to be!' he had stormed, feeling ambushed, abducted, shanghaied, betrayed, rejected.

'It's what your father wants,' his mother had told him.

'Is it what you want?' he had raged at her. Guiltily, she had shaken her head.

'Then why don't you do something about it!' he had cried, knowing it was not what he wanted.

'You don't understand, Danny,' she had tried to tell him.

'You don't understand!' he had flung at her. It had taken him years to reconcile himself to his rage and her submission. He had blamed her for her passivity for years. It had, in fact, been a relief when he had met Phornsiri and discovered that she wasn't the voluptuous witch he imagined. He'd found, to his amazement, that he liked her. Grudgingly, he'd even come to the conclusion that she was much better for his father than his mother had been. She had a zest for life, an appreciation of the extraordinary that had energised his father in his later years.

It wasn't, in fact, until after he had married Irene that his perspective had gradually altered. In their daily conversations, whenever he tended to be impatient or dismissive, it was Irene, the mother of his children, who often reminded him, unobtrusively, 'After all, she is your mother.' It was Irene who helped heal the breach by initiating the occasional visit, the casual call, the by-the-way invitation. It was Irene who would pick up a little souvenir on their trips abroad for her mother-in-law. At first, it used to annoy him. Because it reminded him so tellingly of his mother on that last trip they'd taken together to Disney World. Lindy, like Irene, he realised with a shock of recognition, were upholders of the status quo. Not earthshakers, they. Nor pioneers forging a new lifestyle. Continuity was what kept them going. Family. Familiarity. For the sake of his father. For the sake of her children. That was how his mother had organised her life, along lines he and his sister had never been raised to recognise or accept. It was called destiny. Or peace of mind. It explained why his mother had been able to let her children develop and grow, and to lead separate lives from her own. It explained why she acknowledged but did not claim them. Because, long ago, Lindy had realised that they had their own lives to live, their own destinies to chart.

from The Mother and the Muscle and the Making of Love

Ovidia Yu

Characters
MAY
MARGARET (MOTHER)
NICHOLAS
ALEX
STEVEN

MAY: I'm going to call Nicholas and tell him what's happening here!

(MAY *turns and storms away from her mother.*)

MARGARET: I really don't see what there is to tell him!

MAY: (*On phone*) He's just twenty-something years old! What do you mean what does he look like? He looks like a normal human being *lor*, what do you expect him to look like! Quite tall. His father is dead or something, I don't know. I think he's one of those body-building types. He's got these awful muscles just bulging up all over his body … it's really obscene! What do you expect me to do? You think I haven't tried talking sense into her? Why don't you come back and do something! I'm the one who's been looking after her on my own all this time! I think that it's about time you pulled some of your own weight! What do I want you to do? I want you to buy yourself a ticket, get on a plane and get back here! Never mind what is she going to think. If only you guys came home a bit more often or just called her a bit more often, maybe she would have enough to think about without going off with some gigolo!

(*Lights down on* MAY *and up on* NICHOLAS.)

NICHOLAS: (*Walking around as he talks on handphone*) Don't shout, Jie! I can hear you perfectly well … (*Pause*) Huh? What did you say? Yes, yes, I know I heard you, but just say that again, please, do you mind? (*Pause.*) Well, Jie, I don't see why you're getting so upset about it. After all (*Chuckling*), Mum's old enough to know what's she's doing; you don't want her staying at home and moping all the time, do you? If she's got a man friend who she enjoys spending time with, I think it's just great … in fact, I think that it's wonderful! Especially at her age! (*Off phone.*) Sharon, May says that Mum's got herself a boyfriend! (*Back on phone.*) Sharon says it's great too … (*Off phone.*) What's that, Darling? (*Laughs. Back on phone.*) Jie, Sharon says that maybe Mum is trying to get you to take a hint, as in it's not that hard to get yourself a guy … (*Laughs to a pause.*) Oh … No, Jie I didn't really think that was so funny … Sharon only meant— What do you mean Mum's guy is too young for *you* … He's what? (NICHOLAS *looks at the phone. His sister has hung up.*) My mother has a boyfriend who is twenty-nine years old? (*Exit* NICHOLAS.)

(*Lights up on* MAY.)

MAY: I walked into the living room one evening and I saw my mother standing at the balcony. With him. With his arm. His arm was around her shoulders. What do you mean there's no point in getting so worked up? I'm not supposed to get worked up?

Okay. Fine. But maybe you would like to tell me how is somebody supposed to react when she finds out that her retired, widowed, 62-year-old mother is seeing a man in his late twenties? My mother brazenly tells me that she is going to SSO concerts with a man who's 29 years old. I didn't think anything of it at first. My mother has been a teacher for a long time. She's always going around trying to get young people to improve themselves. I was even glad that she had found somebody to go to her precious concerts with … Then after their concerts they would go to hotel coffee houses where he drinks coffee and she drinks tea. Coffee houses where anybody might see them … any of her friends; any of my friends … Any of *his* friends …) Even that was all right, I thought. Anyone seeing them would probably just think, 'How sweet. Mother and son spending some time together.' They might even think, 'How sweet, Grandmother and grandson spending some time together.'

MARGARET: (*Unseen*) Let's not get too carried away!

MAY: I didn't know that there was all this arm-around-shoulder business going on! And she refuses to say that it's just an innocent relationship. Is it just an innocent mother-son relationship? I asked her. She wouldn't give me a straight answer. All that she would say was …

(MARGARET *appears in a separate spot.*)

MARGARET: I know what I'm doing. I don't see why you're making such a fuss about nothing, May.

MAY: Then you are saying that it's nothing?

MARGARET: May, trust me. Please just trust me and stop being so suspicious! I really don't know what comes over you sometimes!

MAY: That man looks disgusting! I can't describe him to you, you have to see him for yourself. Disgusting! Bulging muscles all over the place!

MARGARET: Alex is a nice boy. He's a very nice boy.

MAY: Huh!

MARGARET: Huh!

MAY: He's noisy! And he's always banging into things. Or playing the piano!

MARGARET: At least, unlike some young people these days, he is polite.

(MAY *turns her back. Lights go out on her.*)

MARGARET: What I remember most about the years when the children were all growing up is the noise. It wasn't a bad noise, but it was a lot of noise. All three of my children were very vocal as they grew up. My late husband always said that they got that from me—I always loved to talk. My husband was always saying that he couldn't get me to shut up ... I remember being glad that May could speak up for herself. I didn't want her to end up getting bullied by men when she grew up, just because she never learned to speak up for herself. (*Small laugh.*) I never thought she would use it against me. (*Pause.*) But I'm still glad that she can speak up for herself. (*Pause. Change of lighting. Change of mood.*) There was always this interplay of different voices, different moods. It worked together like different music blending high and low—getting faster together, building up, getting emotional, reaching a climax, slowing down ... then different voices breaking out, a discordant note claiming its own identity ... but on the whole we got along harmoniously ... me and the children ... When my late husband wasn't at home, that is. Nicholas was always quieter than May, but from the time he started to talk, Steven was a man with his own opinion about things ...

(MAY *enters* MARGARET's *spotlight.*)

MAY: I've spoken to both Nicholas and Steven. I asked them to come back to talk to you.

MARGARET: (*Surprised but pleased*) Nicholas and Steven—are coming? Here? When? How come?

MAY: Nick will be here by next week, I think. He will let us know once he gets his flight fixed up. I told him that it wasn't going to be any use him trying to talk any sense into you over the phone, even though it's for your own good.

(*Pause.* MARGARET *looks at* MAY, *then looks away. She controls herself and speaks calmly and brightly.*)

MARGARET: And Steve? You spoke to Steve too? What did he say? When will *he* be here?

(*Separate lights up on* STEVEN.)

(STEVEN *is laughing, laughing, laughing throughout his piece.*)

156

STEVEN: I know, I know! Let me guess, May—the guy is a vampire or something, right? That's why you're getting so worked up. Only you don't dare to say so over the phone in case it's bugged and they find out that you're crazy and take away your big time ministry job … no, no, no—I am taking you seriously, Jie. I always take you seriously, don't you know? Oh, but the first time you met him with Mum it was in the day time, right? So he's not a vampire … then he must be some other species of the undead. Or no—don't tell me, I know—he's some kind of serial killer, right? All his other wives died horribly under mysterious circumstances and he's got Ma hypnotised so that she won't look at all the evidence that you've collected … I never knew that taking someone out for a concert could be such a dangerous business. Remind me not to stop to help any little old ladies across the road, okay? Somebody should break it gently to this guy that even if he does manage to win the old lady over, she doesn't exactly have a fortune to sign over to him—but wait … actually that's all right, he can always take out an insurance policy on her, hor? I might go into this line of work myself… (*Listening pause.*) Of course I'm *concerned* about Mother, May! I just don't think that you— (*Another listening pause.*) I don't know if I can … right now things are really quite tight … hey, so tell me: Is this guy cute or not? May? May, are you there? (*Shrugs and hangs up.*)

(*Lights down on* STEVEN.)

MAY: I really don't know what Steven's plans are. (*Pause.*) Don't you feel funny being seen with a boy who's younger than your youngest son?

MARGARET: Anybody who sees us together probably thinks that Alex is my son. They are probably thinking what a good, filial son he is!

MAY: Not the way he holds your hand and tries to put an arm around you every chance that he gets!

ALEX: My father also married an older woman. When you consider that women tend to live longer than men, it makes sense for men to marry older women, doesn't it?

(MARGARET *and* ALEX *go for a walk, holding hands, then sit down at a table.* MARGARET *motions to* MAY, *who joins them ungraciously.*)

ALEX: Well, I told you that the curry here was good, didn't I?

MARGARET: I ate far too much!

MAY: A bit too rich for me. Everything here is so high-cholesterol.

ALEX: Well, I think it was good!

MAY: (*To* MARGARET) You should be more careful about your cholesterol!

MARGARET: (*To* MAY) Would you believe I forgot my lipstick ... I knew there was something ... I knew there was some reason why I should bring my purse along with me ...

ALEX: What's wrong?

MARGARET: No, no—it's nothing, nothing ...

MAY: She forgot her lipstick.

ALEX: (*After a pause during which he scrutinises* MARGARET) You look fine to me.

MARGARET: Oh! Thank you.

ALEX: Besides, it's better that you let your make-up get a bit faded than that you do things to your face at the table in front of everybody.

MARGARET: (*A bit taken aback*) Not that touching up with a bit of lipstick is putting on make-up at the table ...

ALEX: You shouldn't be so concerned about covering your face up. You really look fine, you know. My mother always used to say that it was very bad manners to—

MARGARET: (*With a laugh, to* MAY) Listen to him! Quoting the wisdom of his mother to me!

ALEX: You really look very all right, Meg!

MARGARET: Well, thank you.

MAY: If you want to use lipstick I don't think that you should let what anybody says stop you.

MARGARET: Thank you.

ALEX: Anyway, there's still some colour left on. I don't think that you should worry about it.

(MARGARET c*omes forward and sits down on a stool in a downstage spotlight as the rest of the scene fades. She looks outward as into a dressing-table mirror, and holds another small hand mirror in her hand.*)

MARGARET: I was a bit taken aback when I realised that I was afraid to let that boy see me without my make-up on. I really was. Which is so stupid, right? As though I believe that he is so stupid that he can't tell what I really look like just because I put on a bit of colour … (*Small laugh.*) It's almost a standard joke, isn't it? Girls who are so sensitive about their appearances? Women who consider their lipstick an essential along with taxi fare home and money for the phone … (*Puts hand mirror down.*) But it was more than that. It wasn't just a female affectation. I realised there, sitting at the table with him, that I was really afraid of letting him see me without my make-up on. As though I was afraid of giving him too much of a shock … I never felt like that with my late husband. But then I don't think that my late husband really noticed what I looked like … I suppose that that's one advantage of getting married when you're both very young. No matter how much you both change as the years pass, the strongest image that remains is of both of you—young.

MAY: (*to* ALEX) Look, Alex. It's not that I don't like you, you know. I'm just afraid that you are getting a bit out of your depth. I don't want my mother to get hurt. The thing is, Alex, women sometimes get a bit funny in the head around this time … What I'm trying to say, Alex is—what exactly do you know about menopause?

MARGARET: I can't explain, even to myself, why I kept on taking birth control pills after my Robert passed away. In fact, if you think about it, it didn't make any real sense for me to go on taking them for years before he died. After all, we had separate bedrooms and no sex for the last thirty years of our life together. Steve was more or less an accident. And then, once he was born, that was the end of it as far as we were concerned. And now, because I am still taking birth control pills, my change of life still hasn't come. Actually this is supposed to be good for me ... less chance of getting osteoperosis, you know ... But my change of life hasn't come yet. Now my periods are long and very, very heavy ... but in a strange way I am afraid to have them stop for good. As though when they stop I will be leaving one part of my life behind me forever. I will no longer be a biologically functioning 'mother.' I will no longer be a full woman.

MAY: What is a mother, anyway. Somebody who sacrifices her life for you, someone who devotes her life to bringing you up and preparing you for your life. Someone whom you are supposed to owe everything to, because she has done all these things for you ... And how is a girl supposed to repay her mother for all those sacrifices that she has made? By turning around and sacrificing everything for her children, of course. And so on and so forth.

But none of us asked to be born, you know. It was our parents' choice to have us children. So why is it always us that owes so much to them? I think that parents owe their children something too, for bringing them into the world just to satisfy some need that *they* had for a 'complete' family. Maybe they were just some mixed up kids who wanted to add some meaning to their lives and didn't know any other way to do it. So they decide to have a baby that they can unload everything on. An insecure mother, a father who doesn't care either way—but since his wife wants a child so much, okay lah—you need to have children if you want to play happy families. It's not very fair, especially when the parents don't play very well. As well as allergies and bad eyesight, a child can inherit low self-esteem, bad organisational habits and a warped value-system. And then this kid that's been blessed with all this is supposed to go on thinking how wonderful its mother is for the rest of its life.

I try to be glad that I was born, but I don't always manage. Now that my father is dead and I am the only child left in Singapore, I know that I should keep an eye on my mother. But what's the use of being here to keep an eye on her when I can't stop her from doing stupid things like this?

MARGARET: I always respected my mother. She was a very strong woman. She came from a whole generation of very strong women. That was the generation that survived the war that killed their husbands. They survived and they managed to bring up their children on their own. My mother brought up the six of us single-handedly. She had seven children to begin with, but her eldest son was too old when the war came. My dai-koh was almost fourteen years old and he was killed together with my father. So I was left the oldest in the family. And she managed to keep us all together and bring us all up. And I don't think we turned out too badly.

(*Light fades on* MARGARET. *Light comes up on* ALEX, *who is in competition briefs, trying out different poses as he speaks.*)

ALEX: I have found out that having muscles doesn't create the kind of impression that people think it does. If you don't have muscles then everybody thinks that you are a wimp. If you have muscles, then everybody thinks that you are dumb or stupid or something. Or they are always trying to get you to go and do powder milk commercials for them. I used to get bullied in school. That's the reason why I first started working out in the CC. But now when people look at me, especially other people my age … especially girls my age, they always seem to think straight away that I must be dumb. Either that or they think that I am stuck-up. Like only dumb people have muscles and once they got muscles they must be stuck-up.

(*Enter* NICHOLAS *with* MAY.)

MAY: See? That's him over there. That one.

NICHOLAS: But he's huge!

MAY: I told you.

NICHOLAS: You didn't tell me how huge ...

MAY: Of course I did!

NICHOLAS: But you always exaggerate. I thought you were just exaggerating again!

MAY: So what do you think now?

NICHOLAS: He's huge!

MAY: Nicholas!

NICHOLAS: No ... it's just that I—I can't imagine Ma knowing somebody like that!

(*Enter* STEVEN.)

MAY: Steve! What are you doing here! I thought you weren't even listening to what I was telling you—(*Impulsively*, MAY *embraces her brother.*)

STEVEN: Oh, you told me something? Nah ... I just thought it was time to come back and see how everything's going back here ...

NICHOLAS: Good to see you, Bro!

STEVEN: (*Looking at* ALEX) Quite cute, lah. (*To* MAY.) You should have told me. I would have come back sooner!

MAY: Why don't you guys see if you can talk to him? Nothing that I say seems to get through. To either of them.

(*Exit* MAY.)

(NICHOLAS, ALEX *and* STEVEN *sit talking. Or rather,* NICHOLAS *and* STEVEN *are talking while* ALEX *listens.*)

NICHOLAS: Our mother was always very particular about how we looked and how we were dressed and so on.

STEVEN: I don't remember that. Was she?

NICHOLAS: Of course she was. Of course you remember.

STEVEN: I thought May was the one who was always making a big fuss about what we were wearing...

NICHOLAS: There was a time when we our family was quite poor. Even now money is still a bit tight, but there was a really bad period … And then our father had a fight with his boss and decided to quit his job there and then, so things got even worse.

STEVEN: I remember that. Twenty-four hours' notice, I remember that! Mum was screaming at him and you and May were crying. I remember that!

NICHOLAS: No, you don't. You're remembering what we told you much later. You were only a baby then. Our mother was scolding Dad and saying, 'What are we going to do? Are you going to sit there while we all starve?' And telling him that his bad temper was going to be the death of all of us … And all the time that she was going on and on I remember she was ironing our school uniforms. No matter what happened, we had to keep up appearances. She had the plastic sprinkler in one hand and she was waving it around while she was scolding him …

ALEX: Why?

NICHOLAS: Why?

ALEX: Yeah. 'Why?'

(*Pause.*)

STEVEN: Dad hit her. I remember that.

ALEX: I mean, why was it so important to go on keeping up appearances?

[*end of extract*]

Letters

Rasiah Halil

Home is where the heart is, they say
where shall I send my letters
my heart is everywhere
in Singapore, Malaysia, Brunei, US, UK, Canada
shall I make smoke signals
or send the pigeons
or like the eternal wanderer
send my letters
without words
through infinite space
homeless
& seek refuge
in the hearts
of those I love?

Rachel, Her Parents, My Mother and I
Lai Ah Eng

November 1989

It was on a typical winter's day that I sat on the low wall outside King's College, Cambridge, to eat my lunch. Sandwiches again. Egg, tuna, bacon, mayonnaise, even corn and capsicum—there were so many kinds that oh, I could scream at the sight of any sandwich! Nonetheless I ate them almost every day, for they were about the only quick and affordable lunch foods available. And that day, just like every other day, I swallowed my awful lunch stoically and calmly. I did not scream. That would effectively break down the discipline that I had so painstakingly built up over the two years of writing up my doctoral dissertation in a cold windowless basement cubicle. 'You're in the last lap. You can't afford to break down. You have to stay calm,' I reminded myself of this every day. It was as if eating a sandwich every day was part of the torturous process of writing and a test of the persistence, determination and endurance needed to finish the task.

I turned my attention to King's College Chapel. The sun was shining on its stained glass, bringing out their colours to contrast against its grey walls. The last of the autumn leaves were gently falling down from the old tree beside it, and some of them drifted onto the many bicycles leaning against the low wall. Looking at this quintessential Cambridge scene of chapel, tree, wall and bicycles, a sense of tranquillity began to descend upon me. I could feel myself grow less uptight about my sandwich and my dissertation. But all of a sudden, I was startled by a strange familiarity of the view before me. It was not that familiarity that came from my everyday life in Cambridge as a student. It came from a distant past, from my childhood, in a place far away and far different from Cambridge. It hit me as suddenly as it appeared. Why, it was the background scene in a picture I received many years ago! In that picture, Rachel and her fiancé were sitting on a bicycle, he on the seat and she on the bar. They were beside the low wall, and behind them was the

165

tree and the chapel. Rachel had sent me the picture to say that she was getting married to Dirk although she did not say where it was taken. But that day, so suddenly and so many years later, I saw it again. Of course, it was taken here, right here in Cambridge, in front of King's College Chapel right where I was sitting! By the time I had finished swallowing my sandwich, I was almost a quivering mass of shock and excitement at the sudden recognition. And of determination to meet Rachel again. But how?

Just then, who should come along but Richard, my PhD comrade in common suffering. Richard was one of those brilliant young students who cycled up and down King's Parade trying to clear their mental blocks, and who made you feel better when they claimed they had not written a single paragraph in two whole weeks, but only to tell you the next day that they had submitted their dissertations and found jobs.

'You look like you have just made a significant theoretical breakthrough,' he said.

'I have just made the most amazing and unexpected discovery.'

I told Richard my story and that I wanted to trace Rachel. After staring hard and thoughtfully at me, he said, 'My grandfather was in the colonial service in India and he is listed in *Who's Who in Great Britain*. Why don't you check that?' That evening, I did just that. One week later, I was on the train from Cambridge to Brockenhurst, Hampshire, to meet Rachel Wenban-Smith and her parents.

1965

I was eleven when I first met Rachel. My parents, four older sisters, younger twin brothers and I lived in a wooden shophouse of which the front served as a coffeeshop and the back was our living quarters. It was very small—the shop had just six small wooden tables and some chairs, and the living area consisted of one bedroom with three beds (two small ones for my parents and brothers, and a bigger one for us five girls), one bathroom and a wash area-cum-kitchen. Pa and his elder brother had come from Hainan to Malaya to look for work during the economic depression of the late 1920s. For several years Pa worked as odd-job labourer, rubber tapper, coffeeshop assistant and cook in Trengganu, Pahang, Riau and Singapore. Then he and his brother set up their coffeestall in Sentul on the outskirts of Kuala Lumpur, in a squatter settlement of Chinese and Indian immigrants, close to the railway labour lines. That stall was the forerunner of our shophouse. My father's brother died of illness during the Japanese Occupation and my sad father buried him with his own hands. After the war, Pa returned to Hainan only to find conditions there worse than in Malaya. And civil war between the Communists and Kuomintang was already breaking out. He married a war widow and they returned to Malaya. Pa continued to work at his coffeestall, adding plank and zinc extensions to it as his family grew.

Ma first worked at washing and ironing army uniforms at the British barracks near our home. Then she became a domestic help when her tontine scheme partner absconded with the money and she got into debt. I remember how we children, especially my brothers and I, missed her so much when she was away at work. We would jump with joy when she returned in the evening, shouting, 'Ma's come back! Ma's come back!'. Ma left home early at half-past-six in the morning and cycled for nearly forty-five minutes, sometimes getting down to push her bicycle up the steep slopes of Kenny Hill, to get to her workplace. She had a room in the servants' quarters but preferred to come home to her children, unless her employers held night functions. Then she had to work overtime.

I sometimes followed Ma to work. While she cleaned, I would explore the house or watch Peh Deh Teck, the 'cookie' as he referred to himself, fix strange dishes in the kitchen. But I would quickly run and hide in the servants' quarters when I heard Ma's employers come towards the kitchen or their car come up the driveway. Ma taught me to do that. Actually she was not allowed to bring her children to work. Once, I was sitting on the kitchen counter beside the refrigerator, watching Peh Deh Teck cooking. I was so absorbed in observing the strange concoction he was stirring I did not notice that my mother's employer had come into the kitchen. When I did, I wanted to jump off and run away. But it was too late. I was too immobilised with terror to move. He seemed to come towards me, a big, intimidating figure, as if to seize me.

I froze with fear. But all he did was to come to the fridge to get a drink. I think he even patted my head.

It was in no small part through my mother's work as a domestic maid that, as a child, I learnt about the outside world and a world that was very different from the one I lived in. From the leftover party foods Ma brought home, I learnt of the existence of cold meats and salads, stinking cheese, different kinds of jam and pastries, Jamaican rum in beautiful bottles and Cuban cigars much more stylish than the cheap Indian cheroots we sold in our shop. Ma also brought home magazines, cards and stamps with wonderful pictures of European places and paintings, African savannahs with leaping gazelles and grazing zebras, and people in exciting costumes. I developed my interests in reading, painting, designing and stamp collecting in part from these rich discards. Through my secret visits to my mother's workplace, I discovered the convenience and comfort of sitting toilet bowls, thick carpets, washing machines and marbled floors. On those occasions, I often sat on the toilet bowl just for the sheer enjoyment of it. And I flushed it frequently just to watch and hear the water gush—it was music and magic to me. My mother also talked about the strange ways of *ang mo* people, such as the joining of their single beds on Saturday nights, and nude sunbathing in the balcony on weekends. And it was through her job that I came to meet Rachel. For one day, Ma came home from work and announced that '*ang mo towkay*'s daughter' wanted to visit us.

Rachel came one hot afternoon. She came in a little grey Fiat car which she parked right beside our house and promptly caused a stir among passers-by, neighbours and our coffeeshop customers. I was the boldest, most chatty, and spoke the best English in my family, so naturally I acted as guide and interpreter. At first, I was a little shy. But I was not afraid, even though Rachel was quite big and it was the first time I had come so close to an *ang mo*. I noticed the long golden hair on her arms and her greenish eyes. She also had a wide smile and laughed easily. My sisters smiled and giggled often but did not speak because they did not speak much English. My parents hovered in the background, and Ma kept saying, ' Ask her to eat! Ask her to eat lah!' The table in the centre of our shop had been laden with piles of prawncrackers, cakes, peanuts and some Green Spot drinks.

At the end of her visit, Rachel took two photographs—one of my sisters and me, and another of me alone. And like any schoolgirl my age, I asked for her autograph. She flipped through my collection of signatures first. 'Deep in the Ocean, there is a Rock. On it is Written: FORGET ME NOT' made her chuckle. She laughed really loud at this other entry: 'Drink Hot Coffee, Drink Hot Tea. Burn Your Lips and Remember ME!'. Then she thought for a while and penned the following:

> Be good, sweet maid, and let who will be clever,
> Do noble things, nor dream them all the day,
> And so make life, death, and that great for-ever,
> One grand, sweet song.

I learnt it by heart and remember to this day this verse from Kingsley's 'Farewell.'

A week after her visit, Rachel came to take me to my first pantomime. I had attended and even acted in my school concerts before, but somehow I knew that this occasion was different. Ma dressed me in my finest, which was my Chinese New Year frilly frock. It still fitted quite well, as my mother was always wise enough to buy clothes one to two sizes bigger. My sister lent me her imitation pearl necklace and her small purse in which I put the precious two dollars my father gave me for the outing. He said I could buy an ice-cream for myself and one for Rachel with this pocket money, the biggest sum I had ever received. I felt very special, almost grand like a princess, riding in Rachel's car. It was a rare occasion that I got to sit in a car, and definitely the first time I was 'chauffeured' to an occasion specially arranged for me.

It was also the first time I had ever entered the Kuala Lumpur Town Hall. How else could a child from a place like Sentul feel but overwhelmingly impressed and overawed by the red carpet, the velvet curtain, the rows upon rows of plush concert seats and a grand stage with the biggest piano she had ever seen? Especially when her school hall had a cement floor, no seats, no stage, no curtains and a very old piano? Oh, this town hall was absolutely grand, the grandest in the world! But nothing, neither my dressing nor my mother's reminders to behave myself, prepared me for the audience. As Rachel and I walked down the aisle to our seats somewhere in the front rows, I noticed them and they noticed me. By the time we got to our seats and sat down, I had reached the height of self-consciousness and curiosity.

They were the audience. A noisy sea of golden-haired children with their golden-haired mothers and black-and-white Chinese *amahs*. The children looked just like the fairies, angels and little boys and girls in my school's story books. Many had freckles and quite a few were buck-toothed. I noticed especially the girls. They had the loveliest smocked frocks and wore ribbons in their hair. I was equally struck by their English and accents. I knew their language, but they spoke it differently and I could only make out bits of what they said. I knew I stood out among the crowd. Because I felt so many pairs of blue, green or light brown eyes turn to stare at me. I smiled shyly at those who smiled. One girl touched me on my hand. I did not dare stare back at those who stared or made comments, but I stole looks at them out of the corners of my eyes. Throughout the pantomime, my attention fluctuated between the characters on stage and the children around me.

My young heart was completely won over by the Ugly Duckling's music, dances and songs. There were so many children acting, and deep in my heart I wished I too could be on the stage because I loved to sing. I was most impressed by the Ugly Duckling and never quite understood why it was considered ugly. It looked very adorable, just like the yellow and grey ducklings my mother reared in our backyard.

'Was the show good to watch?' Ma asked me when I got home.

'Full of *ang mo kia*,' I replied. But I did not tell her that I felt somewhat like the Ugly Duckling. No, not ugly. But different. I just felt different.

Rachel sent me an atlas as a farewell gift when she returned to England some weeks later. It was British-based, with maps and geographical details about the British Isles but it also had topographical and country maps of all the continents. For years, that atlas was my window to the world and my source of inspiration to travel. I never got tired of climbing mountains, crossing rivers and seas, and visiting exotic places as I poured over the maps of Europe, Asia, Africa, The Americas, Australia. The atlas also reinforced my idea during my early teen years that I would not get married but spend my time travelling around the world with my good school friends. And throughout my school years, I never never failed to score an 'A' for Geography.

I sent Rachel a handmade thank-you and farewell card which had a picture of flowers decorated with silver dust. Over the next few years, we wrote to each other occasionally before we lost touch. Her last letters included the 'bicycle' picture of herself and her fiancé, two photographs of her wedding reception, and finally a note to say that she had given birth to a daughter and was living in Holland.

December 1989

The train journey from Cambridge to Brockenhurst took nearly three hours. When the train stopped at Southampton on the way, I saw a black man with two big bags get off. He looked uncertain and nervous, yet tried to maintain calm and control. Maybe it was his first trip to Southampton, or maybe he was a new immigrant to this country. I don't know why but when I saw him, I thought of my uncle who lived in Bracknell, Berkshire.

Uncle Swang and Aunt Wah Mai were a classic case of the faithful Hainanese husband-wife team of butler-cook and domestic maid so highly regarded by English employers in colonial Malaya. They had decided to follow their *ang mo towkay* back to England to continue working for him, bringing their four young children with them. I remember waving goodbye to them and to my cousins at the Kuala Lumpur railway station where they were taking the train to Singapore, then the boat to England. That was way back in 1963. The next time I saw them was on their first visit back to Kuala Lumpur about eight years later. Aunt Wah Mai's eyes filled with tears every now and then as she talked. And what a sight my mother and aunt were as they stood waiting for a taxi to take my

171

aunt back. One was in her samfoo and clogs, the other in summer dress, sunhat and heeled shoes. After this visit, the two fictive cousins who had emigrated from the same Blue Bamboo Village in Hainan never saw each other again because Auntie Wah Mai died soon after. Uncle Swang came back to Kuala Lumpur once to remarry. He also tried to matchmake me with his son who, much to his displeasure, was dating an *ang mo* girl.

'He's like an ang mo kia now,' Uncle lamented. But I was too busy studying and planning my travels abroad to be at all interested in men and marriage. Besides, would I, or for that matter, my Chinese-British cousin, have agreed to an arranged marriage?

I once visited my Uncle Swang in Berkshire, partly so on behalf of my mother and partly out of my own wish. That was soon after I came to Cambridge. I nearly fell off the steps of the railway station when I saw him. He was in a stiff, immaculate suit of white top and black trousers, complete with white gloves and black bow tie. He had come to fetch me in his employer's Jaguar. We drove deep into the English countryside before turning into the driveway of a grand manor, and went to a small annexe that was my Uncle's home. Throughout, I wondered how he and his family managed to survive in the isolated midst of this very upper-class English place all those years. During my visit, we spoke in Hainanese. But I also overheard him speak in English to the people of the manor. After nearly twenty-five years in England, he still spoke 'cookie' English with the heaviest Hainanese accent.

Rachel was waiting for me when I got off the train. We recognised each other right away, even though she was in her forties and I in my thirties.

'You look just as pretty!'

'And you have the same warm smile!'

We hugged each other like old friends. Along the way to Rachel's farm cottage, we marvelled at my recognition of the 'bicycle' picture, and laughed with deep pleasure at the surprise I was giving her by turning up to visit her in England, twenty-five years after she first visited me in Malaysia. And what coincidence—we were both students of social anthropology in Cambridge! It was only then that I learnt about her fieldwork among the aborigines in the Gombak setttlement when she was in Kuala Lumpur. And was it another coincidence that I was researching the subject of ethnic relations? We almost squealed with excitement at each other's work.

I finally met Mr and Mrs Wenban-Smith in Rachel's home that day, long after I had first known about them. They did not look that big anymore; in fact, they both looked on the small side of average among the English. Nor did they look intimidating at all; on the contrary, they looked extremely kind and warm. And of course I no longer felt like running away on seeing them; I had come specially to meet them, both on behalf of my mother and because I wanted to. We sat by the fireside of crackling fir cones, eating scones and drinking tea as we chatted.

One of the first topics of our conversation was, of course, my mother. I told them her history. 'Nowadays, she spends her time rearing chickens and ducks and feeding stray cats,' I added. Mother had returned to her peasant past after her job with the Wenban-Smiths ended, and sold fat fowls to neighbours and friends for income.

'What about the cook?'

After the Wenban-Smiths left Malaysia, Peh Deh Teck worked for some years as a food caterer on the Kuala Lumpur-Singapore night mail train before he died of an illness. Like many Hainanese immigrants of his time, he lived and died alone, without a family.

'He cooked an excellent version of pork chops and *enche kabin* chicken,' recalled Mrs Wenban-Smith. I told her she had tasted the delicacy and legacy of the Hainanese cook.

Rachel wanted to know if my little coffeeshop-house was still standing. I told them the long story. Which was that it was torn down by a land developer who did not compensate us because we were squatters. My father was so devastated that his hair turned grey within a month and he seldom spoke. For two years, he worked in his friend's coffeeshop as an assistant for long hours, seven days a week, earning a meagre sum of $100 a month. Then he took over a small drinks stall from a former neighbour who wanted to retire home to India. At the age of sixty, my father started all over again. But luckily, this time, he had the help of my mother and sister.

'A few years later, my father felt secure enough to enjoy his one and only luxury each evening—a small bottle of Guinness Stout!' I laughed. That drink was the indulgence of working class men of his generation. They believed it renewed their strength so that they could work their bodies to complete exhaustion again the next day. But at least it was better than the illicit *samsu* distilled for consumption by the poorest of the poor—it slowly destroyed their insides as it made them its addicts. During those difficult years, I did not stop school to help, unlike my sisters. They told me they could manage and that I should continue with my studies. That was the luck and luxury of being one of the youngest in the family. 'But I worked to pay my way through university,' I was glad and proud to say.

Mr and Mrs Wenban-Smith recalled the Kuala Lumpur of the 1960s that they knew. Mrs Wenban-Smith was thrilled that I remembered her driving past my house once a week when she sent Sally and two others from the Association for the Blind back to their home further up the street where I lived. She was then a volunteer with the Association and still kept in touch with Sally. 'Now I sit in the local committee of Amnesty International and work as a volunteer for the United Nations Children's Education Fund,' she said confidently.

I never knew what Mr Wenban-Smith was doing in Kuala Lumpur in the 1960s when I was a child. Then, he and his wife were simply my mother's *ang mo towkay*. It was only when I checked *Who's Who in Great Britain* did I find out about his long and distinguished career. It was in the colonial and diplomatic services, particularly in education and welfare, mostly in various parts of colonial Africa and for a shorter period in immediate pre- and post-independent Malaysia. So quite naturally we talked about the problems of post-colonial societies. About their elites and political cultures. About corruption and nepotism. About tribal, ethnic and class distinctions. About issues of authoritarianism and democracy. We also talked about the May 13, 1969 riots in Malaysia. They had left Kuala Lumpur for retirement in England one month before the ethnic conflict happened, and were shocked by the news. 'My entire family nearly perished and Sentul experienced a "second May 13th" two weeks later.' I told them what happened.

We talked about our present lives. Rachel had three children and the eldest was already twenty. I had married and settled in Singapore, and made frequent trips back to Malaysia to see my folks … And so we chatted like old friends, my mother's ex-employers, their daughter and I. About the places, people, experiences and contexts that had first brought us together twenty-five years ago in Malaysia, and again that afternoon in England.

But all too soon, it was time for me to leave. Mrs Wenban-Smith gave me a hug.

'I am so glad you do not have to work like your mother had to.'

'You know, when Rachel visited us, my mother told me that I too would go to university if I was clever like Rachel,' I replied with a smile.

I hugged Mrs Wenban-Smith goodbye, just like I hugged my mother when I left her to come to England. As a farewell gift, I gave Rachel an copy of my first book. It was on Chinese women in colonial Malaya.

On the train, I cried. For the same unknown reason why I had thought of my uncle on the journey to Brockenhurst, I thought of my father and mother on the journey back to Cambridge. My father who, throughout his hard life, referred to rich people's homes as *ang mo lau* and those like his own as *su kia har*. My mother, who felt the divisions of society so deeply, composed a poem about it:

> *Chiak, chu chiak pui chin,*
> *Siang, chu siang 'satin,'*
> *Sut jip chu 'Lobinsin.'**

I cried over their hardship. But I also felt extremely proud of them.

---

* when we eat, we eat rice balls,
  when we wear, we wear satin,
  when we shop, we frequent Robinson's.

December 1990

Dear Rachel,

This letter will probably be a surprise to you, coming so soon after we spoke before I left Cambridge for home. I have sad news: Mother passed away in late November. She died of cancer. Mercifully, she died quickly and did not suffer much pain. And thankfully, she had all her family members by her side when she passed away, unlike many of her contemporaries who came and died alone.

My father has been rather philosophical in his own way about her death. He just said, 'The Northeast winds blew your mother and I here. Now the Northeast winds have blown her away.' I remember when I was young my father and I used to sweep up the leaves in our backyard when these winds blew. He would have this faraway look and say with a deep sigh, 'The winds blow again.' I think he was reminded of his village and his voyage. This monsoon, the Northeast winds not only remind me of my parents' arrival but also of my mother's departure.

There are also two 'matters' concerning my mother and your parents which I think you and especially your parents would like to know. One arose when I related to her our reunion. I could tell she was extremely pleased. But then she seemed to remember something and looked worried. Later that same day, she told me to write to you and your parents to say that she never stole the portable radio.

The other is something I found while rummaging through her old suitcase just after she died. It is a testimonial from your mother, dated April 5,1969. It said: 'Soon Yoke Lin has worked for us as house and wash *amah* for the five years we have been in Malaysia. She is very hard-working and conscientious. It is a pity that she does not speak any English, which sometimes leads to difficulties if the employers do not speak Malay. In other respects, we can entirely recommend her. Present salary is M$120 per month.' I recall that when she first showed me the letter many years back, she had said proudly, 'I am a good worker. And my *ang mo towkay* are very good employers, they treat me very well. That is why they write me this letter.' My family and I would like you and your parents to know that a copy of this testimonial was among some her personal effects buried with her. We know she would have liked that. It was her only piece of evidence of her identity and worth as a working woman.

Of late, I have often been thinking about the world I have lived in and now live in. Perhaps that is because my mother has died, my father's health is fast failing and I myself am entering another stage of my lifecycle. I think about the people I have known, the things I have done, the places I have been, the experiences I have undergone, the influences in my life. I also often think about humanity, human conditions and human relationships, and about distinctions that divide and ties that bind. And when I do that, I sometimes think about you, your parents, my mother and I.

I have wondered why you wanted to visit my family, took me to the pantomime, gave me an atlas, wrote me letters. A colonial mind? An anthropological mind? A curious mind? But was it any of these and what does it matter? I would probably have done the same if I had been you. And maybe you have sometimes wondered why I wanted to visit you and your parents, twenty-five years later. But I have a feeling you would have done the same if you had been me. You know, after my visit, I felt as if I was the ugly duckling long grown into a swan, and had flown across time and space to meet you and your parents. It had been a long journey but I had finally completed it. And in doing so, I feel a part of my past and my present have been reconnected. But most of all, I have felt a deep sense of pleasure and satisfaction at the journey's end, at having met you and your parents again. Believe me, our first meeting and reunion have been among the most touching and meaningful experiences in my life.

I am not sure when we will meet again. But I have a feeling that we will always keep in touch. And I do hope that your father's frail health does not stop him from writing his memoirs, and my father's from telling his history.

Yours sincerely,
Eng

This story is dedicated to Rachel Wenban-Smith, Mr. W. & Mrs. R.O. Wenban-Smith, and my mother, Soon Yoke Lin.

First Aunt's Solitudes

Leong Liew Geok

When First Aunt failed to wake,
The doctor came in the morning mist:
Warm to his hands she lay
In her corner bed, diapered
Alone and newly dead.

How Aunt loved to pose
Beside, behind, above beds of roses,
Lips smiling a thin curved line,
Eyes seeing past the lens
To places she alone might know.

The rings and bangles, baubled necklaces
She wore for photos Uncle shot
Sit awkward on that bony frame,
Where thick veins course and fan
Into purple deltas on her hands.

She outlived Uncle seven more years,
The last two spent in Corinya Nursing Home;
No sisters or brother from Malaysia ever came.
When Aunt went at seventy-seven, daughter,
Son-in-law, grandchildren had been dead for twelve.

Aunt's letters never told the feel of it
In Chinese greetings when her mother was alive;
And even after Grandma died, and Uncle too,
The English salutations neighbours wrote
For her still came in Ah Phoh's name.

How did Aunt negotiate three
Separate countries of her fate,
Or the chairs and tables in their flat
When, cleaver clutched in hand, Uncle went for her,
Nerves untamed by the Panadols he gulped?

War had come and they had left
Their infant in China in his parents' care;
But when Japan also dogged Malayan
Days, Aunt and Uncle wouldn't remain
And left by boat again, from Singapore.

Fremantle first: a new unthreatened
Land: then to safe Brisbane.
For a Chemistry graduate and a schoolteacher
Who sterilised herself to stay secure,
A restaurant was life and work enough.

Their only child survived the war:
Between two continents the letters moved,
Proof of school, college, career; marriage and birth,
Snapshots of their daughter's growth
Supporting remittances from abroad.

Not a time for exits and reunions,
Decades sealed and stamped long-distance
Love. When in July 1976,
Tangshan's Dragon rose to break the earth,
Its hunger was unleashed

On houses, people, buses, roads,
bicycles, babies, factories,
my cousin; her husband; his mother; their son
And daughter—'All perished!' Uncle wrote of five
From three generations so devoured.

Their only child and daughter;
Her only son, her only daughter;
Uncle dead; Aunt alone—
In two countries torn apart;
Mind going; the last to go.

I keep photos of the dead—smiling
Or intent, these innocents speak in sepia,
Black-and-white or fading Kodak-coloured hues
Of absence, longing, grief: what they knew
And did not know.

from Pink Kisses

Nalla Tan

They were dancing at the Jubilee Cabaret. It was a sleazy sort of a joint, but then what could one expect during the Occupation, that is, the Japanese Occupation? And in a small one-horse town known as Ipoh, nestling in the Kinta Valley. The floor was chock-a-block with people, trying perhaps, to forget that a war was on. Either that or that the war was an excuse for a release of inhibitions.

Certainly it seemed as though dimmed lights added to that feeling of careless abandon. What did it matter anyway. Why think about tomorrow. It could be there would be no tomorrow. Nothing was certain. There was only today. Even that was shaky. Life was so much a matter of chance; the uncertainty of air raids; the uncertainty of wherewithal; the uncertainty of life.

The only certainty, or so it seemed, was the reality of war and with it a 'take what you can while you can' attitude, for only heaven knew what was going to happen next. The kindest thing one could say was that it was deplorably low thinking, only because almost any situation can be credibly rationalised to ease guilt. The concept of low living and high thinking seemed to have got lost somewhere along the way. Whatever it was, to think on those lines during a war would have been the height of stupidity.

The three-man band was playing 'Smoke Gets in Your Eyes' in slow time. There was something soothing and, at the same time, sensuous, about the tempo. He held her close. So close he could feel her heart beating. He wondered, 'Does she feel mine, in oneness, beating in time with hers?' There was no way of telling. Perhaps she did and that was why she made no effort to move away from him. He drew her closer to him, if that was at all possible. She didn't resist. She wanted it that way, that nothing should separate them. Inside of her she felt—no, not just felt—she knew there was something terribly special about him.

She had felt it the moment their eyes met for the first time on that rainy night nearly nine weeks ago. Now, as they danced, she wanted to look at him, perhaps to get some inkling as to whether he felt something akin to what she was feeling, but she didn't. She couldn't. She did not want the moment to end or for anything to spoil it. It was perfect. She wanted it to go on forever.

It seemed like no one else was around—just the two of them. That was all that mattered. Nothing else. Not even the fact that he was married. Steve had mentioned it rather casually, perhaps in a way warning her to be careful not to be hurt. Perhaps intuitively, he saw what was happening. Placating her conscience, she said to herself that sometimes mistakes were made. At the same time, not all mistakes were irreparable. The thought disturbed her and she peremptorily pushed it out of her mind. For the moment it was enough that he was there with her. At nineteen it was heaven.

They moved in perfect harmony, their bodies involuntarily fused. That the band had stopped had not registered. He moved a little away from her to look at her. How young! How very young she was. Too young, he thought. And how very vulnerable, with her lips slightly parted as if to ask a question and yet afraid to, perhaps just in case he gave her an answer that might be different from what she wanted to hear. He then asked himself what this feeling he had for her was. He had to be honest with himself. He did not want to admit it, but he knew he had never before felt anything like what he now felt for her. Wasn't she the reason why he had joined Steve for the weekend? He knew what the answer was; must have known it from the moment he first set eyes on her. He loved her and he wanted to see her, be near her and spend as much time as he could with her; wanted, if he could, to spend the rest of his life with her. It was as simple as that. But alas! It was also as cruel as it was simple. How was this going to turn out?

His mind turned to his marriage: an arranged one. Very oriental in concept. There was no protest on his part. Acquiescence to his parents' wishes was the easier alternative. He was the traditional filial son. Neither was it that his wife and children meant nothing to him. They did. But he asked himself, was it wrong to love as he loved Tamar? This was the third weekend he was spending with Steve's family in Ipoh, and in fact he was infringing on their hospitality, but he just could not get her out of his mind.

The band had started again, and, drawing her to him again, he held her very close. She slid her arms around his neck in a spontaneous and natural way. It was then that he wanted to bend forward to kiss her slightly tremulous lips and in that kiss let her know that he loved her. But he knew he shouldn't, he couldn't, for it would be totally unfair to her. What on earth was he thinking about? Wasn't he forgetting why he was there: that Japan was at war: that he was specially picked for this secret assignment because he was western educated and had a good command of English: that it was a short-term stint here? Was he forgetting he was married and had two children? O God! What a situation! Was he out of his mind? Where would he be tomorrow, in a week, in a month? It was not knowing what the next day would bring, if indeed there was going to be a next day. There was only here and how. The war had brought them together in what seemed to be an impossible situation which could and would cause deep emotional hurt because it was fraught with uncertainty and painful decisions that inherently were part of it.

It was then that he realised they were the only ones on the floor. The band was packing up for the night. It was time to leave. As he walked her back to their table, he scanned the sea of heads, looking around for Steve and Indra. They had come as a foursome but he could not see them anywhere. 'Ah Steve,' he said within himself, 'You never told me about this sister of yours.' And as an afterthought, 'I didn't ever think that I could have feel like this or that I would be so completely bowled over.'

It seemed like an incredibly short time ago when he and Steve arrived at the Raghavan home at the unearthly hour of two something in the morning, drenched to the skin in a heavy rainstorm. And they almost had to break the front door down before any movement from within was heard. A few more moments of waiting and the door opened and there stood Tamar, so beautiful, her skin a honey bronze, her hair reaching down to just below her waist, looking straight at him with her large brown eyes. Their eyes held for a never-to-be-forgotten moment. In that split second, it seemed like a trillion different messages were sent and received, and there and then a silent indefinable bonding was conceived.

He and Steve had just come in from the wartime training centre the Japanese military had set up at Maxwell Hill. The training centre, rather hurriedly established, was really a semi-military/secret service organisation. The recruits, carefully selected, were previously in the volunteer corps established by the British, and were identified from data in British intelligence files left behind at their headquarters when they scuttled down south in what must have been one of the fastest cross-country races ever witnessed. Records of the kind the British kept and the repercussions of such information falling into the hands of the enemy mattered little to them as they fled the Japanese onslaught from the north. These attitudes were indicative of their lack of concern as to what could and would happen to the indigenous population when the enemy came in.

Perhaps all colonial governments were the same and the British were no exception. The most one could say about them was that they saw to it that the young men drafted into their volunteer organisations were among the top intelligentsia in the country, their training extremely good and that the records they kept were reliable. Now recruited by the Japanese, the young men had no alternative but to comply, with no illusions about what would happen if they didn't. Protests were not entertained. No two ways about that!

Juniki Utago—Niki—as all his colleagues and friends in Los Angeles called him, was ordered, at short notice and without any explanation, to return to Japan with his family, about ten days before the war in the Far East broke out. After a brief training period in Tokyo and after arranging for his wife and children to be with his parents, he was posted to Malaya and put in charge of the training school which was, for public consumption and to all intents and purposes, a leave resort for officers of the Imperial Army. A slim, youngish man of average height in his early thirties or thereabout, Niki brought to the centre an atmosphere of camaraderie and mutual trust. The young recruits found him easy to talk to, sincere and where earlier they had viewed him with some distrust, they began to trust him and to forget their in-built prejudices about the Japanese.

184

Among the recruits was Steven Raghavan, highly intelligent and with a keen sense of humour. Somehow the two clicked and in next to no time, without eroding Niki's position of authority, a strong friendship was established. Many an evening, after a rigid schedule of instruction and field work, they got together. Niki, as an officer, had some privileges among which was the luxury of a rationed quantum of alcoholic drinks, something they both enjoyed. Besides that, regular leave from the centre was available to the cadets at the end of every three weeks of training. On the second stint of leave, Steve invited Niki to his home in Ipoh. It was then, on that dreadfully rainy night that Tamar had opened the door for them and when Niki had somehow felt that his life would never be the same again.

As they walked back to their table he thought, this is my third weekend with Steve's family. He had practically invited himself to Steve's home, asking Steve if he could join him again for the weekend. He had one motive. He wanted to see her again and he knew she would be there. 'Of course,' was Steve's spontaneous response. So here they were. Steve and Indra were waiting for them at their table.

'Shall we go?' Steve asked.

'Good idea. Let's go,' Niki responded without hesitation.

'What about some supper?' Tamar asked.

'Let's go back home and scrounge around for leftovers from dinner,' Steve suggested.

'Why not!' Indra decided for them. It seemed to be the sensible thing to do. Drinks paid for, they left. There was no hurry: there was no closing time at home. The night was theirs. Steve and Indra walked ahead. In tow, Niki and Tamar were silent. Niki reached out for her hand. She held it and very spontaneously moved closer to him. 'Oh,' she thought. 'The sweetness of this man whom I've just met. I hardly know anything about him but I know I want to be near him all the time, always. I want to share my life only with him.' All at once she knew that she wanted to belong to nobody else but him. 'Niki,' her heart cried in the agonising proximity of his body, the warmth he emanated and which she returned. 'I'm going through something I have never felt so intensely about before.

I want you with me always. Don't ever leave me.' How little then, had she understood of the vagaries of a war, perhaps too, of the vagaries of love. But who could say ...

As they reached the Raghavan home, Steve and Indra headed for the bench on the side of the badminton court. It was a beautiful, clear May night. The air was moist and cool: the deep blue sky, speckled with the tiniest stars, flickering like fireflies, lent a feeling of warmth. A silent love enmeshed Tamar and Niki as they walked up the driveway. Steve called out, 'Tamar, if you are going in to get the leftovers, while you are about it, bring the pink kisses and the remainder of the sugee cake Mum made the other day. We might as well finish that too.'

'Niki,' she said, without a second thought, 'Come with me.' Obediently, he followed her.

As they made their way to the house, he asked, 'What's pink kisses?' She turned to answer him, her mind in a tizz. Her first reaction was an impulse to go up to him and put her lips on his and to say 'This.' And she then knew how very much she wanted him to kiss her: to be close to him; to be part of him.

Instead, with all the nonchalance that she could muster, she said, 'Oh! They are meringues. Ma had some left-over egg whites the other day. She never wastes anything and so made pink meringues with it. They are so light they simply melt in your mouth. Like kisses, I suppose.'

'You suppose?' Niki asked jestingly.

She looked at him. She didn't answer. Inside she said to herself, 'Oh Niki, I really don't know.' She felt so inadequate, and so inexperienced. Was that because of the conservative, cloistered upbringing Indian girls were subjected to? But somehow, even after two years at Monash, where there was so much, perhaps too much, of an easy availability in short-lived liaisons, she held on to what she believed in. That first kiss, she thought, had to be with someone special. She continued to look at him with those beautiful brown eyes of hers. He discerned a query almost amounting to hurt in them and was sorry that he had caused it. The moment went by. They had reached the small pantry.

They picked up the dinner leftovers, the few pieces of sugee cake and the canister with the meringues. He said, 'Can I see what they look like? The kisses, I mean?' Tamar opened the container and took one out. 'Here, try one,' she said. Without a murmur he took it from her and put it in his mouth. As he did, and as if it was the most natural thing in the world, he reached out to her, pulled her to him and held her close. 'Share this kiss with me,' he said as he bent forward, the unfinished meringue between his lips. Without waiting for her reply, he kissed her. She didn't draw away. Their mouths held: the kiss melted as she said it would. But the real kiss stayed. And the sweetness, oh the wonder of that kiss. It was the unadulterated sweetness of love shared: given and returned.

He moved away from her, and almost immediately drew her again to him, as if he could not have enough of her warmth, her closeness, her lips, of her. And then he kissed her again, slowly and very gently. She closed her eyes and clung to him. It was sheer bliss. She wanted the moment to go on, never to end. He felt her love. He knew he loved her. He simply said, 'Tamar, I love you and I'm not going to let you go.' She moved a little away from him.

'Niki, can't you feel how much I love you, how much I want to be with you? Don't you know I love you: I think I must have from the moment I saw you with Steven on our doorstep, tired and drenched with rain. And since then I have kept waiting for the weekends, hoping you will be here with Steve. I think even on that night when you and Steve arrived and I opened the door for you, I knew immediately that you were different, that somehow you were going to be part of my life. And you are. You are special. Very, very special. You simply became a part of me then. When Steve told me you were coming again, all of me began to be alive and I realised then that I love you.' He drew her close to him again.

They came back to where they were. 'We have to get back to Steve and Indra,' he said. 'They're waiting for the eats.' They returned to the badminton court with the meringues, and what was left over of the cake. Looking at them, no one would have thought anything special had taken place. Indra asked casually, 'When will you both be here again? Perhaps we could plan something special.'

'It's difficult to say.' Steve was being guarded. 'With any luck we might be here in three weeks' time. The situation changes by the hour. We'll try to send word to you.' Both men knew that there was more than a slight change in the situation. B29s were flying over the territory with increased frequency but no bombs were dropped. There were day flights, and air raid sirens wailed the impending presence of the enemy.

The Japanese felt these seemingly benign flights might be indicative of something more disastrous in the offing. But to talk about it was taboo. How was anyone in the East Asia region to know what the Allies were planning, particularly after Germany was defeated? Pearl Harbour had put a different emphasis on the situation. It was an affront to Western superiority that had to be addressed. The splitting of the atom simply had to be accelerated and more Federal Reserves were released to expedite the project known as the Manhattan Project. Some news trickled in on the turn in tide for the Allies in Europe, bringing the Far East into focus. At the same time, Japan's Greater East Asia Co-Prosperity Sphere was gaining a foothold in South East Asia and the Allies now turned their sights to the East. The fall of Singapore had to be redressed. There was much to do to regain their status and there was no time to lose. The means was not of any great importance. The establishment of superiority was. How political expediency affects the lives of millions! This was so in Southeast Asia. Besides, the Japanese had to be taught a lesson. How dare they attack a Western power, be it at Pearl Harbour or Singapore! And how was anyone to know that the bomb that was not used on Germany was to be used with impunity on an Asian country! Asians, it would seem, were and possibly still are expendable. Racial superiority is manifest in many ways under many different disguises.

Tokyo, to some extent, read the signs and had to set its priorities straight, but it wasn't plain sailing. An emergency was in the offing and the usual war-time restrictions were imposed. Travel was curtailed as was casual leave for officers so that Steve and Niki were not able to get down to Ipoh so easily. Sometime in the middle of July they managed, not without difficulty, to get away for two days. The prevailing mood of uneasiness was obvious. Niki felt from what he could gather that things were closing in on them, but he could not say anything to Steve. Neither could he tell Tamar that this might well be their last visit until who knew when. Still, he had to let her know in some way that the situation was not altogether plain sailing.

'Tamar,' he said to her when they were alone, 'I don't know when I shall see you again. Things are moving so fast, it's hard to say anything definite.' Taking all things into consideration it was best to be indefinite. He continued, 'It's going to be difficult to get leave and I'm not sure if Steve and I will be able to come in again. Only, Tamar, no matter what happens, I want you to know I love you. You know that. God only knows when, really if, we will see each other again. It could be a long time. Will you wait for me?'

Within himself and with all the insecurity bred by the unpredictable in times of war, he could not quell the thought that kept running continuously through his mind, that at best, the chances of their meeting again were very tenuous. Somehow the humours were not in harmonious balance and, it seemed, were almost against them. He felt his whole being protesting in futility against so many unknowns. Uncannily and as if in answer to a telepathic insight into the inner workings of his mind, Tamar moved away from him to look at him. 'Niki,' she said. 'You didn't have to ask. I shall wait for you as long as it takes. You know I shall.' Then as if to erase any remaining doubt in his mind, she added, 'Only come back. I know you will.' Gently he drew her again to him and held her very close. In a wordless inexplicable way, they both knew he would.

Rice

Mary Loh Chieu Kwuan

Fluffy white flakes in a porcelain bowl. Steam rises and with it, the particular fragrance. Like a kind of incense, it wafts and weaves so many, many memories.

'Rice is served … Come and eat,' Ma calls to no one in particular. With the regularity of clockwork, dinner at our house is always served at 7:30 pm. Even with the clocks adjusted by half an hour to fit into Malaysian time, everyone in this house leaves aside his particular activity at 7:30 pm, and we are gathered at the table for dinner. The meal is eaten in reverent silence, slowly and with meaningful silence. The plates are emptied and quietly we collect the dishes for washing. This gradually changed, bit by bit as each of us grew busy with work that kept us back at the office. But this I long remember of a family ritual; we've always had rice for dinner. Rice was served even when we had turkey at Christmas. Pa would always have his ubiquitous bowl of rice and Ma would always serve it.

Ma taught me how to cook rice at the age of ten.

'Okay, one milk tin full for four people. Empty the tin of rice into this pot. Now, pick out all the sand and unhusked rice and if you see any little black crawling weevils, pick them out and squeeze them to kill them.

'Now fill the pot with water. You put both hands in the pot and rub the grains of rice gently between your hands. Now pour out the water and be careful that not a single grain of rice spills with the water. Rice is precious, remember that.

'Fill your pot once again and rinse the rice one more time. This time the water should be almost clear.

'Put your hand there, flat on the top of the rice—now fill the water up to the level of the knuckle of your middle finger. Too much water and you'll be eating porridge. Too little, you'll be eating uncooked grains which taste like sand.

'Let the rice boil for five minutes. Stir and lower the flame.

'Stir it to make sure that the rice does not stick to the bottom of the pot. Cover and let it cook over a slow flame until the water dries up. Turn off the fire. The rice is now ready to be served ....'

Thereafter twice a week, until I went to university, I had the duty of cooking rice for the family.

'Ma, please come home ...'

'I c ... can't ... I d ... don't want to ....'

We stood in the middle of the road in the pouring rain, tears streaming down our faces. The cars roared past us and before us, their headlights blinding us. There had been a big fight at home, over what I forget now, but Pa had said something, something about duty and responsibility. Ma answered back. Pa raised his voice. Soon there was shouting and more shouting. A plate was thrown, the crashing resounding through the house. More crashing sounds, more shouting. We covered our ears, trying in vain to block out the noise and confusion. Even then, I heard Pa say, 'Go. See if I care—the clothes you wear, the roof over your head and the food you eat, everything you have you owe to me and you bloody well dare to answer back ....'

Suddenly, there was a silence.

Ma ran out of the house into the rainy night.

'Come home, please, Ma ... please, Ma.'

'Go home, you go home. Your Ma wants to die here.'

'Please, Ma, I don't want you to die.'

'Go home. The others have to eat. Go home and serve your Pa his rice.'

'No, Ma, I won't go home ... I won't go home without you ...'

'Go home, I tell you, go home and serve your Pa his rice.'

We stood there for the longest time, the cars hooting us to warn us from standing too close to the edge of the pavement. I did not dare to let go of her hand. My hands hurt from holding her hand so tightly. Slowly, bit by bit, I could feel the slack, the tension easing. Both of us sobbed in silence. Ma's shoulders drooped and slowly I was allowed to lead her home. We left the main road and slowly made our way through the quiet suburban lanes, the winding alleys and finally reached home.

Pa sat stonefaced before the television, his face grim, his lips set in a straight line. He refused to say a word. I led Ma into her bedroom, closed the door and went into the kitchen. Lifting up the cover of the pot, I spooned the thick white flakes into Pa's bowl and set the bowl on the table.

'Pa, time to eat.'

Silence.

'Pa, eat rice.'

'Don't want to eat.'

The bowl of rice sat on the end of the table, getting colder and colder.

After that, without fail, day after day, for as many days as there were in a year, Ma would place a steaming hot bowl of rice before Pa. Even if she had to go out for her mahjong games in the afternoon, she would return in time to serve the bowl of rice. If she was going out in the evening, she would wait till Pa had finished his bowl of rice and had laid aside his chopsticks. Only then would she pick up her bag and leave on her occasional outings.

I hate eating white rice. White rice is bland and boring. It has to be made more interesting with a variety of other dishes. One hardly eats rice on its own, to savour its full-bodied flavour, simply because it has none. It is a staple, a stomach filler, little else. I make concessions for brown rice, which I eat sparingly, more as a health fad rather than as real food. I am, my Ma says, 'western-educated' and prefer *hong-mo sek*. Pasta is a definite favourite, all kinds of it, from capellini to fettucine to lasagna, smothered with thick creamy sauces, and yes, I love cheese—the Bleus with their coloured blue green ridges and sharp-smelling Bries which turn Ma green with disgust. Parmesan toasts had me turned out of the house because no one could bear the smell of the cheese I was eating—which is a continual joke to my neighbours who see me sitting in the garden in the evenings, chewing on foul-smelling toasted bread. Of course, I like breads, French, Danish, Manoucher deli-style sandwiches with pickles and relishes, sandwiches which are so large that two hands are required to grip the bread together while large mouthfuls are chewed vigorously and then swallowed. Yes, don't forget salads. I am the resident rabbit in the office—please pass the greens over. Healthy crunchy lettuces with loads of lovely dressings make my day. But rice … I cannot take rice two meals in a row. I'd rather go hungry.

I remember that Ma was very particular that we never wasted any rice. Not a single grain was to be left on the plate or else, every single grain left would appear as ugly marks on the face of our eventual Intended. Certainly not wanting to marry any man with a scarred or marred complexion, we faithfully cleaned out plates and through our dating years, every close encounter with men with chronic acne resulted in real guilt that perhaps, just perhaps, this might be retribution for that one plate of rice we had not finished.

When I went to University and did Philosophy, the logic of this underwent severe examination. Did some, say, scientists in China, gather up two separate groups of women as a test case for this hypothesis? Did they force one group to finish their plates of rice clean? And the other, not? Did they then observe and track the progress of both groups through life till marriage and deduce conclusively, based upon empirical findings, that girls who did not finish their rice would marry pock-marked husbands? Why did this rule never apply to men? Or did it?

I hate that bowl of rice. I hate what that bowl of rice means.

I remember my grandmother's favourite rice-bowl, the one from which each noonday and each evening she would lift to her face and shovel the white rice into her open mouth. It was a creamy white bowl with a swirl of blue outside. It was grandmother's special rice-bowl, one with which she associated fond memories, memories which she did not share with any of us. I remember gingerly handling it when we held it over the basin of soapy water. My older sister would carefully rinse it, wipe it dry and put it into the great wooden cupboard, only to take it out again, at the next mealtime, to scoop the soft white grains gently into the bowl.

It was an accident! We didn't mean for it to break, Grandmother's precious bowl. It was an accident, the bowl slipped. We clutched desperately, our fingers barely missing the rim and finding only empty air. The silence in the kitchen reverberated with the crash as the bowl shattered into a thousand pieces. We looked shamefaced at each other, before Grandmother came bursting in.

We left the house that day, Pa, Ma, my sisters and my brother. In silence, we gathered up our belongings and stepped through the old gate of the family home without a backward glance. I remember the last word my grandmother said, a word which I had heard her mutter under her breath for so long: *fan-thong.*

In Cantonese, a fan-thong or vessel for rice is used as an epithet. It implies that a person is of no more use than a receptacle of rice, that all the rice that has been consumed is wasted and therefore such a person is useless.

We never saw my grandmother after that, not even when she passed away.

So I married Brian Worth, an Englishman whose idea of great cuisine was bangers and beans and whose face was as smooth as a baby's bottom, though he swore he had chronic acne during his teenage years. Aside from his wit, his love for the same kind of music and writers drew us closer, making us more than good friends. When he proposed, I thought, what a relief, I can handle bangers and beans and the occasional steak and potatoes. Heck, I could even do a turkey at Christmas, complete with cranberry sauce and pudding. I won't have to serve him rice every day, seven days a week, every week of the year.

There was rice sprinkled at our wedding, instead of confetti. As we ran down the aisle, the rice was scattered like rain. Afterwards, like monkeys, Brian and I picked the rice from each other's hair. The sprinkling of rice was symbolic of fertility, just as in Singapore they had forced us to drive around with a pair of chickens, one male and one female. In the heat, one poor chicken expired, leaving the other one alone to weather the storms of marital pomp and ceremony. This, I hoped, was not a bad omen.

'You are marrying a *kwei-lo!* Why do you want to bring more *chap-cheng kia* into the world?' Pa snorted in disgust.

'Pa, Brian is not a kwei-lo. Brian is Brian. I'm not marrying a race. I'm marrying a man.'

'I tell you, they are all the same. Your Pa has seen how they always behave, so smelly and dirty, always getting drunk. You think they are getting serious with you. So many Chinese girls have been fooled. They are all alike, these kwei-los. All the same.

'And I tell you, your Pa drives the school bus around for so many years, I know the chap-cheng kia are the worst. All like monkeys, climbing here and there and always fighting. They never respect their parents. Your children will be exactly the same.'

'Pa, I think you're wrong. Brian respects you and he respects Ma. Look, he is always helpful and kind to Ma. He is not a tourist or a sailor and even if he were, not all sailors or tourists are the same.

'Pa, he cares about me. You dislike him because of the colour of his skin but Pa, underneath we are all the same. I am marrying a man and not a race. He loves me and he will look after me and he doesn't treat me as if I was an inferior. Nothing you say will change my mind about marrying him.'

'Do what you like. Your Pa has nothing more to say. I am an old man. I have eaten more salt than you have eaten rice. You wait and see ...'

Fan thong. My father called me fan-thong and said he regretted the day I was born.

Italy was wonderful. We dined on sunkissed green terraces, on the best pastas, cheeses and wines. Along old cobbled streets, we wandered, the strong smell of spiced breads baking. We picnicked in the old squares, the misty spray from the ancient fountains rising up to refresh us. As the sun went down on the city, we sat on open rooftops and drank wine from each other's lips.

'Darling ...?' I murmured into his ear.

'Hmmm ... what?' His strong suntanned arms snaked around me. The dull light of a dying day filtered through the drawn curtains, casting dim shadows around the bedroom of our new flat.

'What would you like for our first meal home?'

'I'd like you for dinner.' His teeth sank playfully into my shoulder.

'Ouch, stop it, Brian, that's ticklish ... Stop, don't bite!' I squealed in protest. 'Stop, I'm serious ...'

He sobered and looked into my eyes. 'Well, after that long flight and that nap, I am hungry ...' He paused. 'Actually, darling, I miss your mum's cooking. It would really be nice if you learnt to cook like she did. Do you think you could rustle up one or two Chinese dishes ... and a bowl of rice? Please?'

David's Story

Claire Tham

He loved her, of course he did, in his own way, not in Wai Keong's way, perhaps, that faithful, deathless, romantic way that was as potent and useless as a dead jellyfish, but in his own way. For him, love was an adjunct of manipulation: he'd manipulated her because he loved her, and he loved her even more because he'd manipulated her. Seeing her in Wai Keong's room in London, he'd felt that premonitory crackle of electricity down his spine, the stirrings of battle. He'd heard that covetousness was a sin. Heard that, in the dim, sleepy religious service he'd endured through his teenage years in the good school he loved to hate. What nonsense, he'd always thought. Covetousness was second nature to him, so ingrained a reflex he'd practically ceased to notice it, like an intestinal worm with which he'd long since made a medical accommodation. He had coveted Wai Keong's life, for as long as he could remember.

She hadn't liked him, that first time. He was unperturbed. He knew her type. Clever, middle-class, a good deal more sheltered than she looked, paid lip service to feminist principles but probably liked having a good man to wind around her finger. Wai Keong, he could tell, was completely felled by her. 'I hate smart women,' he'd said, to provoke her. It had been as simple as that: he'd wanted to see just how far he could go in testing her limits. She was a woman with a battery of limits; enticingly, she could be provoked.

At that stage, he could not have said, quite honestly, whether she was good-looking or even what she looked like. Unlike Wai Keong, he simply didn't notice these things, until they were practically under his nose. His first instinct, on meeting people, was to probe their frailties, the things that made them wake with a start in the middle of the night. It was only after he'd unearthed, and filed away, this information, that he could turn to the comparatively unimportant (for him) business of ordinary socialisation. He only noticed that Li was small, that she had long, smooth waterfall hair which didn't really suit her, and a stare that almost razored him.

He'd set out quite cold-bloodedly to win her, and falling in love was the last thing he expected. He'd enjoyed the campaign, the lightning visits to London, seeing her startled, unsettled expression, the questions scuttling transparently through her mind, *should I tell Wai Keong, should I not?* Like many inherently secretive, or calculating people, he was perversely attracted to honesty in others. And Li was honest, her inability to mask her feelings giving her at times an almost *faux naif* quality, as if she were some wild child that had wandered out of a wood and had to re-learn the rules of ordinary discourse from scratch. He felt almost sorry for her sometimes, for her total lack of defences, yet found it hard to resist himself. 'What's the worst pain you've ever experienced?' he'd asked her, knowing that anybody else would have turned on him at that point. Instead, she'd answered him, quite seriously, biting on her lower lip in that way she had, and wrapping strands of hair around her finger. And he'd wanted so badly to reach out and touch that lower lip of hers, tell her that she couldn't always trust people, that they were not going to be as tender with her vulnerabilities as he was. He'd refrained, only because he knew it was too soon, and he didn't want to scare her. The impulse had been out of character for him, and when he got back to Oxford, he'd sat in his low chair by the soaring windows of his room for a long time, nursing what felt like an open wound cankering somewhere in his body but was only the realisation that he was done for, totally and absolutely, and that he had never planned for this.

She *got* to him, in a way that no-one had ever done before, or ever would. What started out as a game became serious. She had probably cost him his First. Almost every weekend of that third, crucial year, he found himself taking the coach down to London, drifting, almost against his will, to the places where he knew Li would go, either alone or with Wai Keong. He watched her in Chinatown, shopping for foodstuffs. He watched her going to the library, books carried with both hands in front of her, her chin tucked low into her muffler. In spring, he watched them in the park, picnicking, reading the newspapers, throwing sticks for dogs to catch. He saw Wai Keong lope an arm around her waist, and kiss her on the ear, and Li frown, and wriggle away. She hated public displays of affection, he knew; it was one of the reasons he'd camped it up with Clarissa, who loved a show, for her benefit.

He suspected that Li, at least, was aware of his presence; often, while walking along the street, she would look back, suddenly, and he would have to duck into doorways, alleys.

She never actually caught him, though; he was too good for that. During his army service, he'd always been the scout, the navigator; he had the uncanny ability to see in the dark, to materialise, unseen, in places where he wasn't supposed to be. Twice, though, he could not resist appearing before her, like a tawdry jack-in-the-box, just to remind her that he still existed. To keep his hand, as it were, in the till.

He never doubted that he would prevail, although he hadn't counted on her stubborn loyalty to Wai Keong. That was the other thing he liked about her, her scruples. 'That's because you haven't any,' Clarissa told him. 'You're constantly looking for other people to compensate for your deficiencies.'

'It's called the principle of equilibrium,' he said.

He and Clarissa understood each other. She, like Li, was also completely honest, which was why he'd liked her instantly. She was also, as he had cause to know, unnervingly sharp. The night after the dance, she'd said to him, 'I saw you looking at her tonight.'

Innocently: 'Who?'

She'd surveyed him out of those bottomless green eyes. White people's eyes fascinated him, they had an unbearably naked quality in their transparency, as though you could see clean through their skulls. 'She's not your type,' Clarissa said. 'You'll be *miserable* together, darling. Not to mention that it seems rather hard on that poor sap.'

He shrugged. There had to be winners and losers after all. At the time, he simply took her prediction as a challenge.

Following her to Calais had been an inspired impulse. He was tiring of the chase, and was seriously considering sitting them all down for a *talk*, God forbid. It would have been the civilised thing to do, but it was not his way, and the thought of it made his hair stand on end.

Not once did he consider himself as being consciously duplicitous towards Wai Keong; he had the capacity to rationalise all his actions, questionable ones included, and to launder them cleanly in the only guiding principle he acknowledged, which was that the ends justify the means. He knew she was not in love with Wai Keong. That correct exterior of hers hadn't fooled him; she was someone on the cusp, waiting to be made real to herself. He knew her better than she did herself. At school, it was not the wild girls who had interested him, though he had taken full advantage of them, but the others, the shadowy ones with the banked-up fires.

He told himself he was doing Wai Keong a favour: a relationship where the feeling ran all in one direction would collapse under its own unequal weight. He was relieving them of future misery. Not wanting to concede that one-sidedness might have its advantages: the party with the deficiency of feeling would have no illusions, might have tried harder, out of compunction, if nothing else, to hide that deficiency and to make things work. And conveniently forgetting, for the moment, the case of his own parents: each had been in love with the other, and neither, it seemed, had been particularly happy.

He'd lost them both, in that strange crush at the crossroads when that drunken girl had gone berserk, or so it seemed. The girl awakened an uneasy memory of another girl he had known in school, who had hung around him like a limpet, and couldn't be shaken off. She too had that same saucer-eyed emaciation, the same hunger for self-abasement. He had not been nice to her: he had told her, in the crudest language he could think of, that he didn't want to see her. She hadn't heard a word he said; she'd followed the motion of his lips, with her eyes, and then she'd pulled his hand under her blouse. Snatching his hand away, he'd backed off, staring at her as though she were an untamed animal that might maul, or bite. She'd upset him more than he'd cared to admit; for the first time in his life, he'd crashed up against a stronger force than his own will, something he couldn't control. Even now, he didn't like to think about it.

He had searched for them for a while, then given up. There was no point going to their room at this hour. Confrontations were not his style. He knew where to find Li, if he needed to. He knew he'd won. He'd seen it in her face, at the beach, when he'd cracked his stupid joke and fallen off the wall: she hadn't been able to look at him. He slept, dreamlessly, on the beach, under the stars.

In the event, neither he nor Li had been required to break the paralysis: Wai Keong had done it all. Something had pierced his obliviousness, and no explanations were necessary. They met him at the door of the *pension*, bags packed. He announced he was leaving. 'See you in London,' Li had proffered, brightly. Betrayal made her glib, frantic; she looked fearlessly into his face, and it was he who had to turn away. Not once did he look in David's direction; it was as if he simply didn't exist. David said nothing. He didn't underestimate Wai Keong's pain, but he did believe in quick deaths and not prolonging hope unnecessarily. Someday, he telegraphed silently to Wai Keong, you'll understand.

from Kaleidoscope Eyes

Theresa Tan

Synopsis

Clare is a 27-year-old Chinese Catholic woman in search of the ultimate Sensitive New Age Guy. Along comes the tender and handsome Ben, they get married, and for one year things seem all right ... until Ben breaks the news that he is in love with another. Another man, that is.

Clare takes a harrowing journey on her own—through the seas of Chinese tradition and church dogma. Her parents and her relatives blame her entirely for the breakdown of the marriage—of course it must have been she who drove him into another man's arms. Not just that but Clare has to suffer through trying to find an explanation herself; only there is none to be found.

Later she discovers she is HIV-positive. Then she meets the man that Ben has left her for, who has full-blown AIDS and is dying. Against the inexplicably cruel blows life deals her, Clare has only one shield: her kaleidoscope eyes.

In this scene, Clare visits her mother. One month ago, her husband left her, and now her mother wants to know why her daughter isn't pregnant yet. Today is the day she must tell her mother the truth. Or should she?

Characters

CLARE
MOTHER

MOTHER*'s house. The living room is simply, but expensively furnished.* MOTHER *is seated on the divan, engaged deeply in a phone conversation.* CLARE *enters, unannounced, and stands eavesdropping on her mother's conversation.*

MOTHER: (*In Teochew*) She gets married for one year, I see her, what, five times? She doesn't call, she doesn't visit, it's like she's forgotten all about us ... (*Listens.*) ... She was my favourite daughter! ... Yah *lah*, she is my only daughter, but you know how mothers love their daughters more than anything else, right?

(CLARE *puts her bag down, walks to the back of the room and gets herself a drink.*)

MOTHER: (*Still in Teochew*) And that husband of hers, so handsome, so young. But I don't know what kind of parents he has, never teach him about respecting elders. Of the five times Clare visited me, he came with her only once ... (*Listens.*) ... I know she loves me. I know my daughter cares for me ... I just wish she would give me what I want. (*Laughs.*) I don't think I'm being unfair what. Your daughter was pregnant right after her wedding, right? I was pregnant with Clare four months after David and I got married. Why can't she be like her mother?

(CLARE *crosses over and sits next to* MOTHER. MOTHER *starts, realising her daughter has heard all her complaints.*)

MOTHER: (*In Teochew*) Ah Ping, I will call you back. (*She hangs up the receiver and sits back, looking at her daughter.*)

CLARE: (*Cheerfully*) Hi Mom.

MOTHER: Your life very long. I was just telling Auntie Ah Ping about you.

CLARE: I heard. (*She takes out a box and hands it to Mother.*) Happy birthday, Mommy. I'm sorry, but I was out of town that week.

MOTHER: (*Opens the box and lifts out a lovely pearly white sweater*) Wah! I can wear this to San Francisco! Your father will be very happy!

CLARE: (*Drily*) I'm sure he will take many many photographs of you.

MOTHER: Why? You don't like those photos of me?

CLARE: (*Laughs and kisses Mother*) Don't be silly. So are you going to try it on or do I have to put it on you?

MOTHER: (*Standing up and pulling sweater over her head*) Clare-girl, you better don't work so hard. I see your face, you look so tired. Those dark rings— (*Reaches over and rubs under Clare's left eye.*) ee-yer! So ugly!

CLARE: Can't help it Mom. I need the money.

MOTHER: Say until like you're some kind of prostitute like that.

CLARE: (*Grins*) Hey, journalism is prostitution of writing, Mom!

MOTHER: (*Showing off*) Nice or not?

CLARE: (*Examines her carefully*) Very nice. Ten points for Clare-girl.

MOTHER: (*Pulling off sweater*) Thank you very much, girl. (*She kisses* CLARE, *and hugs her, and then pushes the hair from her daughter's forehead.*)

MOTHER: Still my little baby.

CLARE: (*Laughs*) I thought Chris was your little baby.

MOTHER: Have you seen your brother lately? He looks like a tank. He is so fat, he can't even fit through that doorway anymore. (CLARE *laughs uncontrollably.*)

MOTHER: I'm not joking! I don't know where he got his genes from. The three of us are very thin and nice what.

CLARE: I think he inherited Grandma's eating skills.

MOTHER: (*Crossly*) Eh, don't anyhow talk about the dead like that.

CLARE: (*Still laughing*) Okay, okay.

(*There is an awkward pause.* MOTHER *gets up.*)

MOTHER: You want a drink? I made bird's nest this morning.

CLARE: Wah, don't mind some.

(MOTHER *shuffles off in her bedroom slippers to the kitchen, while* CLARE *sits and stares at her fingers. She starts playing with her wedding ring, slipping it off and putting it back. Eventually, she takes it off and puts it in her pocket.*)

MOTHER: (*Offstage*) So where is Husband?

CLARE: (*Softly*) No bloody idea.

MOTHER: Hah?! I said where is he?

CLARE: I don't know, Mom.

MOTHER: Working ah?

CLARE: I DON'T KNOW.

(*Rapid shuffling in the background as* MOTHER *hurries back to the living room.*)

MOTHER: (*Puzzled*) What do you mean you don't know?

CLARE: (*Nonchalantly*) I think he's working or playing tennis. The usual.

MOTHER: (*Hands her the bowl of bird's nest*) Oh. (*Sits down.*) How come he doesn't come to see us?

CLARE: Don't worry, Mom, he doesn't even see his own parents.

MOTHER: (*Huffily*) Doesn't mean he doesn't have to come and see his in-laws once in a while. We are not like his parents, you know, so easy.

CLARE: Yes, Mom, he knows.

(MOTHER *looks like she is about to begin berating.*)

CLARE: (*Mouth full*) Mm! This is really good bird's nest! Who gave you?

MOTHER: Your Auntie Ah Ping lor. You know how good she is at buying all these nonsense things.

CLARE: So … Priscilla is pregnant?

MOTHER: (*Pleased that the subject is broached*) Yes. Five months already.

CLARE: Wow, should call her.

MOTHER: So?

CLARE: (*Smiles cheekily at Mother*) Yah?

MOTHER: So? Are you all going to or not?

CLARE: (*Feigning ignorance*) Going to what, Mom?

MOTHER: Clare, you know that your duty to God is to reproduce.

CLARE: (*Shouts with laughter*) Mom! Since when were you God?!

MOTHER: (*Hisses*) Eh! Don't be sacrilegious!

CLARE: (*Smiles*) I was only joking …

MOTHER: What I can't understand is, why it's taking so long. I mean, it's been—when did you get married? Last January? That's one and a half years, girl. It only takes seconds for the sperm to enter the egg!

CLARE: Mom, I know how babies are made.

MOTHER: (*Accusingly*) You are not using contraceptives, are you?

CLARE: No, Mom. I would not dare disobey the church like that!

MOTHER: Good. Because you know good Catholics …

CLARE: Yes, Mom. Ben is a really good Catholic when it comes to contraceptives.

MOTHER: (*Not entirely grasping her meaning*) Good. I think young people these days don't listen to the church, that's why there's so much disease and divorce in the world.

CLARE: Mom …

MOTHER: So, is it because you all are practising NFP?

CLARE: No Mom. We're not the natural family planning type. (*Pauses.*) We sort of follow the urges that God gave us.

MOTHER: Then, is it your period? Are they irregular?

CLARE: No, Mom. They have never been irregular.

MOTHER: Did you see your gyny?

CLARE: Yes. He says my womb is fine.

MOTHER: Maybe Ben's sperms are weak. Or maybe he has low sperm count.

CLARE: Then, Mother, that is God's way of deciding what is the best thing for us, right?

MOTHER: (*Confused by Clare's statement*) I don't know what you mean lah.

CLARE: Mom, I'm just not pregnant. And I don't think I'm going to be pregnant in the near future.

MOTHER: (*A new realisation dawning, but it's the wrong one*) Oh. Are you having the problem already?

CLARE: (*Now it's her turn to be puzzled*) What problem?

MOTHER: You and Ben are not having sex.

CLARE: (*Thinks over her answer very carefully*) You are right, Mom. We are not having sex.

MOTHER: (*Greatly dismayed*) WHY?!!! Is it your work? You are too tired all the time, don't feel like it, right?

CLARE: Uh, Mom …

MOTHER: Or is it Ben has one of those problems? Those premature ejaculation problems?

CLARE: No, Ben is—

MOTHER: He has a problem getting aroused, is it? (*Panicking.*) *Aiyah,* I told you you shouldn't cut your hair! Men like long-hair girls, they look more alluring, more sexy. And look at you, you've put on weight! You better start your aerobics again …

CLARE: (*Pissed off*) Mom. Stop. Stop it. It's not my weight. It's not my hair.

MOTHER: I'm telling you …

CLARE: (*Shouting*) Mom, it's not my fault, okay?! Ben left me, okay?

(MOTHER *stops her hysterical outburst, stunned.* CLARE *is wondering how to soften the blow she just dealt.*)

MOTHER: What?!

CLARE: Mom, it was for the best.

MOTHER: Why?! It's only been a year …

CLARE: Because things just didn't work out, Mom.

MOTHER: Were you a bad wife?

CLARE: (*Gently*) No, Mom. I followed your example. I was not a bad wife. I did everything right.

MOTHER: Then was he a bad husband?

CLARE: (*Thinks*) Well. He never hit me or anything—

MOTHER: Another woman? A third party?

CLARE: (*Very slowly*) Uh. I guess you could say it was a third party.

MOTHER: Where? Who? … How?

CLARE: Yup, that's what I said too.

MOTHER: Why are you so calm?

CLARE: I'm not, Mom. I've been walking around in a daze for one month since he walked out. I have been trying to explain to myself how all that could happen.

MOTHER: *Aiyoh*, girl, this will kill your father.

CLARE: Mom, let me tell Daddy myself. I want him to hear it from me.

MOTHER: (*Stares at Clare*) Okay. Okay.

CLARE: Mom, Ben didn't really know himself, you know.

MOTHER : What do you mean? He didn't love you?

CLARE: (*Starts to tear*) I think when we got married, he did love me. I loved him very much. But when we tried to be a married couple, that's when things went wrong.

MOTHER: He's a horrible boy, I never liked him.

CLARE: (*Smiles*) You liked him, Mom. If you didn't like him I wouldn't have married him.

MOTHER: But I didn't know he would be like this. Who is this girl?

CLARE: Mom, it's very hard to tell you, so please let me tell it my way, okay?

MOTHER: Who is she? I'll get your brother to go and make sure she knows what she has done.

CLARE: (*Laughs despite herself*) Yeah, I can see Chris now, threatening her through the gate that he can't fit through.

MOTHER: Don't make jokes! How can you make jokes! This is serious.

CLARE: Mom, there is no other way for me to deal with this. I never in my entire life imagined this would happen to me.

MOTHER: (*Suddenly seeing her daughter's distress*) Girl. Come here. (*Hugs* CLARE.) It happens. I know it happens. Marriages don't always work out like your Daddy's and mine. People change.

CLARE: Yes they do.

MOTHER: Get hold of Ben. We can talk to him. We can make him change his mind.

CLARE: No, I don't think so, Mom.

MOTHER: When a man is attracted to another woman, it's usually because this woman reminds him of his own wife. (CLARE *opens her mouth but* MOTHER *outtalks her.*) No, it's true. I read *Readers' Digest.* It's true. So there is a chance when the man realises that his wife is the one he truly loves, he will return.

CLARE: Mom, I know all that is true. But it will not work in this case, not with Ben.

MOTHER: Nonsense! Ben is a smart boy, and he's gentle and understanding also, and I know he will come to his senses once I talk to him.

CLARE: Mom, you are making this so hard for me.

MOTHER: (*Startled*) What do you mean?

CLARE: There is something you must understand about Ben, Mom. And it's not easy to explain.

MOTHER: He's stubborn, right?

CLARE: Yes, and a lot more than that.

MOTHER: It's just another woman, Clare. The Other Woman never wins, one.

CLARE: No, Mom, it's not another woman.

MOTHER: Then? He wants to be a priest?

CLARE: No, no. It's much harder than that. Oh Mom, how can I tell you?

MOTHER: Tell me what? Tell me what?

CLARE: Ben left me for another man.

MOTHER: (*Pause*) What do you mean?

CLARE: He is now living with another guy. From our church. But they are not going to church anymore.

MOTHER: You mean Ben is homosexual?

CLARE: In so many words, yes.

MOTHER: HOW CAN?!

CLARE: He never really wanted to admit it to himself. I know he loved me, Mom, but he didn't love me like a man loves a woman.

MOTHER: But you had sex, right?

CLARE: Yes. We had sex.

MOTHER: And that also cannot change his mind?

CLARE: No, Mom, it's much deeper than that.

MOTHER: How can a married man suddenly decide he doesn't even like girls?

CLARE: It happens more often than we realise, Mom. Since last month, I have met women whose husbands are gay or bisexual, and have been having affairs with men behind their wives' backs.

MOTHER: (*Crushed*) I can't understand. I cannot understand.

CLARE: There is nothing to understand, Mom. It just is. At least Ben had the courage to tell me the truth when he finally faced it.

MOTHER: (*Furious*) You give me his telephone number! I'm going to call that boy and talk to him! How dare he!

CLARE: Screaming at him won't change anything, Mom. I already tried! It won't help matters.

MOTHER: If he thinks he can just walk away and leave my daughter like this, I'm going to teach him a thing or two.

CLARE: It's done, Mom. It's done already. He's gone. There's no way to get him back, and I don't want him back.

MOTHER: Why? He's your husband.

CLARE: But what will I do with a husband who doesn't love me, and will never be able to be the kind of man I want in my life? Or the kind of father I want for my child?

MOTHER: Girl-girl! Why do you let these things happen to you?

CLARE: I didn't exactly have a choice, Mom. I didn't know. Ben himself didn't even know!

MOTHER: Then how?! What will happen now?

CLARE: I have to get a divorce, Mom.

MOTHER: (*Horrified*) You cannot! You are a Catholic! How can you even think about it?!

CLARE: What choice do I have? I'm not about to become a nun. I don't want to be lonely all my life, thinking about my gay husband. I want my life to carry on! God gave me only this life, and I must use it to the fullest!

MOTHER: Don't be sacrilegious! You cannot get a divorce!

CLARE: Mom, I love you. I love God. But this is what I am going to do. My life cannot end here. I refuse to stop living because of this.

MOTHER: You will burn in Hell!

CLARE: If God let me make the mistake of marrying a gay man, God should jolly well give me the chance to start over again.

MOTHER: (*Slaps her*) Shut up! Don't talk like that!

(CLARE *looks at* MOTHER *in tears.* MOTHER'*s face flickers between righteous anger and doubt. Doubt wins out, and she grabs her daughter and holds her tight.*)

MOTHER: Oh my girl! Oh my girl!

CLARE: Mom …

MOTHER: Mommy never meant to let this happen to you.

CLARE: It's not your fault, Mommy. It's nobody's fault.

(*They weep quietly.*)

[*end of extract*]

Under the Bell Jar

(for Sylvia Plath)

Lee Tzu Pheng

i
Did even poetry fail you?

I understand it well.
For we who have let the unutterable
etch crazy lesions on our hearts
think of redemption in terms
of the saving word:
that the word could make things new,
or gather up our griefs so
to hang them on a nail outside us
for dispassionate review.

But the word is itself
living, a tortured thing;
both death and life we crucify again.

ii
Now I am forced to watch
asphyxiation of your hopes—
as one looking in upon
a moth trapped
under a bell jar—
you say it was not your choice
to be in the throes
another ten years, that you would
have made certain that first escape,
had you known it would come to this.

I am forced to ask:
why was your death postponed? Was it
to teach decisiveness?
What if the source in you
of children, poems, felicities
of spirit, is made mockery of
by what sorrows survive?

iii
I pick the troubled path
through shards of your broken life,
the bafflement of biographers,
the guilt of those you loved;
and I think how there must be
something to keep us living
through the deserts of our faith,
the culpability of writing.

You chose to close the book
when the ink ran near to blood;
you lost your nerve at last.

I take up mine in hand
to understand yours whole,
open up a vein to stare
despair in the eye.
For poetry itself must speak
the power of helplessness;
else, Sylvia, too many of us
surrender what is beautiful
to that most faithful lover, death.

in the proximity of humans
(the case for bird space)

Ho Poh Fun

birds may still base
a style of living on trees

track an insect
peck at a worm
warble, mate, and
in a manner truly enviable
scale the lengths, the breadths, the heights …

this, by itself being never infinitely irrepressible

once, the rude shock might have come
some nasty but reparable bump
product of extrapolation
'midst sentries of a kindred green

now that timber's yielded to concrete
sand, gravel, cement in continual increase
crowd of high sky-scouring scenarios
habitats more congenial
to crows than to sparrows

what ebullience surrounding presences
On swings of winged exuberance
swerving, gauging, negotiating distances?

for one flier at least

inevitable collision
up at high windows
hard walls of indifference
to palpitating feathers

a beak shattered
a wing crushed

no ambulance for birds in sight ...

civilizations aspiring ever higher
propagating greater human worth, growth and endeavour
preach no democracy to birds

leave concern for a more equivocally-definable sky space
a conscience for sustaining wider un-breach-able birdspace

to rot

March 1995

The lady to her scholar

Heng Siok Tian

dare she
weaving words to feelings
each willowy night,
bring him her
enshrined embroidery?

dare she un
furl
her mute emotions
to him who pines for
a scholarly scroll?

(strip pining of symbols,
it makes you real sick.)

China Girl Not Picture Bride

Leong Liew Geok

Getting a bride from China did not pose
A problem for a man with *guanxi*.
He was happy she reached his ears
And, a dozen years younger, was good looking.
Where in Singapore, pretty twenty somethings,
Taller than a furniture dealer, look past
Little-educated runts, here was a love match,
Ambition struck true by luck: a young and beautiful
Woman taken indeed with him. After Suzhou and Shanghai
And a third nuptial feast in Singapore for his family,
Friends and associates, Mr and Mrs Chua settled
Into becoming loving husband and dear wife.

Their flat overlooks twenty storeys down, a small park
Planted with rain trees, neat benches and a fountain;
Not the gardens of Suzhou or its river of bridges,
But some green and water to contemplate
While her Singapore family is still giddy
With a lightning marriage, three receptions, and busy
Selling furniture. Her mother's been settled
As a permanent resident, for a sum very handsome
By Chinese standards; a son-in-law's gift
To the mother of the youngest daughter.

She means to be a real *tai-tai* with a maid
For her needs and her mum's, and a business
To her name, for she didn't leave China to be some
Little wife at home. A businessman like her husband
Can surely afford a maid; then he won't need to do
His laundry at night, or take them out for dinner
After work. In Singapore, he spends too little time
With her. Tonight, sharing his pillow, she will
Whisper eight weeks, so he will agree to six
Instead of the four he's promised her in China
Each New Year. His family can mind the furniture;
Meanwhile, he should own a new Mercedes, like his brother.

The Matchmaker

Geraldine Kan

Characters
SUSIE, Single woman in her late twenties, early thirties
WOMAN, A matchmaker
RICHARD, Bachelor number one
MENG, Bachelor number two
TONY, Bachelor number three (if there's enough time to change,
   the men can be played by the same person)

*A modern, airy bachelorette's pad. Not opulent but tastefully furnished.
Modern, uncluttered. Evening.*

SUSIE, *dressed in T-shirt and shorts, maybe glasses, hair messed up.
Attractive. Home alone and working intently. There's a knock on her door.
She tries to ignore it but the person is persistent. She finally throws up her
arms and goes to the door, opening it slightly.*

SUSIE: (*Through the crack in her door*) If you're a boy scout I've
   already contributed to Job Week—and I didn't even charge the
   kid for the vase he broke. If you're the Avon lady, I've bought
   an entire year's supply of make-up and if you want money I'm
   already a monthly contributor to the Community Chest.

WOMAN: No, no, no. I've got nothing to sell. What I'm offering
   is a lifetime of happiness and prosperity.

SUSIE: Oh. I've already bought life insurance. And I already have
   a stockbroker. And I'm busy.

   (WOMAN *pushes her way into the apartment with her black umbrella.
   Closes it and dusts herself off. The two women eye one another. The
   woman is dressed in conservative nanny's garb. Black—like Mary
   Poppins, but a little more modern.*)

SUSIE: What are you? Mary Poppins?

WOMAN: Goodness, no. With the abundance of maids here, the
   nanny business is simply not economically viable. Besides, ol'

220

Mary was just a bit too prim for my taste. I was a convent girl you know ... for a while anyway. Then my father moved to Japan and I had to go to finishing school. Boy, was that culture shock.

SUSIE: OK, OK. So uh ... who are you and what do you want from me?

WOMAN: Tut tut. It's actually what I can do for you.

SUSIE: Really. You mean you can clean up this apartment in a single bound, balance my checkbook, take care of my mortgage, write this report due tomorrow AND tell me the meaning of life?

WOMAN: Close, very close. I can't do all those things for you, but I can find you someone who can—well, except for the housework and the meaning of life.

SUSIE: Huh?

WOMAN: A husband, my dear child. I can get you a husband.

SUSIE: What's this? Who says I want a husband? And what are you anyway? The freelance SDU door-to-door service?

WOMAN: You insult me. I have nothing to do with the government matchmaking unit. I cater only to a select few.

SUSIE: Great. Which agency are you from?

WOMAN: I'm not from any agency.

SUSIE: And why me?

WOMAN: Quite simply, you were on ... the List.

SUSIE: The List?

WOMAN: The List. One of the few singled out for special attention. For starters, you've already exceeded the age at which the average Singapore woman gets married. Also, you are highly educated, with degrees from two of America's top universities ... of course, some men would say you're over educated, but I'm sure we can remedy that unfortunate perception. And most of all, you are still of child-bearing age, which makes it worth my while to bring you back on the right track.

SUSIE: Jeez! Who sent you? The head of the population planning unit? My boss? My mother? Wait, wait. I know. (*Starts smiling suspiciously.*) I'm on Candid Camera—I mean, Gotcha. Right?

WOMAN: No, no, no. Just hear me out. What have you got to lose?

SUSIE: My sanity?

WOMAN: (*Puts her reading glasses on and flips open her laptop*) According to my data, you have a tendency of dating men less academically qualified than you—I guess with your qualifications you can't help it; but you don't have to let them know about the graduate degree. The last date you had described you as over opinionated, over capable and over ... assertive.

SUSIE: God, What's this? A joint project between the SDU and the ISD?

WOMAN: I keep telling you—I'm not with the government. Listen Susie, you're not getting any younger. At least let me tell you what I can do for you.

SUSIE: OK—since this is a 10-minute play, you have (*Looks at her watch.*) about six minutes left.

Woman: Done. My job, quite simply, is to identify your prospective partner based on certain demographic criteria and personality traits. Then I diagnose your weak points, make you over, and viola! you're walking up the aisle. Based on my charts (*Flips open laptop, punches a few keys as if she's looking into a database.*) your first weakness—you waste your time on futile questions wondering about things like where your place in society is, how you fit into the system and whether or not you have a role in changing your society to suit people like yourself.

SUSIE: People like me? What am I? A social statistic?

WOMAN: Yes—English-educated Western liberal female who keeps asking questions. Your need for individualism and independence is at odds with the society you live in. Especially when it comes to finding a spouse. Men here, as a rule, don't like such intellectual wandering.

SUSIE: I see.

WOMAN: You're obviously not very date-smart, despite your being a high flyer at work. Remember that doctor you decided you weren't interested in? Well, you can't even use him as a back-up now because he's getting married in six months. And did you know that his PEP level …

SUSIE: PEP level?

WOMAN: Potential earning power, silly—his PEP level is $150,000 a year—at age 30. That includes his investments of course. And he's very good at those. And your children! They would have been equally adept at both the arts and the sciences because of your two different backgrounds. Plus he consistently scored 'A's' in his second language, which would balance out your—ugh—'C5's' in that subject.

SUSIE: Excuse me, but have you MET the guy? All he could talk about was SALARY SCALES in the government service and how far he can rise in the system because he's an overseas scholar. And he couldn't stop talking about his stocks! Plus he had sweaty palms. PLUS he has never washed a single dish in his life.

WOMAN: For goodness sakes. He had been wondering for three months how to make a move on you—so by the time he decided to hold your hand, of COURSE he had sweaty palms.

SUSIE: Great—I can imagine our wedding night. I'd be in bed with a groper—I mean, a garoupa.

WOMAN: At least you won't be in bed alone.

SUSIE: Listen. Instead of treating the symptoms why don't you treat the root of the problem? There's just too large a gap between the way men and women here think. The men are just too damned conservative and chauvinistic.

WOMAN: I do try to do that—I tell the men whom I matchmake to uh … help out with the housework once or twice a week.

SUSIE: Oh yes—and at the same time you tell women to lower their expectations right? That's great. Just great. (*Taps her foot impatiently and looks pointedly at her watch.*) And you have two minutes left before this play is over.

WOMAN: All right. What I've done for you is to have identified three men who would suit your social and intellectual scale. You have a choice of viewing them first or meeting them later.

SUSIE: Viewing? You run a video service?

WOMAN: Even better—a telepathic computer conference. Their personalities have been programmed into my computer— actually, my secretary did a rush job for you this morning. You know temps ... never take their job seriously—labour shortage and all ... Anyway, with this conference, it'll be like you're talking to them—but of course they won't remember your conversation—and in a telepathic computer conference, they can't lie either.

Shall we begin? We have Richard, an investment banker; Meng, a civil servant on the fast-track ... went to Oxford or something; and (*Taps on computer.*) hmmm, Tony ... we don't seem to have his biodata here—my secretary must have forgotten. (*She types noisily into her laptop and a smoky spotlight appears. There's a desk and a chair and a checkered tablecloth.*)

You can ask them three questions. Can we have bachelor number one, please. (*Drumroll or gameshow music. Man appears at table.*)

RICHARD: (*Adjusts his tie, clears his throat, speaks with pseudo Brit. accent*) Hi Susie, I'm Richard, age 33, current income ... well, I shouldn't say—I don't want a woman to marry me for my money you know, since I do have a rather high net worth. So, what would you like to know about me?

SUSIE: What do you do on Friday nights?

RICHARD: That's easy—I go to Boat Quay and hang out with the guys. I knew Nick Leeson, you know? Knew the whole Barings thing was going to happen even before it blew up. Wanna hear a joke? Nick Leeson is sailing around some island aimlessly—so this guy comes up to him and says: 'What are you doing here, Nick ol boy?' And Nick says, 'I've lost my bearings but I'm keeping my options open.' Get it? Options. Derivatives ... get it? See? Who says Singapore men don't have a sense of humour?

SUSIE: What kind of woman are you looking for?

RICHARD: Actually, I don't look for women; they look for me. Hey, I'm only being honest. But I do want someone who can carry on an intelligent conversation when we have dinner with the bosses. And someone with a golf handicap would be good, but I can always teach her. I'm good at uh ... strokes.

SUSIE: Suppose I get posted to Vietnam. How would you react?

RICHARD: Why would you want to go there? Nothing works in Vietnam. It's so much more comfortable here. Plus if you go overseas, you lose out on promotions here. (*Looks at his watch.*) Hey, that's all, right? I've got to go meet my property agent. Going to look at some showflats in District 15—near the beach you know ... god knows you can't live here without a good piece of property. Despite the restrictions, they're still a necessary investment. Kinda like a woman with good career prospects—high maintenance but solid returns. Ciao, baby. You can send me your CV on the Net.

WOMAN: See? A man with a plan. Good networker that one. If I had a daughter I'd fix her up with him. (*Taps on computer again.*) The next one's not too bad either. (*Spotlight again.*)

MENG: (*Fiddling semi-nervously*) Hi Susie. I've seen your biodata. Can't wait to meet you. You have good genes you know ... I've checked out your parents' medical/social history too, plus their secret IQ test scores ... (*Looks over at the matchmaker who is frantically and obviously trying to shut him up.*) Oh ... she's not supposed to know about the IQ tests? OK.

SUSIE: So—what do you do?

MENG: Genetics research. Eugenics. Working on a project to predict the intelligence of offspring. Intelligence is very important, you know. Men are said not to like brainy women, but I do.

SUSIE: Right. So what do you do for fun?

MENG: Discuss genetic theory with other researchers. That's why someone with a medical background is so important to me. But you'd do too—all you have to do is to read up on the stuff, so we'd have some things in common to talk about ... (*Fade light.*)

SUSIE: I think I've had enough.

WOMAN: (*Sensing her dissatisfaction*) One more—just one more.

SUSIE: Really, I've seen all I want to.

WOMAN: Just wait. (*Spotlight. A guy in a grey T-shirt and jeans comes out.*) Oh shit. How did this guy get in here? This one is supposed to be sent for reconditioning. (*Taps a few keys.*) Can't put him away. My stupid secretary must have put him in the wrong file.

TONY: Hi Susie. How're you? I'm Tony. I gather I'm not very popular with Mrs Matchmaker here.

WOMAN: Susie, he's not one of the men for you—just ignore him.

SUSIE: (*Ignoring her*) Hi Tony. So tell me about yourself.

TONY: I teach 'O' and 'A' level music right now ... I know it's not much compared to the other guys, but I like it. (*Matchmaker is seen trying desperately to adjust the controls.*) What I really want to do is open a cafe and play jazz piano there at night, and have poetry readings. But that's for later—I can't afford to do that now.

SUSIE: A cafe? Really? Where?

TONY: I don't care—anywhere. Here's fine, but there's life beyond the island too.

SUSIE: (*Spotlight is flashing*) What else do you do?

TONY: Rollerblade, go to the beach, read, go stare at the stars, play the piano, all that kind of juvenile stuff. (*Spotlight flashes even more.*) Look, I don't earn as much as you do. Would that be OK with you? It's a problem with some women ... OK, quite a few women.

SUSIE: That's OK—I'd rather be with someone who has a life.

WOMAN: (*Brandishing a remote control*) This ought to work. (*Spotlight flashes, then fades off.*)

SUSIE: HEY!

WOMAN: So, what do you think—Richard? Or Meng? Bachelor number one or two? Let me know and I'll tell you which parts of your personality to suppress to get them.

SUSIE: Neither. I want bachelor number three—Tony.

WOMAN: That is NOT an option.

SUSIE: (*Grabbing her handbag, looking like she's ready to get out the door*) Too bad.

WOMAN: Hey where are you going?

SUSIE: OUT. I'm tired of you barging in here and telling me how to live my life and telling me what to do with my genes. You can take your genetics and social engineering and shove it. (*Starts walking out the door.*)

WOMAN: If you're going to look for Tony, forget it. He won't remember your conversation and you won't be able to meet him because you don't move in the same social circles. Your probability of bumping into him is one in a million.

SUSIE: I'll take my chances. I'm leaving. Most of all, I don't want to be in the same room as you. (*She leaves, slamming the door behind her.*)

WOMAN: (*Packing up*) Singapore girls. So damned choosy! Found her two perfectly nice and capable guys and what does she want? Someone who's ... aiyah, never mind. It's not easy being a sam gu luk por these days. Last time, just introduce them and it's

OK. Now they must have these high faluting things like common values and chemistry. CHEMISTRY! What do you want that for? (*Starts to gather her things.*) I'm going to ask for a transfer, I tell you. Get me to some faraway village in the country where the girls don't go to school. Makes my life easier. (*Starts walking.*) Now, who do I have next? (*Checks filofax.*) Oh GOD! Another one. Angela Tan, 29, lawyer. Another tough case. Why me? (*Runs her finger down Angela's CV.*) Wah liau! Ex-member of debating team some more. Big paycheck and smart mouth. God help me. That's it. I need to quit this job. (*Continues talking as she exits.*) I'm going to withdraw my CPF money and retire to a beach in LA. (*Exits stage, voice fading.*) I hear the men in LA are good looking. Brainless too. Easier to control. Why not?

end

For Tze, July 1993

Angeline Yap

'what shall I bring you?' you ask
as I make my list
of children's sock and T-shirt sizes

'what shall I bring?'
conscious that you leave me to manage
    runny noses,
    piano lessons,
    the clamour of impossible simultaneous questions
    asked by three young kids.

(we've promised ourselves
to someday lease them out
to a childless couple
if only for an afternoon's peace
—but I've deferred drawing up the papers)

'what shall I bring?'
you are loathe to go. I know.
and I
am trying not to think
of the parting that draws near.

If you could I would ask you
to bring back our first year—
the smell of summer
from our walks
to Brattle Square,
and the whales
that leaped off Nantucket
(remember how the dolphins played?).

I'd ask
for the leaves
that bronzed
the Harvard Quad,
the squeeze of your hand
by Walden Pond,
and the hours
spent browsing
amongst old books.
I'd ask
for that summer day
we fled from bees
attracted by our lunch,
or for the strains
from the lone bagpiper's vigil
by the frozen Charles.

but bring again
what you have brought before—
the sights and sounds and smells;
the stone mosaics in Morocco,
the way the cars
make way along the autobahns;
tell me what your eyes have seen,
your ears have heard—
about ice cream in Rome,
the flower fest in Rotterdam
and snowfall in Japan.

but most of all bring back
the squeeze of your dry broad hand.

Kumari

Denyse Tessensohn

The whole staff at the branch of the NTUC supermarket in Telok Blangah could not help discussing the scandal at every break and in between the aisles. That mousy girl, Kumari Govindran, had been arrested for criminal breach of trust. She had been stealing frozen goods!

'No. Actually, money from the till was missing.'

'Perhaps it was true that she took both.' The speculation was rife, and Kumari did not report for work. The management had a headache on their hands, all right. Action had to be taken, and quickly, but the circumstances were a problem the Manager of the branch, Mrs Ho Ai Ling, would rather not have had to deal with. The rule book was no help in this.

'Kumari, you must have known that this is not right. You know that this is a police matter and you can go to jail for stealing. Why did you do it?'

'Why?' Kumari echoed slowly to herself. 'I'm afraid of what is going to happen. Maybe it was going too far, but what else could I do? Next time I won't do it again if it causes such a big fuss. But … was it really wrong?'

None of this was spoken aloud to Mrs Ho, or later to the Inspector who came to question her, nor to the policewoman at the station who questioned her yet again. She maintained a silence that was variously interpreted as being sullen, unrepentant or defiant.

'Look, I can't help you if you don't answer me. You want to help yourself, then speak up!' the fed-up policewoman threw at her. That did not work either.

Mrs Ho had realised her problem when her accomplice had become quite agitated on being caught, because he kept shouting that, 'Miss Kumari is a good girl. She did not keep anything for herself. It is all for the old people.'

'Well, tough! Stealing from the supermarket is still thieving, whoever it is for. What makes people think they can simply help themselves?'

As no further fuss was created by either culprit, she reported the matter routinely to the Committee, and there it rested while the police investigated.

Kumari Govindran, aged 26, was charged with criminal breach of trust against her employers, the NTUC Co-Operative, that operated their popular supermarket branch at Telok Blangah. The goods she was accused of taking were staples—rice, tinned sardines, milk powder, Milo and Maggi mee. There were 148 separate charges against her, because the value of the items totalled $2278. It had been going on for six months before she was caught, with her accomplice, who also faced criminal charges.

The accomplice was one Ariff Mydin, aged 71. A small, thin man of the darkest shade of brown, bespectacled and neatly dressed in the cheapest clothing, he was one of life's victims who had all but given up, but in sheer self-preservation just managed to stay alive but with no noticeable degree of physical comfort.

Who was Kumari Govindran that she should get herself into such a mess?

A nobody. Poor grades at school, close to missing the marriage boat for being without a decent dowry, and plain to look at. Her second worst fault, as far as the few prospective suitors' mothers were concerned, was her complexion which was dark and dull.

'At least learn to cook and keep the house properly!' she was exhorted by her elder sisters. She did her best, but somehow she was not inspired as a homebody, and the food she cooked was just edible.

So she went out to work, here and there, glad of a little independence, such as it was, only in the hours she was away from home. Her parents were barely literate, ultra-conservative and without any hope of better times to come. Kumari's teenage years dreaming of bright possibilities evaporated slowly and she found herself sinking into the same feeling of uncomplaining hopelessness.

Since they had so little themselves, the family did not think at all about their neighbour's problems, mostly correctly assuming that theirs were similar.

Kumari first noticed the old Chinese lady by the staircase on the ground floor, eyeing the steps stoically. But Kumari, who was not really thinking about it, thought she would have a hard time of it, seeing how thin and frail she was. She walked past her up the steps and went on to her flat on the third level.

Coming down later to retrieve a blouse that had blown off the clothesline, she was not too surprised to see the same old lady sitting on the steps, seemingly unable to go up at all. That was when Ariff Mydin returned from his evening walk and went up to the old lady, speaking to her in a mixture of broken Malay and words in a Chinese dialect.

He called out to her to help him.

This was something outside her usual experience. She hesitated, and he spoke to her in Tamil, urging her not to delay, as the old lady should be at home as soon as possible, seeing her so tired and pale.

Kumari, still feeling unsure of herself, Ariff Mydin and the whole situation, went reluctantly forward. Between them they got the old woman up to her flat on the second level at the far end of the building.

The flat was small and rather dark, and occupied by two other old ladies. It was filled with stacks of what appeared to be bundles of clothes. There were three makeshift beds, also piled with bundles.

Ariff explained to her that the old ladies collected discarded clothes and sold them by weight to a dealer who came about once a month. It was how they made money to live on. As their movements were necessarily slow, and the clothing was heavy, it was a tiring process. At eighty cents a kilo, they did not make enough to buy proper food, after the rent was paid, so that left them weak and less able to collect the used clothes. Their monthly stipends were not enough.

'Thank you for helping the old lady,' Ariff said softly to her, as they were leaving. 'Do you work?'

She paused before answering him, not being used to interpersonal communications outside the workplace, with strangers.

'Yes, I work at the NTUC supermarket.'

'That's very good. Your family can buy their food at a discount, right?'

'Yes, that is one of the benefits we have.'

She walked beside him for some time along the corridor, her mind wandering as she looked in doorways and low windows, observing the food preparation and evening activity of the families within.

'What is your name?' he asked politely.

She told him, and he introduced himself. And then they parted ways as she headed for the next level and home.

The very next day, she bumped into him at the supermarket, and he greeted her with real pleasure. As she gave him his bill at the check-out counter, they both realised that he was short of two dollars to cover all the few purchases.

He looked at her. Toothpaste, can of sardines, tin of condensed milk, single bar of soap, packet of cream crackers, two cucumbers and a box of tea leaves made up the items.

'Which do you want me to reverse?' she asked him, taking out a calculator to work out exact deductions.

'Miss Kumari, I don't know. We need everything here.'

She looked stolidly at him. 'Well, make up your mind.' She thought, 'People should not waste our time by going out shopping with not enough money. At least they should know how to choose with the money they have with them.'

'I leave it to you,' he said to her.

'You can't do that!' she exclaimed, surprised.

'I have no more money, and all this is needed at home. How can I choose? You help me decide.'

For the first time in her life, Kumari reached into her own pocket in the uniform, took out two one-dollar coins from the purse she ought not to have had with her, and asked him for the rest of the money to settle the bill.

He looked at her, thanked her, and said he would try to see her that evening downstairs.

It agitated her tremendously, the incident. The idea of Ariff meeting her without purpose was too unusual to be comfortable. She went home deliberately late.

He was waiting for her. He had brought some sweetmeats which he had made himself to thank her once more. She took them very shyly, not wanting to offend him by refusing.

Which is how it all began.

Kumari learnt of the many near-destitute people who lived in the vicinity. She, who had felt without money for a good dowry, became familiar with what it was really like being without money. Being old made it far worse.

So she gave, a little at a time, by buying foodstuffs using her staff discount privileges, knowingly, against regulations.

She found life more interesting, her clandestine activities proving rather enjoyable. A strong satisfaction came with the service she was rendering. The Nobody was becoming well known to a small network of old people whom she visited with her occasional gifts of food.

It grew from there, with Ariff's active encouragement. But it took many months of serious soul-searching before Kumari, who could hardly be called a deep thinker, made a decision to work out the scam with Ariff.

'Don't worry, you are taking nothing for yourself. You are not really doing anything wrong. '

She did not quite agree, but trusted to fate that they would not be caught.

The *modus operandi* was easy. Ariff would go shopping at the supermarket, and Kumari would check out his purchases; only, he would not be charged in full for all the items.

It took the supermarket supervisors months to trace the loss, and then Kumari had to face the consequences, as did Ariff.

They had not had time to work out a story. It had never occurred to them to work out the story 'in case,' as they never expected to be caught. So Ariff tried to take the entire blame, and in so doing confused the investigation.

But both of them had not reckoned with the anonymous, unimportant twelve old people who had been the beneficiaries of the acts.

Jointly, they went to see their Member of Parliament, who was that day having the press to tea, so they could observe the work at grassroots level.

It did not take long for them to get excited and loud, one old man dramatically offering to cut his wrists there and then with the small knife he had brought along for the purpose.

The press loved the photogenic possibilities of the situation and made it a Home Story that exploited every angle of the pathos displayed.

NTUC hastily found out all the unusual details and themselves declared that, while they did not approve of the crime committed in any way, Kumari Govindran was a conscientious worker who had an unblemished record for the five years that she had worked there. They would, of course, support their own worker in every possible way.

There were letters to the press. Offers of assistance to the two accused in the form of money and legal counsel were generously extended. People gathered money and gifts for the twelve old people who were featured by the media in the most poignant manner.

Appeals were made to the Attorney-General's office for leniency, and distinguished people wrote in for the charges even to be dropped.

While all the hoopla was going on, Kumari received a proposal of marriage from a young man, who had read all about her and refused point-blank anything by way of a dowry. Her parents accepted the marriage offer with her bemused consent.

Everyone is hopeful about the outcome of all the appeals being made in the case.

Till Bankrupt Do Us Part

Lin Hsin Hsin

it surely will
empower some & bankrupt others

armchair shopping
is available twenty-four hours

supermarketing the food
& browsing the goods
can all be done at a click
& in the thick of your goodwood
without even leaving your door & exit
to the stores in your neighbourhood

invoice will be quickly sent to you
& you can pay the bills
by inserting your *smartcard*
into the friendly terminal in front of you

alternatively, you can pay
by your favourite charge or credit card
accumulate bonus points
or get a free massage

armchair shopping
is more than an art
it's a *techno-logical-shopping-bug*
that binds & hugs

for richer or poorer
for better or worse
in sickness and in health
till bankrupt do us part!

from Exit

Eleanor Wong

'Exit' was produced in 1990 by Action! Theatre as part of a doublebill with Chua Tze Wei's 'Trine.'

Synopsis

Chen Tze Wen's seemingly ordinary and unexceptional life takes a bizarre turn when he is arrested one night by members of the mysterious Foreign Affairs Department 'dealing with exit problems' (Part I: The Arrest). He undergoes a terrifying and baffling interrogation during which it is slowly revealed to him by his nameless interrogators that he is being investigated for alleged treason because of his desire to emigrate and at the end of which, broken, he confesses (Part II: The Interrogation). In Part III: The Trial (which appears below), Chen is prosecuted for, and must defend himself against, this charge of treason.

Characters

DEFENCE COUNSEL
PROSECUTOR
COURT CLERK
CHEN TZE WEN
STEWARDESS
MUM
FRIEND
ANNA
BOSS
WIFE
YAP
ARTIE
PRESS
STAGEHAND

Production Note

The script calls for the play's performance area to be in the centre of the audience, with audience seats surrounding the performance area in a square or rectangular formation.

Casting Note

In Part III: The Trial, certain members of the ensemble cast play multiple roles, i.e., all the witnesses (STEWARDESS, MUM, FRIEND, ANNA, BOSS, WIFE, YAP, ARTIE, PRESS) are played by ensemble members.

Part III: The Trial

As the lights come back on, COURT CLERK *enters carrying a chair which he deposits in the centre of the stage. He also has a rope around his neck, hung like a noose. He walks across the central area. At the edge of the audience, he secures the edge of the rope to a chair and proceeds to fence the 'court area' in. When he has come full circle, he indicates to the trial participants (except WEN) to enter, then steps into the court and secures the other end of the noose.*

PROSECUTOR *and* DEFENSE COUNSEL *tango to centre stage together.*

> (*It is envisaged that each major participant will have a signature dance. Every now and then, he moves, using his dance step. E.g., the* PROSECUTOR's *could be a little march.*)

DEFENSE: Fifteen years for rape. Congratulations.

PROSECUTOR: Thank you. The drug trafficker?

DEFENSE: Off on a technicality.

PROSECUTOR: Masterful.

> (*They twirl.*)

PROSECUTOR: The Chen case, I suppose.

DEFENSE: Yes. You too?

PROSECUTOR: Aha (*as in affirmation*).

239

(*At that, they abruptly break apart and take up opposing positions.*)

CLERK: Bangun. (*All rise.*) The Supreme Court is now in session; the honourable Justice See Yew Lai (*As in 'See you lie.'*) presiding. Public Prosecutor against Chen Tze Wen.

PROSECUTOR: May the charge be read to the accused.

(WEN *is outside the fence trying to get in, but there's no way. During this scene, while the witnesses are giving testimony, the flow of question and answer should be as uninterrupted as possible, i.e., there should be some overlap as* WEN *responds to what is going on, but everyone else ignores him.*)

CLERK: (*Addresses the empty chair*) You, Chen Tze Wen, NRIC No. 0878271D ...

WEN: You're going to start without me?

CLERK: Quiet in the court.

PROSECUTOR: Just a minor disturbance outside.

WEN: What's going on?

CLERK: (*Ignoring* WEN *and addressing the empty chair again—his dance could be a sort of military tattoo*) You. Chen Tze Wen, NRIC No. 0878271D are charged that you on or about the _____ day of _____ 1990 (*i.e., one day before the date chosen for the arrest in Part I, the intention being for the producer to insert a date close to the date of the production*), in Singapore, committed the offence of treasonable disloyalty in that you wilfully harboured, singly or in consultation with another or others unknown, a prohibited intent, to wit, the intention to quit the country without lawful excuse, and have thereby committed an offence punishable under the Deportation Act of 1990.

DEFENSE: He pleads not guilty.

PROSECUTOR: (*Strutting with a great deal of flair ... in the style of Susan Dey of 'LA Law.' Everyone in the court has seen this act before and, rolling his/her eyes, is not that impressed.*) Please the court. The accused, ladies and gentlemen, was given every opportunity;

afforded every advantage. Yet, *he* decided (*Long, long pause for effect.*) to leave. (*Horrified gasp from audience.*) Yes. Mutiny. Desertion. Betrayal. (*Long pause.*) And we have the evidence to prove it.

(*The ensemble cast members who take on the roles of witnesses have been standing quietly at the four corners of the performance area from the start of Part III. Some of them, such as FRIEND and ANNA, could speak their lines from their respective corners or could move forward into the performance space. Spotlight on Witness Number 1, AIR STEWARDESS. Could either sing some airline jingle like 'We love to fly and it shows,' or 'Fly the friendly skies,' or pose in typical air stewardess style while the theme song of an airline is played. Should be slightly silly in character.*)

PROSECUTOR: Prosecution Exhibit 1, please.

(STEWARDESS *holds up a blown-up airline ticket. Concerted gasp.*)

PROSECUTOR: And what, (*Looking around with satisfaction.*) is Exhibit 1?

STEWARDESS: An airline ticket.

PROSECUTOR: To whom is it issued?

STEWARDESS: Mr Chen Tze Wen.

PROSECUTOR: You mean the accused?

STEWARDESS: Beg your pardon?

PROSECUTOR: Chen Tze Wen, the accused.

STEWARDESS: Yes sir.

PROSECUTOR: When was it purchased?

STEWARDESS: _____ (*The date of the charge*)

PROSECUTOR: And what sort of ticket is it?

STEWARDESS: Sorry?

PROSECUTOR: What sort of ticket is it? Return?

STEWARDESS: Oh no. One way ticket, sir.

PROSECUTOR: Thank you. (*Pauses, as if the conclusion is self-evident.*)

CLERK and WEN: Is that all?

PROSECUTOR: Not at all. My second and only other exhibit (*Dramatic pause.*) is the accused himself!

(*Another gasp from audience.*)

PROSECUTOR: Through the testimony of witnesses, we will paint a picture of the accused; a man with no reason whatsoever to leave, a man sparing no thought save for his selfish and unreasonable whims, ungrateful of the effort and expense devoted to him by the country of his birth, and unwilling to shoulder his responsibilities as a loyal citizen. A traitor, ladies and gentlemen.

WEN: It's not true!

PROSECUTOR: (*To* DEFENSE) Did that come off all right?

DEFENSE: Yes, yes. Quite dramatic.

WEN: Who would say these things about me?

CLERK: Call your witnesses.

(MUM *waltzes in.*)

MUM: From the time he was a child, I tell you.

WEN: Mum???

MUM: He didn't like to play with other children. Such a serious boy.

FRIEND: (*Eager type*) I can confirm that. I can. Not a group person. Good chap. Friendly. But had his own ideas.

PROSECUTOR: Uh, thank you. I'll call you when it's your turn.

FRIEND: Oh. Just wanted to help.

PROSECUTOR: Yes … thank you. (*To* MUM) Bookish, was he?

MUM: Not really. But we had a garden where he spent all his time. He likes solitude.

WEN: I was happy there.

MUM: We used to worry about him, his Dad and I.

WEN: Why?

PROSECUTOR: Why? Did you feel his behaviour was unusual?

MUM: He would talk out loud sometimes. As if there was someone else there.

WEN: There was.

PROSECUTOR: SOMEONE ELSE?

MUM: We just wished he had more friends, lah.

FRIEND: Oh, he did. Like me. (*Proudly.*) Just liked to have his own space, you know.

PROSECUTOR: Please.

FRIEND: Oh. Yes. (*Shuts up.*)

PROSECUTOR: You were saying, ma'am?

MUM: Not healthy, you know, to spend so much time alone.

WEN: But I loved those times. Freshly mown grass, clean from the rain, prickling at the back of my neck while I lay looking at the sky.

MUM: Couldn't tell what he was thinking, you see.

FRIEND: That's what I mean. Just had to have his own private space.

PROSECUTOR: For the last time!

FRIEND: Sorry.

PROSECUTOR: Or I'm not going to call you at all.

FRIEND: Oh no, don't be a spoilsport.

PROSECUTOR: (*Wearily turning to* MUM) So you believe that might have been the start of it?

WEN: When I was twelve, I followed the monsoon drain behind our house, to the forest reserve. If I needed to think, that was what I'd do. Sneak out, crash through the dead brown leaves and sit at the water's edge.

MUM: Hah? What is that?

PROSECUTOR: Do you think that might have been when he started to lose touch with reality?

WEN: No.

MUM: (*Considering*) Maybe.

WEN: That was when I was most clearheaded. Clearsighted. It broke my heart when we moved.

FRIEND: I remember that.

PROSECUTOR: Okay, that's it. (*Spotlight goes off on* FRIEND.)

FRIEND: (*From the dark*) But don't you want to know about … (*He is cut off abruptly, as if someone has clamped his mouth shut.*)

PROSECUTOR: Did this behaviour continue into adulthood?

MUM: We hoped he had settled down. Good job, promotions, marriage.

WEN: There was no longer anywhere to go.

PROSECUTOR: (*To* MUM) Thank you. By the way, what was his favourite colour?

MUM: Blue. (*She walks off.*)

ALL: BLUE!

PROSECUTOR: (*Indicating that he has another witness*) And what, Professor Anna Lis, (*As in 'Analyst.'*) are the implications of this?

ANNA: It is my considered opinion that people whose favourite colour is blue are dangerously disposed to individualism.

WEN: That's total bullshit.

ANNA: My conclusion is supported by research showing that subject uses the word 'I' or some variant thereof 8,329 times in his conversations over the past two weeks.

WEN: I can't believe this.

ANNA: 8,330.

(BOSS *dances in.*)

PROSECUTOR: Sir, you are the accused's employer? (BOSS *nods.* PROSECUTOR *indicates that he proceed.*)

BOSS: Yes.

PROSECUTOR: So. Did you think the accused was dangerously individualistic? Selfish even?

BOSS: No, I wouldn't quite say that.

PROSECUTOR: Oh. But was he lazy?

WEN: I worked my butt off for you.

BOSS: No, I thought he had potential.

PROSECUTOR: But couldn't make the grade?

BOSS: Wouldn't say that either.

PROSECUTOR: Lacked commitment?

WEN: It was a job, dammit, not the search for the Holy Grail.

WIFE: (*To* BOSS) How can you say that? Wen used to work late sometimes.

WEN: What more did you want? I did my job. I put in the hours.

PROSECUTOR: Mrs Chen!

DEFENSE: Objection. Uncorroborated testimony of an accomplice.

WEN: But she's speaking up in my defence, you fool!

WIFE: Actually, I didn't want to go. We just moved into a new flat.

Then I managed to get Bobbie enrolled in pre-school. But Wen insisted that we had to leave.

DEFENSE: Objection!

WEN: Let her speak.

PROSECUTOR: Oh, it's all right. I don't need her anyway. Sorry about that, your Honour. Can't always control these non-legal types, you know. They want to tell you everything. Now, where were we .... Soft?

BOSS: No. I can hear you.

PROSECUTOR: I mean the accused.

BOSS: Oh. No, no, that's too extreme.

PROSECUTOR: Then how *would* you describe him?

BOSS: Don't mistake me, but he always seemed a little restless.

PROSECUTOR: (*Settling for whatever crumb he can get*) Ah, restless!

BOSS: Don't mistake me. It's usually the case, you know. From my experience. After a few years, when the ... er ... learning curve, you know, levels out. Three years, that's my estimate. The younger ones get restless.

WEN: I ran a glorified postal service for stocks and bonds, for God's sake. Learning curve? We never got off the ground!

PROSECUTOR: One final question. Speaking with the benefit of your experience, is there any lack of opportunity for advancement for a young person with initiative and drive?

BOSS: Oh really. No doubt at all in my mind. Of course not.

PROSECUTOR: Thank you.

WEN: (*Shouting at* DEFENSE COUNSEL) Aren't you going to ask him any questions? Aren't you going to ask him what the point is?

DEFENSE: No questions for this witness.

WEN: Six days a week, I wake up, brush my teeth, shave, match ties to shirt and pants. I rush to make it in before the traffic snarls, my hair still damp from the shower. All day, I sit in an office with windows looking out over the garbage collection ramp. I leave work late, have dinner, watch TV. Sleep.

PROSECUTOR: That's my last witness.

WEN: What's the point?

CLERK: (*To* PROSECUTOR) Closing address?

WEN: That's enough?

PROSECUTOR: I submit that the witnesses' testimony is crystal clear. The accused had every reason to stay.

(PROSECUTOR *gathers the witnesses into a conga chain. They take turns to sing, Caribbean style, the following lines, each line being echoed by the rest of the chain after the soloist:*

> *What de problem wid living here?*
> *Plenty comfort and plenty cheer.*
> *Think about it, it very clear,*
> *Only traitors be leaving here!*

They chant 'traitor, traitor' at empty chair, volume rising to fortissimo. They abruptly stop. There is a stunned silence. They slowly return to their places at the four corners.)

DEFENSE: We accept that the accused voluntarily decided to go.

WEN: What? Are you trying to get me convicted?

DEFENSE: But, Sir, as you well know, nothing is an offence which is done in the exercise of private defence. Necessity, in other words, completely excuses. The defence shall call expert witnesses to testify that the prospect of life here was so intolerable, the accused had no choice, indeed, was compelled, to leave.

CLERK: Not calling him, ah? (*Indicating the chair.*)

DEFENSE: No.

WEN: Why not?

CLERK: Carry on.

WEN: Why not? (*He runs around, trying to get in. Finally, in desperation,* WEN *jumps over the rope and runs to the centre of the stage. The timing for this sequence must be very fast, so as to create a sense of confusion and escalating chaos.*)

DEFENSE: What are you doing here? Let me handle this.

CLERK: Who is this?

DEFENSE: No one important.

WEN: I'm the accused.

CLERK: Then who's *this*? (*Indicating the chair.*)

DEFENSE: This is most irregular. You must trust your lawyers to map out the best strategy for your defence. Truly now. You pay us for that.

WEN: But you're screwing it up! Who are these experts?

DEFENSE: Precisely what I'm coming to. Mr Yap Pi Man (*As in 'Yuppieman.'*) …

YAP: The problem is, there is ABSOLUTELY NOTHING to do here. Quality of life. Totally missing. Art? Culture? Films? Books? What a joke. I have to subscribe to the *New York Times Book Review* to find out what the latest in good reading is. It's disgraceful.

PROSECUTOR: Ooh, let me at him.

WEN: What has any of this got to do with me?

CLERK: Order. Order.

YAP: Material comfort isn't everything, you know. After a certain stage, you want something more. Graciousness. Class. Why don't people stand aside to let you off trains in this country?

WEN: You want to know why? I'll tell you.

YAP: Yes. Why? It's so rude. They crowd the entrance. You can't get out without shoving their shopping bags aside.

WEN: (*Interrupting*) I didn't mean that. I meant … I'll tell you why I'm leaving.

YAP: See? He doesn't know.

DEFENSE: (*To* WEN) Please. Sit down.

(*As* WEN *looks around.*)

CLERK: (*Indicating the empty chair*) Sorry, that's taken.

WEN: What?

CLERK: You can't sit there. It's taken.

WEN: I don't want to sit.

DEFENSE: Sit!

(WEN *doesn't sit. Instead, he starts pacing.*)

CLERK: Cross-examination?

PROSECUTOR: Mr Yap. Isn't it true that you frequent Hannigan's (*Consulting his notes*), an 'American-style drinking hole boasting ambience, good music, flowing drinks and the chance to meet other young, upwardly mobile professionals'?

YAP: Yes.

WEN: No.

PROSECUTOR: Also, hang around the Village? A 'quaint assortment of pubs, small shops, cafes, fast-food joints and karaoke lounges offering everything from Mexican food to Asian antiques'?

YAP: Yes.

WEN: No.

PROSECUTOR: Member of the sailing club?

YAP: Yes.

WEN: No.

PROSECUTOR: Gym?

YAP: Of course.

WEN: No.

PROSECUTOR: Attend the Film Festival, Drama Festival, Arts Festival every year?

YAP: Yes, except that the Arts Festival isn't every year, you know that.

PROSECUTOR: Hardly a barren lifestyle, wouldn't you say?

YAP: (*Splutters a little*) Perhaps not. But far from being truly gracious.

PROSECUTOR: (*Proudly to everyone, as if saying, 'You see?'*) Not enough, I submit, your Honour, to amount to a legal excuse for desertion!

WEN: I don't care!

DEFENSE: You're distracting me!

WEN: Please, let me tell them about the mountain.

(*Abrupt silence. Pause.*)

ALL: Mountain?

DEFENSE: You see? You're confusing them. Err ... I'd like to call my next witness. Ms Artie Fah. (*As in 'Arty-fart.'*)

ARTIE: Where, I want to know, can a person go for intellectual stimulation in this blasted place? Government censorship keeps out the best works and this *local* stuff. I mean. You're kidding me, right?

PROSECUTOR: Your Honour, it's clear that Ms Artie is going to repeat the same evidence as the previous witness. The defence, your Honour, must prove legal excuse. Not this spineless griping. Must we waste further time?

ARTIE: Much as I hate to be associated, in even the slightest way, with Mr Yap, on occasion, I must agree with him. This is a cultural desert. Where is the vibrance? The push and shove of ideas? The excitement of creation? The refinement of history?

WEN: That's enough! If you want to see pictures of nude people having sex hung on our museum walls, more power to you. I don't.

DEFENSE: You don't seem to understand. I am trying to build a case here. And I haven't even gotten to the political repression.

PROSECUTOR: WHAT?

WEN: Maybe there is a case to be built. Maybe there are people who leave because of a case. Everything that's been said today sounds like some perverted echo in me, so maybe, deep down, I'm leaving because of a case.

DEFENSE: Exactly. I wish to call Ms Press. Ms Florence Press.

PROSECUTOR: Objection. Lack of standing!

WEN: Wait. Let me finish.

PROSECUTOR: Ms Florence Press has no standing to comment on this case. Interference in domestic politics.

PRESS: This is a city of fear and repression. Public opinion is stifled in the name of order, silenced by the heavy autocratic hand of the powers that be.

PROSECUTOR: Slander. Defamation.

PRESS: There is no freedom of information or press …

PROSECUTOR: Gazette her!

PRESS: … without which a free society is impossible.

PROSECUTOR: Stop her. Immediately.

WEN: What are you afraid of? If there is a case to be built, let's hear all sides of it.

DEFENSE: That's the spirit. Carry on, Ms Press.

WEN: No!

DEFENSE: No?

WEN: If there's a case to be built, we should hear every side there is to it. Loudly, without fear. There's a place for that. But now. Here. I'm the one being tried, not your case.

DEFENSE: You laymen! Forever getting it all mixed up. (*Turning to* PROSECUTOR *for assistance.*) Would you? Please? ...

PROSECUTOR: The *only* thing being tried is your case. It's what the judge gets to see. (*Pause.*) Oh dear. You expected him to judge *you?* How endearingly innocent.

DEFENSE: We'd have won with him (*Pointing to chair.*) but no, you *had* to barge in.

PROSECUTOR: Oh, I wouldn't overstate my position if I were *you.* We have an airtight case.

DEFENSE: Nonsense. A trifle over the top, even for you.

PROSECUTOR: (*Anxious for approval*) You think I shouldn't have gone that extra round in my closing, don't you?

DEFENSE: Oh no. That was a nice touch. Not my style, naturally, but ...

WEN: This is a bloody masquerade.

(*Both* DEFENSE *and* PROSECUTOR *stop their intimate discussion.*)

PROSECUTOR: What did you say?

WEN: It's a farce, a charade. It's ludicrous.

PROSECUTOR: Contempt of court!

WEN: And what is your precious process but contempt of me?

PROSECUTOR: Arrest him.

CLERK: He's already under arrest.

PROSECUTOR: Do it again!

PRESS: Another example of official oppression.

PROSECUTOR: Arrest her too!

DEFENSE: Now see what you've done?

MUM: *Aiyoh*, why so stubborn, Wen?

BOSS: What a waste of potential.

ANNA: Bordering on delusionary megalomania.

YAP: Just can't understand why they don't stand aside and let us out first.

PRESS: (*Scuffle*) Get your hands off me! I demand the right to an attorney.

DEFENSE: Here, have my card.

ARTIE: Crass. Too crass.

(*There is a scuffle as* PROSECUTOR *tries to restrain* WEN.)

WEN: Let me go!

(WEN *punches* PROSECUTOR *to the ground where he sits in sudden bemusement. This exchange shocks everyone else into silence.*)

WEN: Listen. The first time I saw a mountain, it seemed that tears grew from my belly, rose up and lodged in my throat.

DEFENSE: Not mountain talk again.

WEN: But you see, before that, my heights had always been mildly sloping or, if steep, had to be scaled in smooth, silent lifts. Sometimes the lifts spoke. Ground level. Good Morning. Going up. (PROSECUTOR *says, 'I've seen those …' The effect should be of murmuring and remarks at the beginning of the monologue that gradually fall silent as* WEN *proceeds.*) But always they were steel and glass and concrete. Always I was caged. Now, this mountain spoke. It too called. Ground level. Good morning. Going up. But it was earth and wood and snow. And at the top, when we stepped out, it let us run about its aged white crown. Imagine. It LET US RUN. So I did. Paddling my legs in the soft sinking snow. Waving my arms. To keep my balance, you know. Like a mad person.

Yah. Really.

Not used to the snow. Never been this cold. I kept falling …
running, running, falling, running, falling, running, running
…

And that's when I met him again. After all those years. Under
blue sky and blazing white sun. His colour was high, his voice
excited. He shouted at the trees in the valley. Happy things,
angry things, stupid things. Lay in the snow till his head started
to ache from the cold but he could feel his nose peel with
sunburn. Weird, right?

I knew then. I would only find him in wideness and open
space.

Some months ago, I was riding in the MRT. Just gone shopping.
The wife wanted to. Weekend crowd was everywhere, pushing
at me. Not anyone's fault. NOT ENOUGH SPACE. That's all.

I suddenly realised we hadn't seen each other for a long time,
and if I didn't watch out, I would forget how to get in touch
with him.

After that, every time I was in the train, I would stand at the
doors and stare out the glass. Maybe a mountain would speak.
But the black tunnel only reflected my face.

So that is the reason. Very simple, actually. I am leaving to meet
an old friend again.

(*There is a short silence. Then some of the onlookers start clapping;
hopefully, this will set the whole theatre off.*)

SOME: Bravo. Bravo.

DEFENSE: (*Dancing in joy*) Excellent. So touching. I'm really rather
miffed at you. Why didn't you tell me you could do this? I would
have put you on the stand from the very beginning.

PROSECUTOR: I don't see what the big fuss is about. Who is this
friend? Sounds fishy to me. Is he going to corroborate the
testimony?

DEFENSE: Your Honour, you heard my client. I submit the Prosecution has no case.

PROSECUTOR: Not so fast. When has a social engagement constituted a defence to treason? In fact, the accused stands convicted by his own testimony.

CLERK: Ooh, a confession. Always much more fun with a confession. (*Rubs his hands in glee.*)

PROSECUTOR: You heard him. In open court. He decided to leave to meet an old friend again. NO EXCUSE! Guilty.

DEFENSE: He has a point there.

WEN: Damn you all.

DEFENSE: I told you to leave it to the experts.

WEN: How is my decision evil? Why was it wrong?

DEFENSE: That's quite beside the point.

PROSECUTOR: I submit. The accused's own confession proves the charge of treason. Conclusively.

WEN: Tell me. What would have been a legal excuse?

PROSECUTOR: Also, your Honour will recall, you witnessed the accused in the act. Contempt of court, and might I add, assaulting an officer of the law while in the conduct of her duty.

WEN: Tell me. What reason would have been good enough?

CLERK: Any previous record?

WEN: *Nothing* would have been enough, right? That's what you're saying. *Nothing.*

PROSECUTOR: Nothing known.

WEN: It's so perfect here? It's paradise? No reason could be valid? Every leaving is a treachery?

CLERK: Any submission on sentence?

WEN: TELL ME! (*Everyone stops for a while, then ... everyone ignores him.*)

CLERK: Any submission on sentence?

WEN: We don't all need the same things. (*Tired now, disheartened.*) Sometimes they just aren't here.

PROSECUTOR: The prosecution recommends a deterrent sentence.

WEN: Do you want to drive us away altogether? (*Pause.*) Very well, (*Resigned.*) find me guilty

DEFENSE: Beg your pardon?

PROSECUTOR: Make up your mind.

WEN: Find me guilty then.

CLERK: (*Very alert suddenly*) Does your client wish to amend his plea after all?

DEFENSE: I suppose so. Are you sure?

WEN: I told the truth. Nothing I could have said would have excused me. So I must be guilty, mustn't I?

DEFENSE: Well, actually, the process isn't really about the truth.

WEN: And I am sick and tired of your bloody process.

PROSECUTOR: We're amenable to a plea of guilt, I suppose. He could have said so sooner.

CLERK: You realise the implication of your plea, do you not?

WEN: I really don't care anymore. What can you do? Lock me up? I'm already caged.

CLERK: (*Notes down*) Chen Tze Wen. You plead guilty to the charge against you?

WEN: Yes.

CLERK: Sentenced to deportation.

DEFENSE: (*To PROSECUTOR*) Lunch after this?

PROSECUTOR: Your treat?

> (*Everyone packs up and starts to leave. The court clerk grabs* WEN *and pulls him.*)

WEN: Wait! Where are you taking me? How long is the sentence?

CLERK: Life.

WEN: Life! (*He's totally stunned. Slumps. It's all been too much for him.*)

WEN: You can't do this. Not for life! Please.

CLERK: You heard the judge.

WEN: Don't lock me up like this …

DEFENSE: There you go again. You're all mixed up. No one's going to lock you up.

WEN: What? (*Perking up desperately.*)

PROSECUTOR: Didn't you listen?

DEFENSE: You wanted to leave? You get to leave.

WEN: What?

CLERK: The sentence is deportation.

WEN: I get to leave?

CLERK: Yes. Yes. That's right.

WEN: I get to leave? (*He starts laughing hysterically.*)

> (*Everyone breaks out of character and gets up to go.*)

WEN: Wait! (*They stop with a 'now what?' attitude.*) The term is life? What does that mean?

DEFENSE: You don't know?

CLERK: Exactly what it says. DEPORTATION … FOR … LIFE …

WEN: Does that mean I can't return?

DEFENSE: Amazing. And I thought his strategy so brilliant.

PROSECUTOR: Strategy?

DEFENSE: You know. Got to be cruel to be kind ... guilty to escape ...

PROSECUTOR: That *would* have been brilliant.

WEN: I can't return ever?

CLERK: Of course not. You think we want traitors here?

WEN: But I'm not a traitor.

CLERK: Well, you're not welcome anymore.

WEN: This is my home. You can't keep me out forever.

DEFENSE, PROSECUTOR and CLERK: Oh yes, we can.

WEN: Look. Call the judge. This is a mistake.

CLERK: Sorry ...

WEN: I HAVE TO CHANGE MY PLEA.

CLERK: Too late.

WEN: No, no, no, no ...

DEFENSE: Speaking of which, lunch reservations don't keep ...

> (PROSECUTOR *and* DEFENSE COUNSEL *tango out.* COURT CLERK *sashays contemptuously behind them.* WEN *is left on stage, on his knees. Long pause before house lights are turned on. A stage hand or janitor comes in, sweeping, picking up props.*)

STAGEHAND: Excuse me, sir. You have to go now.

> (WEN *breaks down. Sobbing.*)

[*end of extract*]

The Rap

Rosaly Puthcheary

I hear a stutter of consonance
an acoustic rumble
a connotation of violence
enshrouded in rhyme.

I listen to a clatter of a street
in the drum of his lips,
splatter through the beat
in the images he records.

I watch the terror of anger
as the phonemes splutter fury,
the rhythm relays a horror
hammered on his psyche.

I see the coil of his rancour
in the rattle of his ballad;
the rap embodies power
in the ramble of sound.

Not All Babies Have Endearing Faces

Lee Tzu Pheng

Not all babies have endearing faces.
Often, I'd say, the truth of this
impresses. I've seen quite a few
really ugly ones, where
the proportions are troublingly askew;
or where, familial beauty notwithstanding,
the least appealing features reappear
in eyes too close, a concave brow,
slack mouth, or gibbous nose.

Or, as with some, a face beyond their years—
little old gnomes, grandparents' miniatures.
It's not the blemishes of skin, or pallor
of complexion that can ruin
the young face, but the impression
that nature's waywardness holds sway,
or else her perplexing variety.
I saw an infant once, my blood ran cold:
face of Lugosi's Dracula in a four-year-old.

Thank God, the human heart is less deceived!
—holds dear a gift, however plain the wrapping.
For just as certain is this observation:
the child dismissed from winsome angeldom
is centre of his family's attention,
the one you see his siblings fighting over,
the one dandled with total tenderness,
and perfect in the proud gaze of his mother.

Gareth's Room

Elizabeth Su

The sun burst into his room. It entered with a great rush of light and exploded into a hundred beams of radiant energy, bathing his bed in a warm, yellow glow. It bounced off the pale-blue walls cheerfully, fell upon his favourite Mortal Kombat action figures with gusto and devoured every single empty space. Gareth was annoyed. Why hadn't Nita drawn the curtains? She knew he didn't like to be woken up before it was time. What time was it, anyway?

He looked at his G-shock watch and saw that it was ten o'clock. He was rather proud of his watch. It had been the last G-shock in the shop at Takashimaya and he had been the envy of his gang of friends when he wore it to school. G-shocks were the latest fashion, and he was lucky to have gotten the watch when it was most popular.

Gareth rubbed his eyes. Why did his room have to face the sun? His mother had said it was good fengshui. He did not really know what that meant. He only knew that it was supposed to be good for your health or something, and if you placed your bed and slept in it, with your feet facing the door, that was bad luck and meant you could be dying sooner than you had expected. His mother had invited the fengshui man to come into the house just after they had moved in, and he had ordered the furniture to be shifted around as if it were his own house.

'Now, Mrs Tan, why would you put the oven there? The fire will not be good in that dark corner. As for the family altar, it should go there—that position will please your ancestors because they can get to hear your prayers more directly and see the offerings you place on the altar.'

And when he had come to Gareth's room, he had paused and for a brief moment, Gareth thought, *Ah! He has decided to leave my room alone.* But no such luck. The fengshui man had merely stopped to take a breath—he had been talking non-stop for nearly half an hour.

He surveyed Gareth's room, and shook his head most perceptibly. 'Mrs Tan, you should think twice about letting your son sleep in a double-decker bed. First of all, it is not good fengshui to place it in that position where it faces the door. You know, it is so important that the feet do not face the door. If you remember, that is the way we place our dead, feet first through the door. And next, why a double-decker bed? You have only one child, and he does not need a double-decker bed.'

Boy! Gareth thought, That wasn't fengshui. It was dis-crim, discrim-ation. What was that word he had heard the adults use? That word that meant that it was so unfair, and he was receiving unjust treatment. Never mind whatever that long word was, the fengshui man was using it now on him—Gareth. It had taken him two weeks to coax, cajole, persuade, threaten his parents to buy him a double-decker. He had gone for one night without food, just to show how determined he was that he should get the bed he coveted. And now, all it needed was for one big-mouth fengshui crook to cheat him of his well-deserved double-decker. Why, the new spaceship 'Enterprise' was still waiting to be launched from the upper deck, waiting to roam the vast expanses in the universe. Why couldn't this man bother about Nita's room? Why his?

Gareth prowled around the fengshui man restlessly, hoping his mother would not listen to all this stupid mumbo-jumbo. He needed his double-decker bed. He had to have space to launch his new supersonic laser weapon. It was an awesome thing. And he needed to use it to attack the enemy territory in the south where Lord Zed's army was located. Besides, how was he going to be Tarzan if he did not have his tree and the cliff from which he could jump into the waterfall pool (his fibre-filled cushion was going to double-up as the pool; it was nice and soft when you jumped into it).

Gareth noticed his mother looking uncertainly at him. He put on his best mutinous face and stood with his feet apart, looking ready to do battle. If this strange man was going to deprive him of his bed, Gareth was not going to stand idly by. He was going to fight. He'd call upon his forces that were even now awaiting his instructions. He would order his little army to position themselves right in the path of this intruder so that this enemy would fall hopelessly all over the floor. Wasn't that what that kid in 'Home Alone' had done? He had placed his toys strategically so that they would frustrate the robbers entering his house.

But luckily, he could see his mother having that look. It was a special look, as if she felt uncomfortable and wanted to squirm and wriggle to get that beastly insect out from under her skirt. Actually, the first time she'd had that look, at least as far as Gareth could remember, was when he had played that trick on her and put a little earthworm on her leg. That trick had earned him three spanks on his little six-year-old bottom. Later, his mother had had that same look when his uncle had made a joke about the American President and his wife, and talked about a bush or was it no bush? Anyway, his mother's face had turned a little pink, and she had shifted her seat on the sofa so she was a little further away from Uncle Mark, as if she did not want to associate too closely with a man who seemed to like bushes. Now, Gareth noticed that same look on her face, and he was encouraged. He decided to change his tactics.

Quickly, he dropped his pose of angry young man. His face gentled into lines of disappointment. His mouth drooped appealingly at the corners and he allowed a teardrop to pool into shimmering brightness in his eyes. His father had always said he was a good actor. 'Gareth takes after me,' his father would tell his friends who visited them at their old HUDC apartment in Clementi. 'He is so dramatic, a chip of the old block. You know, I was in the Literary, Debating and Dramatic Society for four years in secondary school, and I was a school debater in the inter-school debates.'

'Maybe Gareth will make it to "Triple Nine." I hear they are auditioning for a child actor in one of their next shows,' volunteered Mavis Chow, his father's old secretary who was now pregnant with her third child. She had always resisted the idea of having more than one child but since the government had changed its two-child policy to encourage couples to have more than two children, she had rallied valiantly to the call to be a good citizen and produce more babies.

'This is my national service,' she used to laugh and pat at her growing stomach. Gareth could never understand how her stomach could grow so grotesquely huge. She must be having the wrong kinds of food in her diet, he thought a little pityingly. His mother and father were so careful with what they ate. They had even taught

Gareth to read the labels on cans at the supermarket to watch out for additives. And they had bought a calorie counting book which they sometimes would surreptitiously take out to consult.

Mavis Chow normally was not a very intelligent woman, Gareth thought, but for once, she had said something interesting and true. He was his father's son. Hadn't his father patted him on the shoulder and said so? His father heard Mavis' suggestion and looked a little pleased, flattered that Mavis considered his son acting material. Then, almost immediately, he drew himself up to his full height of five foot ten inches (their family had not turned metric yet; there had been some unspoken but stubborn resistance to change their system of weights and measures, even when the metric system had become official) and said, 'Gareth will be too good for "Triple Nine." He's in training now,' (Gareth had told his father he wanted to join the Acting Workshop run by Act Three in the June holidays) 'but he'll be in top form soon. He does not need all these small distractions. Watch and see. My son will be the next James Lye!' And everyone had laughed goodheartedly. And Gareth had felt a warm glow in his heart at his father's praise.

Now, when he was facing this great threat from outside, it was time to put his great acting skills to use. So Gareth pouted gracefully, and looked woeful and dejected, sending his mother mournful looks. He knew she was soft-hearted. She would notice he was not happy and she would give in to his wishes, never mind what the fengshui man said. Anyway, they had struck a bargain. His parents had agreed to buy the double-decker for him if he scored a Band Two in his Chinese. And he had done that. So they could not go back on their word. It was a contract and if they broke it, he—Gareth—would sue them. What could he sue them for? Oh, maybe, for another ten Sony Playstation games, and a new remote-controlled racing car. But these toys would not make up for the loss of his dearly beloved double-decker bed, with the wonderful ladder and the springy mattress on which he practised his trampoline jumping. And he could never be Tarzan without his 'tree' up on the upper deck! What a great loss! Thinking this succession of depressing thoughts of deprivation and loss spurred Gareth into another spurt of masterly acting.

'No, Mr Lee, thank you for your advice. But we have promised our son his double-decker, and we will not take it away from him. I am sure it would not be greatly harmful if he is allowed to keep his double-decker.'

Whew! Bless his mother! He wanted to run over to her and give her a big hug and kiss. But she had turned away from him and was pointing to another part of the room.

'What do you say if we move the bed from its present position to here? Would this be better fengshui?' his mother asked the disgusting Mr Lee. Gareth controlled his first impulse and patted himself mentally on the shoulder. Actors were supposed to be controlled people anyway, not running around, giving their mothers kisses.

After five minutes of gesturing and talking (Gareth had counted the minutes diligently on his G-shock), the hateful Mr Lee stopped at the doorway to take a last look at Gareth's room. *Good riddance! Goodbye, thank you, and don't come again.* He delivered his last salvo. It was like shooting a man in the back. So unfair. So stupid.

'You said your son is a fire child, didn't you, Mrs Tan?' His mother nodded warily, unsure of what prediction would come next. 'The sun is going to come into this room. It is a good room. It will be full of light and brightness, very auspicious for a young, intelligent man like your son.'

Gareth did a mental doubletake. Maybe, Mr Lee wasn't so bad, after all. 'But I think that we should take care there is a good balance between the hot and the cooling elements. The walls in this room are white in colour. The white will enhance the light but it might be too strong. Why not have a bit of water in this room, to counter-balance all the sun?' Gareth thought, *Wow! I'll have a real pool in my room! Tarzan will be happy!*

'What do you mean?' his mother asked. 'Should we get him a water bed or something like that?' Gareth's parents had bought a water bed for their new semi-detached house in Sixth Avenue. It was supposed to do wonders for back trouble. But Gareth didn't want a water bed. It was yucky! It made him seasick.

Mr Lee looked a little surprised. 'Oh, no. I don't think a water bed is necessary. Why not do something simpler? Why not paint the room blue or some colour that looks like water?' Gareth gave a snort beneath his breath. Water was not blue. Mr Lee obviously did not know what he was talking about. He'd known from the start the man was a fake.

'What a lovely idea,' his mother said. She turned to Gareth. 'What do you say, Gareth? Would you like a blue room?'

Gareth actually was quite happy with his room the way it was. But since his mother was so nice about it, and he had his double-decker bed after all (and that was the important thing), he nodded.

'That's it, then. We'll paint this room blue,' his mother declared.

The next week, his room was a pale shade of baby blue. It was not bad at all, Gareth thought. It made his room feel a little different. Perhaps, it was the visual image Mr Lee's words had planted in his mind. He imagined himself Captain Nemo, and he was patrolling the seas for dangerous vagabonds. Somehow, Lord Zed had managed to go underground and was surfacing in Captain Nemo's territory as a water bandit. At night, the moonlight played on the soft blue walls, and made them shimmer with a whispering kind of gentleness.

Gareth thought he might like to develop his water kingdom further. He asked his parents if he could paint on the wall facing his bed. He had a great idea he could populate the wall with some exotic fish like the piranha, the blue whale (More blue, Mum. Mr Lee would be pleased) and of course, the giant octopus who is the real terror under the sea. At first, his parents were hesitant. What if they did not like the paintings? Walls were not supposed to be drawn on. But luckily for Gareth, the Montessori school helped him in his appeal. He did not really know what Montessori was but he had seen the advertisements in the newspapers and had heard his parents talking about how good the ideas on child development in the Montessori school were. And they had agreed to his idea of painting his wall the way he liked it because Montessori was all about encouraging children's creativity. And Gareth's suggestion was certainly creative. So why not?

So it was that on that Tuesday morning, when Gareth blinked his way into wakefulness in the glare of the morning sunlight streaming into his blue room, there was a blue whale impaling onlookers with its baleful staring eye while next to it, the outreaching tentacles of one gigantic grey squid stretched lazily. Gareth hadn't quite managed to capture the bell-like form of the squid which now looked more like a grey carrot. But he was going to work on it today. Then it struck him. Shucks! How could he do any serious painting on his wall when his grandmother was coming to visit?

She was sure to want to come and visit his room. And on entering, she would probably make some belated gesture of appreciation at the great masterpiece that was taking shape on the wall. But more likely than not, she would probably exclaim in horror. Gareth wanted to pretend it would be mock-horror but he had seen and heard enough exclamations of surprise, and let's face it, shock, from the visitors his mother had paraded through his room, to know that their voices exclaimed in real, not pretended, horror. They just did not understand great art. Even his father and mother had been a little disturbed. 'But Gareth, do you think your whale should have so many stripes on its belly? It looks a bit like a zebra crossing, but on the wrong side!' And then, they'd laughed sillily. Parents needed to be educated. Wasn't that what his school teacher had been saying? Boy! He hoped it wouldn't take a long time. It was very tiring for a ten-year-old to have to endure, not only strangers' comments, but his own parents' misguided remarks.

The sun was still miserably cheerful. Why couldn't it go away for once, and stop bothering him? *I suppose I have to get up now. It's already 10 o'clock*, Gareth thought. There was a soft knock at his door. Nita slipped in quietly, like a shadow—if shadows were dressed in a green dress that some people like his mother and Nita called a uniform. His mother had not wanted the standard blue and white stripes, or pink stripes that were the usual maids' attire. She had selected green because it was her favourite colour. Well, Gareth thought, no other maid he knew (not that he knew plenty) had a green uniform. Nita looked like a wood nymph who had gotten lost in his water kingdom.

'Gareth, time to wake up. Your mummy says grandma's coming in half an hour. She wants you to bathe and be ready when Granny comes.' Nita bustled around Gareth, pulling away the blanket and fluffing up his pillows.

'Humph!' Gareth tried to snort. He had heard his hero, Zorro, do that wonderful scornful sound yesterday on television. He loved 'Zorro.' It was on TV at 11 a.m. He had not watched this programme until his school holidays because he had been in the morning session and had been at school every time the series was shown on TV. But now, school holidays allowed him to watch it, sleep late and do other things he normally would not have done. Like paint his beautiful sea. And Gareth began to sulk a little, as he remembered he would not be able to indulge in his painting today since his grandmother was coming to visit.

Why did his mother have to invite Granny? She was so old. She was nearly seventy years old, too old to play his games with him or take him shopping. Besides, she was always dressed in that funny old two-piece suit, that looked so old-fashioned and well—just old. His mother had explained it was a samfoo, and that older people in China used to wear it all the time. Well, his granny wasn't living in China so why should she wear those out-of-date clothes? He liked her glasses though. They were a tortoiseshell frame, and had small lenses. He sometimes thought his granny looked kind of cute, peering out of those little windows at the world around her. His mother had said that tortoiseshell was in fashion. At least, his grandmother was wearing something that was fashionable.

'Come on, Gareth. Hurry up! You haven't seen Granny in two months,' Nita fussed. 'She'll be so happy to see how you have grown. I think you grew an inch this time.' Gareth was momentarily distracted. Had he really grown? He was hoping to be tall enough to make it to the NBA basketball team and so he had been eating a lot of long beans (Nita had told him that eating long beans and other vegetables might make him grow taller, faster) and jumping a lot (his mattress looked as if it had a permanent dent in the middle). Michael Jordan was his hero—and 'Space Jam' had been great!

Gareth got out of bed, and went to the bathroom. Since his room was in blue, his bathroom had tiles that were beige—'some earth colours to make up for all that blue,' his mother had said. Boy! She was even beginning to sound like the fengshui man. Had it really been two weeks since that fateful day when his underwater kingdom had been declared? Gareth gave a gasp when the water hit him. Captain Nemo or not, he did not like cold water in the morning. And the water was cold—brrrr …. 'Nita!' he called, shivering, 'Did you switch on the water heater?'

Twenty minutes later, Gareth presented himself before his mother. She had taken leave that week to spend some time with him on his vacation, and do a few things in their new house. His mother loved ornaments and glass. She had been trying to decide where to put a Bohemian glass crystal vase (that had been a housewarming gift from her office colleagues), and when he greeted her, she gave him a bemused look, and turned back to positioning her crystal, first on the dining table, then on the coffee table, then on the mantelpiece she called a *tokonoma* which she said, was Japanese for alcove, a small empty space to put a painting or a vase in a Japanese home. What's in a name? Gareth thought. It's nothing but a hole in the wall, waiting to be filled with something. And now, his mother would most probably fill it with her crystal vase.

'Where's Granny?' Gareth asked.

'She'll be here very soon,' his mother replied. 'Be good now. Greet her nicely and ask how she is.' Gareth suddenly remembered that his grandmother had been sick until very recently. Two months ago, his mother had been very frightened because she thought her mother was going to die. Grandma had had a sudden heart attack after she got off the bus, in his aunty's house after she returned from a mahjong game in Albert Street. She had had some old ladies there she played with. And she was a stubborn one, insisting on taking the bus home although aunty had wanted to pick her up from the mahjong place after work.

'I can take care of myself,' Granny had said. Gareth remembered because he had been there when the argument took place. His mother had been on his aunty's side, telling granny that she was old and might get on the wrong bus, and it was hot and the car was air-conditioned, and so on. But his grandmother had remained stubborn to the end. And so, she had taken a public bus and had gotten a heart attack.

She was in hospital for a week. The first night Granny was sick, Gareth heard his mother crying in the sitting room. His father was hugging his mother, telling her it was all right; granny would be fine. The best doctors were looking after her. And she had had a good life after all. When it was time to go, it was time. But she wouldn't die, his father said, because it wasn't time yet. All this talk about time confused Gareth. He knew his grandmother was very sick. And because she was sick, his mother was worried. That night, his mother came into his bedroom. (The walls were white then, and he had put up a few posters of WWF*: Shawn Michaels and Lex Luger, but he'd taken them down when they turned bad. The fengshui man had not appeared then. He had only made an appearance a month later when his mother got excited after hearing her friend's good luck at the national lottery. 'Alice had the fengshui man come to her house, and he advised her to change her doorway because it was blocking all her luck from entering the house. And now, see what has happened. Alice's luck has come back home. She's won a thousand dollars at the lottery.' His mother told this story to his father, and on the phone to his aunty and her friends.)

'Gareth, let's kneel and pray for Grandma, okay?' And because it was so seldom his mother wanted to kneel at his bed and pray with him, Gareth felt happy. He was sorry, of course, that Granny was sick but he was glad his mother wanted to pray with him. He had concentrated a lot of his energy on praying that night, wishing Granny better. His mother had said a few words, and then bowed her head, praying her silent prayer. And Gareth felt united with her. It was a special feeling. Gareth felt his mother needed him and only he could comfort her. And so after she got up from the floor, he hugged her fiercely and gave her a big kiss. And his mother hugged him back, a little tearfully. She loved Granny. Gareth knew that.

'Granny has been sick, and now she is better,' his mother spoke again. 'But don't jump around her too much, okay? We mustn't frighten her with loud noises. Her heart is weak and tired, and she gets a little excited when there is loud or sudden noise.' Gareth decided Granny wasn't going to be much fun. Why couldn't she be like his friends' grandmothers? Those grannies bought ice-

---

* World Wrestling Federation

cream for the boys, gave them money to buy tokens for the video games arcade, and gave them lots of toys, even when it wasn't their birthdays.

The doorbell rang. His mother reminded him, 'Remember now. Be kind to Granny.' As if he needed reminding. He wasn't a wicked boy. What could he do to Granny, anyway?

When Gareth saw his grandmother, he had a little shock. She looked pale and tired. It looked as if something had gone out of her body, leaving her a shadow of her former self. Was she going to die? And he had prayed so hard for her too.

'Gareth, come and say hello to Granny.' Gareth stood before his grandmother, feeling a little awkward. Should he kiss her on the cheek? But her skin looked so thin and papery. Should he hug her? But mum had said no sudden movements. While he was deliberating what to do next, his grandmother reached below her samfoo shirt (she had a bulky wallet in her undershirt—Gareth had seen it once, this white, sleeveless shirt that had three buttons down front; it looked like a cotton vest) and took out a folded red packet. 'I haven't seen you for so long, Jia Wei. Here's a little angpow for you.' Gareth was happy. It didn't matter that his Granny could not pronounce his English name. She had always called him by his Chinese name. He had always known his Granny was real cool. *I wonder how much she gave me. Maybe I'll have enough to buy that Power Ranger I wanted; guess I'll have to add my own savings to it but that's okay.* He took his angpow and gave her a little peck on her right cheek.

'Thanks, *Po-po*.'

'He's grown a lot since I last saw him,' Granny said. Gareth stood up a little taller. She had noticed!

'How are you, mother?' his mother reverted to Cantonese, which was the language Granny spoke. Gareth could speak a little Cantonese but he understood more than he could speak.

'Oh, I'm fine. I'm taking the doctor's medication. Don't know what the fuss is about. I feel all right. A little tired now and then. But that's natural. I'm an old woman.' While his mother and grandmother were talking, Gareth thought to himself, *Why, Granny has never said she's old before. She must be ill.*

271

Gareth remembered the time his mother had had to travel to Hong Kong for her work. When she came back home two weeks later, she had brought presents for him, and even some new brand of hamster biscuit for his pet hamster, Sonic.

'Where's Sonic?' his mother had asked.

'He's in the cage, Mum. Here, let's give him his new biscuit.' And Gareth and his mother knelt before the hamster cage which was in a corner of the house (the sun was not good for hamsters, so he had placed the cage in a shadowy corner of the room).

'Sonic, here's some food for you.' When Sonic ambled out to sample his new food, his mother had cried out in shock.

'What's the matter with Sonic? Why does he look like that? Is he sick?'

Gareth had looked at Sonic, and he did not see any great difference between the Sonic of December 1996 and the Sonic of January 1997.

'Mum, you haven't seen Sonic for some time. He's okay. He's just growing older.'

'But why is he limping? And why is he losing his hair? He looks bald. And there's a black spot on his back. Has he always had it? Is it cancerous? Oh, poor Sonic.' And his mother had suddenly, dramatically, burst into tears.

Gareth's father had ambled over from his favourite reading chair then, and asked, 'What's the matter, Susan? Why are you crying?' And his mother had sniffled like a kid and pointed a finger at Sonic (Poor thing! He couldn't help growing older. They'd had him for two years now, and that was a pretty good record for a hamster. The man at the hamster shop had told Gareth, when they bought Sonic, that normally, hamsters lived only for two human years. They had a short lifespan. His classmate, Andrew, had a hamster that had died after only one year.)

His mother cried, 'Sonic looks so old. Is he dying?'

'It's all right, Mum.' Gareth patted his mother's shoulder. 'Sonic's all right. Don't worry.'

It was funny why Sonic should come to his mind now, Gareth thought. It had only been a week since Sonic died. That was why he had enjoyed his painting project—it took his mind away from his pet. They'd had some great times together—Sonic and he. He had let Sonic run on the floor in his bedroom and had made a fence with his storybooks so Sonic wouldn't get lost. One friend had had a hamster that had run out of its cage and gotten into the washing machine by mistake! And Sonic had loved to do the treadmill when he was younger. It had been fun to see him running in the middle of the night. The first time he learnt that hamsters were night creatures was when he had heard a scuffling noise from the corner where Sonic's cage was, and on investigating, had found Sonic hard at play, burrowing his body into the trough of grains and running around on the treadmill.

Gareth realised, without really knowing it, that his grandmother reminded him of Sonic. He was like his mother now, reacting to a picture of someone he had not seen for some time and suddenly, noticing that that person was getting old.

'Gareth, why don't you show Granny your room?' his mother asked. 'He's got a very interesting wall you must see, Ma. It's blue in colour and right now, he's painting fish all over it.' His grandmother took Gareth's hand in hers when she walked upstairs. He noticed her hand was small and firm, very tanned brown with fine lines. When she walked, however, he felt a pressure in his hand, as if she were leaning on him for support. And suddenly, Gareth's heart filled with love for his grandmother. She was such a gentle and giving person, his mother had said. And Gareth knew she was kind. She had looked after him when he was a baby, and had often come over to stay with his family so she could take care of him when his parents went to work. They had only gotten the maid two years ago, and that was when granny decided to stay with aunty, who was mother's elder sister and who had a new baby grandson. His grandmother had wanted to help aunty with the baby, since aunty's daughter and son-in-law had to work full-time. Nothing like family, Granny used to say.

When his grandmother entered his bedroom, Gareth waited for her to make some comment. He was surprised when she was silent. Was it that bad? He looked at her, and was relieved to see she was smiling gently. 'Jia Wei, it is a beautiful colour. Reminds me of my home near the river in China.' And his grandmother sighed softly.

'Really, Granny? Did you live near the river? What was it like?' Gareth had never known this before. When he was younger and his grandmother stayed with him, she had told him lots of stories about heroes and kings in China. But he had never heard her story about herself. He did know, though, that she couldn't read numbers. When she started learning to take the public bus, she was sixty-five years old. Her children—his two aunties, his mother and one uncle—had gotten married and started their own families, and she had been busy looking after their children. Then, the children had grown up, and granny had been left with a lot of time on her hands. His own mother had gotten married when she was twenty-eight years old. But she had waited four years before she decided to have Gareth. His grandmother had been twenty-eight when she had given birth to Gareth's mother, her youngest-born. His grandfather had died when Gareth was two years old.

Gareth knew his grandmother did not know how to read numbers because he saw his mother teaching her to count strokes as numbers. When his grandmother answered the telephone and took messages, she would write down the numbers on a piece of paper as lines—three lines for number three, seven lines for seven, and so on. And when she wanted to take the bus, his aunty and mother had to teach her to recognise the numbers and remember them by writing down the bus numbers on a small piece of paper which his grandmother would keep carefully in her vest pocket. Sometimes she would have this funny bulge sticking out of her shirt, and it looked as if her breasts had shifted downward to her stomach. And Gareth's mother would ask his granny to use the handbag she had bought for her, but his grandmother always refused, saying she would forget her bag and then, she would lose all her documents and money.

Now, in Gareth's sunny blue room, his grandmother sat down on the lower deck of his bed and said, 'My, what a nice, soft bed. I could almost sleep in it.'

'Tell me more about yourself, Po-po. What was it like in China? What sort of toys did you have?'

'Toys? We didn't have many toys. No time and no money.'

'What was it like near the river?'

'Oh, it was nice when the river was calm. The river was the source of life. People bathed in it, drank from it, swam in it. We travelled along it too. I remember taking a trip up from Chongqing to Wuhan. It took several days. But the scenery was wonderful. The cliffs were like in the pictures. Kind of funny shaped,' his granny paused, at a loss for words to describe the scenery, 'like the way you sometimes mould your plasticine, you know.'

Gareth couldn't quite imagine it. Now what else could he talk with his granny about? Hearing about scenery was boring. He looked at his wall. The whale looked back at him sympathetically. 'That's a good, strong fish you have painted there, Jia Wei. Why, I would never be able to draw like that. You'll make a good artist. Maybe, you'll be an architect, just like your father.'

'What other kinds of fish do you think I should have in my picture, Po-po?' Gareth asked humbly.

'Oh, I don't know. You've got a good mix there. Your squid looks interesting. Is it going to be a fierce and scary squid, or is it a kind and friendly one?'

Gareth hadn't really thought about the character his sea-world creatures would have. But it was an idea to play around with.

'I think my squid should be a nice one. I think I'm tired of monsters under the sea. It might be a nice difference to have a friendly squid to wake up to, and play with.'

His grandmother smiled. 'Have you been to the Singapore River, Jia Wei?'

'Yes, Po-po. Why?'

'Well, there used to be bumboats and *tongkangs* around. These were small flat-bottomed boats which travelled along the river. Did you notice the small green and red boats that are called *sampans*?'

'Yes. Why? What's special about them? They are just put there for decoration, aren't they?'

Granny laughed. Her laugh was a little raspy and hoarse. When she was younger, she had rolled her own tobacco and smoked a good number of home-made cigarettes a day. When she was in her sixties, she developed a bad cough, and the doctor said she could not smoke cigarettes anymore. But Granny was stubborn. She cut down the number of cigarettes she smoked from ten per day to four, but she still smoked. Her cough became a little better but it stayed on.

'Do you know, my child, that when I was a young mother, I took a big boat to go from China to Malaysia? The journey from Kwangtung took five whole days.'

Gareth leaned forward. 'Were you the only woman on board, Po-po? Was it safe to travel by boat then?'

'Well, I was one of the few women aboard. Many people got seasick because the sea got rough. But me? I took my firstborn—your Aunty Pei Fen …'

'You mean, Aunty Rachel, don't you, Po-po?'

'Ah yes. As I was saying, your aunty was only then a small baby. I took her with me and stood by the prow of the boat and felt the seaspray splash against me when the boat rolled against a big wave. I wasn't afraid. I liked the water. Remember, I grew up beside the great river in China.'

'Why did you travel across the ocean, Po-po? Where was *Gong-gong?*'

Gareth's grandmother looked at him, a little sadly. 'It was because of Gong-gong that I left China. He had gone to Malaysia more than half a year ago, to seek his fortune and to work hard so he could send money back for us. Life was hard in China, you see, and many Chinese men left their villages to seek the better life in Nanyang. Your grandfather left when I was expecting your aunty. He had not even seen his baby. We all had such high hopes. Ah …'

'What happened, Po-po?' Gareth was interested. He'd been prepared to be bored when he was asked to bring his grandmother up to his room. But now he was intrigued by the story she was telling.

'Your Gong-gong got mixed up in some bad company, and was getting involved with someone else. He was lonely, you see. It was hard also, in Nanyang. When we got word of his behaviour in Kwangtung, his mother told me I should leave to join him in Malaysia. A man should have his wife with him, she said. His aunty, who was a lady of some means living in Shanghai, furnished me with the boat fare. She was very kind. Before I left my hometown, my mother-in-law gave me a parting gift. You see this jade bangle?' Gareth's grandmother lifted up her right hand. The bangle Gareth had seen on her since he knew her as his grandmother shone in the morning light, like a piece of green jewel.

'I was my mother-in-law's favourite daughter-in-law, you see. And she wanted me to have something special. She told me to be strong and to love your Gong-gong. Men will be men, she said. They need women to help them be strong. This jade has protected me for many years. It is a part of me now.'

Gareth remembered his mother telling his father excitedly one day a year back about his grandmother's fall. It seemed that granny had been cleaning the staircase and mopping the floor when she had slipped and fallen. She had been told not to do any mopping but she had always mopped for as long as she could remember. Being old, she could have suffered serious injuries but her jade bangle had saved her. 'Do you know that her bangle cushioned her fall? It cracked but did not break. Imagine—she could have landed up with a broken arm!'

Gareth looked at his grandmother's bangle in the light in his blue sea room. Yes, there was a crack, very faint and brown-veined. So it was true, after all. The bangle had saved his granny's arm.

'What happened next, Po-po?'

'I managed to meet up with your Gong-gong. We had a talk and everything was all right again.'

'What really happened, Po-po? Did you two have a quarrel? Did you shout at him? Mum and Dad sometimes shout at each other when they are angry.'

Gareth's grandmother looked at him. 'No, we did not shout at each other. Your Gong-gong has respect for me. I have respect for him. We talked and settled the matter once and for all.'

'And then? What?' Gareth was curious.

'We decided to take up bigger rooms at Jonker Street in Malacca. That was where your Gong-gong landed up, selling cars. Malacca.'

Gareth knew about Malacca. His parents had driven him to

Malacca last December and they had met up with some relatives. It was a boring place, except for the beach, Gareth thought. And even then, there wasn't much of the beach. A lot of it had been reclaimed for development.

'And then we came to Singapore. It was so thrilling when I took a boat along the Singapore River. It was one of those sampans I mentioned. Your Gong-gong was working for a businessman on the River, and he was supervisor of the deliveries the coolies brought up the river and into the warehouses along the riverside. I had missed the boats and the river in China. And one day, on our wedding anniversary, your Gong-gong arranged for me to have a sampan ride up the Singapore River.'

Wow! Gareth had not known his grandfather but hearing his granny speak of Gong-gong made him wish he had been known him. Maybe then, he could also have gotten a ride in a sampan up the River.

'There was so much traffic on the River then. Now, it is quiet and empty. The sampans have disappeared. The only ones left behind are the decorations. Still they are real sampans, with that special colour combination—red, green and white.'

'Po-po, why is it that those sampans look so strange?'

'What do you mean, Jia Wei? Strange?'

'Yes, they've got eyes painted on their sides. Funny-looking eyes. Looks like crocodile eyes.'

Granny laughed again. 'Oh, those. You should know, Jia Wei, that those eyes offer special protection for the boat. When a new boat is launched on the water, the owner has the privilege of "dotting the eye" in a ceremony. Yes, he literally paints the dots in the eyes. And then, when the boat goes on the water, the people on board are protected from dangers in the water by the eyes which guard over them.'

'Wow! Real cool, Po-Po.' Gareth looked at his wall. He noticed his blue whale, of which he was very proud. Then, he looked at his squid. It did look a bit squishy. Then, an idea struck him.

'Po-po, do you know that my squid has no eyes yet? Do you think if you dot his eyes, he will be able to protect me in my underwater kingdom? I've got enemies all around. Look.' Gareth pointed to

Lord Zed hiding behind a rock. 'And there,' and he pointed out more enemy soldiers surrounding his double-decker bed. 'I can be attacked from all sides. It's a really dangerous time.'

His granny looked tenderly at him. Her eyes shone as bright as the morning light that greeted him every day. 'Are you saying you would like me to dot the squid's eyes?'

'Yes, Po-po. It would be really great if you could do that. I bet no one's granny has ever done this to protect a grandchild. It'll be real special.'

His granny asked him, 'Where's the paint and brush?'

Gareth hurried to his cupboard and took out his set of paints. He could not find his cup for the water, so he went to the bathroom and took his rinsing cup. Nita did need have to know he was using it to paint, did she? His grandmother waited on his bed.

'Here, Po-po. Everything you need to paint the eyes.'

His granny stroked the picture of the giant carrot squid. 'Nice squid. You will make a good protector of my grandson.' She lifted the brush and dipped it in the black paint Gareth had prepared for her. Slowly, she drew the outlines of the eyes. Gareth stood by her side, silently watching in almost breathless anticipation. The eyes were shaping up nicely. His granny couldn't read but she sure could draw.

'Where did you learn to paint, Po-po?' he asked.

'Oh, in secret. My brothers in China went to school but I never did. My father thought that boys deserved to go to school but girls should stay at home and learn needlework and do housework. But when I saw my brothers use the brush, I tried it secretly. And found I could do it. I had to hold the brush upright, like this.' And she showed Gareth how. 'And then the firm hand.' And she painted a lovely oval-round eye.

Gareth whispered, 'Po-po, it's beautiful.'

She smiled. 'Here's the other eye.' And she did another perfect oval. 'And now, let's help your protector see.' And she positioned her brush in the perfect centre of the eye. 'Here goes.'

Gareth held his breath. He saw the squid come alive. It was the most perfect squid possible. The eyes became alive, bright pools of mysterious dark light. He could almost imagine they were smiling at him.

'And now I charge you, O great squid, with looking after my special grandson, Jia Wei. Protect him from all the enemies and dangers around him. Guide him along the right path. Teach him gentleness and kindness. And serve him well.'

His grandmother's soft voice intoned these words with dignity and a certain power. He could almost believe she had some magical power. He looked at his squid. It was complete.

'Thank you, Po-po.'

'My pleasure, grandson.' And his granny took him in her arms and surrounded him with her age, her wisdom, her love. Gareth felt as if he was all lit up. Was the sun shining in again? It felt so warm and good, as if the sunlight was pouring in.

His G-shock watch beeped the hour. He was a little surprised it was only noon.

His mother appeared at his door. 'Ma, it's time for lunch. Have you been enjoying Jia Wei's company?'

His granny put her hand in Gareth's. Her hand felt small and warm, and familiar. 'Yes, we have been talking about his underwater kingdom. It is truly an exciting world he's painted.'

They walked downstairs to the dining room. It was wonderful to have family, Gareth thought. He had never thought his grandmother would be so spontaneous, and yes—young. He felt happy. The day was turning out better than he had expected. Yes, he was enjoying himself.

That night, Nita gave him his cup of hot cocoa while he was in his pyjamas in bed. His mother came in to kiss him goodnight. 'Did you have a good time with Granny, Gareth?' He nodded sleepily. 'I'm glad, darling. Goodnight. Sleep well.' After his mother left, Nita started drawing the curtains.

'No, leave them open, Nita. I like the sun.'

Gareth snuggled into his treehouse. He was going to have a busy day tomorrow. He had to help the starfish give birth. And the plants needed to be planted. He'd need some more paints tomorrow. He yawned and suddenly, the image of his grandmother came before him. Her small face, her gentle smile, her workworn hands. His heart filled with love and pride.

'Goodnight, Po-po,' he whispered. He looked around his room. His was a beautiful kingdom. There was much to do. 'Goodnight, whale.' Bluey, the whale, seemed to wave his tail. Gareth looked at the giant squid. It no longer looked like a carrot. It had a nobility and specialness that was all its own. Especially since it got its eyes.

'Goodnight, friend.' And Gareth thought he saw his Protector wink.

Quartet: Grandmother's bun

(for mom and sisters)

Heng Siok Tian

early each morning
you retire
to favourite corner
of the kitchen
with comb and hairpin
neatly wrapped in batik
handkerchief,
you uncover
with firmness of age
slowness of wisdom.
your fine hair
so carefully unravelled
after the thin black netting comes away

bit by bit
taking care to preserve
as much as you can,
fine strands
that lightly touch
the kitchen linoleum,
your care distilled from years
of gentle routine,
as quietly
as you let your hair down
you put away stray strands
beneath benign bun
like pain
neatly tucked away
camouflaged with black pins:

all this in memory
as startling

as i found mother
last night
retiring to your corner.
from where i was in my room,
book in hand,
her remote quiet
haunts me.
do books teach me
to be
half as brave as you
half as strong as mother
as she hunched over rubbing her aches
with the sour-black ointment
you gave her?
(both of you do not sing
your wisdom which i need.)

On bare feet

Agnes Lam

a psyche escaping
across Freudian borders
cannot care
if strangers stare

from thickets of
interior within burst
thoughts untaught
feelings unmannered

children of refugees
running through fire
orphans straying onto streets
on bare feet

hair in knots
unbathed unfed unclothed
bruised skin showing
eyes still searching

26 March 1985
Kent Ridge

daddy loves me

Nirmala PuruShotam

the Body comes
darkening the Dark
again the Body comes
carrying midnightmare smells
bristle-textured cologne
re-trace the graffiti
of Shame on this body.

the Body dresses
in thin translucent Shadows
the Body dresses again
to hide and play Bare seeking,
the fingers undulate
a paintwork of smearing colours
dank Dye brines this body.

the Body leaves
the cradle stolen
again the Body leaves
unburdening the Dark
this otherbody sighs
a Space for sleep to seep
inside the skin of Shame

cologned and bristled
bristled and cologned
this body waits:
daddy disguised in daylight
weaves crayonned coloured play
for his very good little girl.

A Reel

Rosaly Puthucheary

You don your costume
and take on your role
to the demand of the director.

You watch the silence
to catch the pause
in the sound of a gesture.

You stage an emotion
to scatter your rage
in the control of a feature.

You act feeling no action
till time pulls you out of joint,
and spatters you on the public page.

Never Mind Father

Tan Mei Ching

Father never got angry with me. He was the calmest person I knew. He would go off to work early in the morning, and return just before sunset. He worked in a large antique shop, selling his prized pottery and ceramics to people who were 'romantics' and liked 'old stuff.' Sometimes halfway through dinner, Father'd say just that, 'Someone came in today, looking for "old stuff,"' and he'd give a little snort.

When Father sold a piece of ancient Ming pottery to someone who truly appreciated its value, he'd join us after dinner in front of the television with his evening papers which he'd read during commercials. Occasionally he'd ask us to explain why this and that happened in the drama series. Mother would sigh because she'd have to tell Father the whole story, from the very beginning, for Father to understand all the nuances and heartbreaks. Life, Father then said, was made to be simple; only people like those on television made headaches attractive and exciting. What was exciting was seeing a sixty-year-old man take a century-old pot and watching his eyes light up as he gently turned the pot in his liver-spotted hands and caressed the designs on the pot as he would the head of his grandchild. That was love, you see, not this sensational rubbish they portrayed on television. Why do you watch then, Mother would ask. But he'd already returned to his papers, and we would have missed a whole big chunk of some character's life.

Sometimes he'd come home and not say a word to anyone, although I told my sisters that he'd tell Mother when he thought we were asleep. With our ears stuck to the wall separating our room and theirs, we would hear murmurings and sometimes sharp words, but we couldn't tell who was talking at any time.

Father didn't work on Sundays and he'd take us to the park. Mother would wear her soft sandals and walk beside him, her short, quick steps catching up with his long strides. We ran ahead of them, chasing pigeons and tearing into the playground like hooligans, scraping knees and getting dime-and-penny-sized blue-blacks when we climbed trees and played One Leg. Ya Mi had the most blue-blacks because she was always tripping over sticks or grass or her own feet. Father and Mother sat and watched, sometimes smiling, sometimes holding hands. They were not too worried about our scrapes. Mother just told us, from time to time, to be careful.

Besides the park, Father liked sitting by the kitchen window reading the newspaper, in the pool of sunlight that fell across the table and made the old kettle sparkle like new. He would look up now and then, when my sisters and I got rowdy with the dog or with each other, and give Mother a look from under his eyelids. Mother would tell us, quietly, to stop it. We never listened. When she raised her voice, Father would say, 'Never mind, they're just kids.'

That was why we never persuaded him to play pick-up-sticks with us, or asked him to inspect our mudpies, or wear a towel on his head for our theatre. He wouldn't have been interested. He was an important man with a lot of responsibilities, and when he was home, he would want rest from the world, so we didn't want to bother him. Anyway, he never seemed to have much to talk with us about. When Mother went to the market, and he had to look after us, he'd tell us to be good and play by ourselves, and then bring a pile of catalogues of antiques onto the kitchen table and study them. Sometimes, I'd stop playing Old Maid or Snap or Monopoly and sneak a look at him. He'd be totally absorbed, and it was as if we weren't even there.

When we scrambled down the hallway, our feet would automatically slow down and soften as we passed his room. Sometimes he would nap with the door open for ventilation and we would stop altogether and look at his peaceful face. Where did all the lines go, we wondered. Father looked like Grandfather, whose portrait was on the living room wall. He had the same eyes and ears and face shape as Grandfather. Mother would touch our noses and say we had noses like hers, but Father never mentioned such things. Sometimes when he was asleep, I would get my little pocket mirror and we would compare his features and ours, and wonder if we were a part of him, a part he never put to bed and told stories to, a part he saw but never reached to touch. Once, on a television show, a father slapped his child and said, 'I did that because I love you.' We were mortified. 'Lucky our father is not like that,' Ling Ling said. 'Then he's like what?' Ya Mi asked. We looked over at Father with his newspapers, oblivious to our discussion. It was better he didn't mind us so much, he just let us be and never got angry with us, not even the time we floated his favourite slippers in the roadside drain and they sank and disappeared. Perhaps they weren't that important to him.

One Sunday, Mother sat at the kitchen table with a pile of socks to darn, and Father sat across from her with a pile of catalogues to read, and since nobody suggested anything better to do, we sat on the floor and folded pieces of coloured paper into animals and airplanes. I was very particular about having the edges of the paper meet perfectly, and they never did. I pushed my papers away, one after another, until they scattered around me like autumn leaves around a tree. Ling Ling told me I was too fussy. I told her to mind her own business. She shrugged and turned back to the green paper she was just beginning to fold. Beside her was a little pile of red and yellow papers. Since I had used up all of mine, I took hers. She screamed at once. Mother looked up, told me to give the papers back, and returned to her socks. I turned up my nose at Ling Ling and she had to get her papers from Ya Mi. I couldn't make this pile of papers do what I wanted either, and one by one I pushed the papers away. I tried to take some more from my sisters, but Ya Mi sat on her pile and Ling Ling turned her back to me. I pinched Ya Mi's backside and got her papers. She yelled. Now both Father and Mother looked up. From behind her socks, Mother said, 'Don't bully your sisters.' I slapped hard at Ya Mi's hands as she tried to get her papers back. Ya Mi winced. Father slowly straightened from his seat. 'Are you listening to me?' Mother asked in her soft voice. I stuck my tongue out at Mother, something I'd never done before, and pulled my sister's hair. Ya Mi started to cry.

I heard Father crossing the tiled floor to me. He took me by the shoulders and shook me, jiggling my head like a puppet. I lost all my breath. Then he grabbed my ankles, slid me off the floor and lifted me, dangling me upside down. My paper slipped from my hands and fell in with the rest of the vagrants. Blood rushed to my head and I saw that Father had quite a number of legs and the kitchen table was an octopus. I could feel my head rolling away from me. 'You listen to your mother and do not hurt your sisters, do you hear me?' Dangle, dangle, my head involuntarily jiggled 'yes.' When Father put me down, I cried. All I heard was Father's step-stepping away and the air was heavy with stillness.

I collected all my papers and threw them into the dustbin. Mother said nothing. My sisters said nothing, for fear that my fragility would break into a thousand pieces they couldn't collect and glue up again. Cocoa, our dog, came and sniffed my knee. I pushed him away, went into my room and sat on my bed hugging my pillow; only its softness could shrink and absorb me into nothingness. I watched the little lights in the insides of my eyes as Cocoa licked and licked my ankles sorrowfully.

I got up when light outside started to mellow, and the sky streaked rose and orange. The day got ready to leave. I went into the kitchen to get a drink, but Father was there, sitting by the table, tapping his foot on the floor. I hesitated, then walked the long way around the table. Once at the cabinets, I took out a glass. Father glanced at me while I balanced a jug of water and poured. His foot tapped away as I drank and looked into the images of my face in the water and in the inside of the glass. As I was finishing, Father stopped his tapping, cleared his throat and called me. I went to him slowly, looking at my feet.

'Would you go for a walk with me?' he asked in his low voice. I nodded.

We walked along the little dirt road with yellow flowers and parachute seeds. I asked him if he liked mudpies and he said yes. He lifted me onto his shoulders and I could see the roofs of the houses we passed, and the tops of people's heads who passed us. And we just walked and walked and walked.

Turning Thirty
Minfong Ho

'She did it. Of course she did it.'

'But how do you know?'

'I know her type.'

'Really, dear. You need proof, you know. Hard evidence.'

The Old One was only half listening, in the way that she did when English was spoken, understanding by intuition through a mixture of the tones, the gestures, the context, and only incidentally a few of the English words.

When her son and his wife spoke together in English, as they usually did, they acted as if she wasn't there, or at least was there only the way the television was there—something that could talk at them when switched on by them, but incapable of absorbing and taking part in their conversation.

She finished watering the kumquat bush, and quietly plucked a few of the withered leaves off. They must be talking about that Filipino maid again, she thought absent-mindedly, not their own maid Rosa, but that other one whose picture was in *The Straits Times* the other day, the one who was supposed to have drowned the baby and killed the other maid in charge of him.

'Proof? She never looks me in the eye these days. Just slinks about looking down at the floor. And when I asked her about it yesterday, she pretended not to hear me, and just left the room. Isn't that proof enough?'

The Old One plucked off another leaf. Wait, this wasn't about the maid in the newspapers. It was about Rosa after all. She listened more carefully, her back taut with attention.

Her son laughed. 'Not really, Beverly. Not looking at you in the eye isn't really hard evidence. Why don't you sit her down and ask her about it point-blank?'

'Because I know what she'll do. She'll just look away and probably start mumbling something in Tagalog or Cebuano or whatever it is that …' Abruptly she stopped, as Rosa stepped into

291

the living room.

'Dinner is ready, ma'am,' she said quietly, standing in the doorway.

Beverly shot a meaningful look at her husband. 'See, just like I said,' she continued, switching smoothly over to Cantonese. 'Coming and going, not a sound she makes.'

By way of a reply, Ah Liong folded up his newspaper and stood up. 'Ah Mah, let us eat now,' he said in Cantonese, and taking her elbow, gently steered her into the dining room.

The Old One liked the touch of her son's hand on her arm, firm and gentle and yes, kind, like the boy she had known and raised and loved. It wasn't that many years ago, that he guided her the same way down the aisle of the Hwa Chong Junior College auditorium, showing her to the seat from which she could watch him receive his diploma. She had worried that he might not want to be seen with her, not to acknowledge that the plain woman in her grey samfoo was his mother, when most of his classmates had mothers who glided by in rustling dresses and high-heel shoes. But if he had minded, he had not shown it, not to her nor even to those other, by far richer and more elegant, mothers. For hadn't he introduced her to them all, standing by her as she smiled and bobbed her head mutely at them?

Seated at the dining table, her son helped her to a piece of chicken before taking one for himself. When she had first moved in with them, he had tried to talk his wife into just such a gesture—the token serving of the first morsel to her plate before they started to eat. But Beverly had raised her eyebrows, and said, 'We never did that in our family.'

'I did,' said Ah Liong, 'when I was growing up.'

'Well, I didn't,' Beverly said, and that was the end of that.

Ah Liong had said no more. Quietly he helped his mother to the first bit of food, while his wife sat across the table stonily.

Beverly waited until Rosa had finished pouring the water and left, before continuing in English, 'What's the use of asking her point-blank? She will just lie and deny it.'

'Look, maybe you just misplaced it. Have you tried looking for it—I mean, really looking?'

'No, but a video camera isn't just something you "misplace."
Besides, I always put it in your desk drawer. And it's not there now.
You know that. You said you've just looked.'

'Maybe Billy took it and played with it.'

'He couldn't reach that drawer. Don't always be blaming
him.'

'Well, it'll probably turn up sometime,' Ah Liong said. He
spooned a bowlful of soup—pork bone and pickled cabbage, one
of his favourites—and started to drink it.

'Not in time for your birthday party, certainly,' Beverly said.

'Birthday party?' Leon said suspiciously. 'We're having a
birthday party? For me? When? Why?'

'Tomorrow night, Leon. Really, I've told you at least a dozen
times. It's an important event—the day you turn thirty.'

'What's so important about turning thirty?'

'Because you've made it, darling. A four-bedroom condo, a
good son, a good job, a new car, an attractive wife,' Beverly paused
and pouted prettily, 'Isn't that reason enough to celebrate?'

'I've worked hard for it. I don't see any reason to celebrate it.
It's just showing off.'

'So what?' Beverly countered. 'We do it as a country. Why can't
you do it for your own birthday? The National Day parade this year
was much more lavish than usual, Singapore is thirty this year too.
You also deserve a big party too.'

'I don't like it,' Ah Liong said. He spooned up a piece of pork
bone from the soup and sucked the marrow noisily.

Beverly winced. 'But think of how far you've come, Leon.
Twenty, even ten, years ago, you were just a nobody, fighting to
survive in a rough world, barely scraping by enough to live on, let
alone live graciously. Well, now it's time to live graciously.'

'There's a difference between gracious and ostentatious,'
Leon said, in his serious, lawyer-like tone. 'I don't like things
ostentatious.'

'Well, like it or not, there's going to be a party. The caterers
are coming, the people have all been invited. And I want that video
camera to record everything.'

So that's it, the Old One thought. No wonder she's so bent on having the video camera by then. She wanted to forever record this big dinner party. Record and then replay those bronze platters of food with little gas flames burning under them, the centrepiece of foreign flowers, the starched tablecloth and uniformed waiters, all courtesy of the caterer.

The Old One could see that her son understood the situation too. 'Have it your way, Bev. You always do anyway. But about that video camera—if you want it, you track it down. I don't want to have anything to do with it.'

'But if Rosa …'

'I said, I want nothing to do with it.' He picked up the bone and sucked it again, emphatically.

Beverly's lips pursed into a tight line. 'Rosa!' she called. 'You can clear the table. We're done. And by the way,' she added as the maid slipped into the room, 'Come see me before you bathe Billy tonight. There's something I want to talk to you about.'

Bathing Billy was one of the things that the Old One really enjoyed doing, and one of the few chores that she actually envied Rosa for. The others—scrubbing the laundry, washing the dishes, mopping the floors, always the cleaning up, everything she did as a maid herself years ago—she had not missed, not even when it was in her own home, for her own family, for a change. She had even, as her joints became more swollen and arthritic, been genuinely glad to have been relieved of them. But she had missed bathing the baby, missed soaping his thick black hair and running her hands down his smooth round belly. It reminded her of the times she had bathed Ah Liong when he was a little boy. So when she realised that Beverly and Rosa were engaged in a long, serious conversation, she quietly—almost stealthily—ran the bathwater, and started to undress Billy.

She put the toilet seat cover down, and sat on it, contentedly watching her grandson splashing in the tub. Above the sound of the running water and the baby's laughter, she could hear Rosa's voice coming from the living room. Soft and hesitant it was at first, a halting murmur in between Beverly's sharp questions. Then louder, sadder until it broke down into a series of sobs.

The Old One frowned. Rosa, sobbing? But the girl was usually so reserved, so self-contained. What was going on? The Old One considered stepping out to the corridor to listen, but she didn't dare leave the baby in the tub alone. She turned off the faucet, and gave Billy his rubber duck. In the ensuing quiet, she could make out some of the English words coming from the other room.

'It was my husband, ma'am ... took all the money ... yes, ma'am, the salary I sent back all these months ... some bad drug, white powder, he smoked it ... I thought he was making the payments for our house with it, but he smoked it away, ma'am. Yes, the letter last week. Two, ma'am, two children, and my mother—the bank is going to take away the house. Where will they live now, I don't know ma'am. I work and I work ... for so long now ... for nothing, ma'am ... for ...'

'But what about the camera? Rosa, the video camera?'

'For four years now I work. First in Kuwait, ma'am, now here ... in just seven more months, the house will be paid for. When ...'

'Rosa, did you or did you not take my video camera?'

'Please, ma'am. May I borrow some money from you? Three months pay, and I will work without pay for four, no, five months. Please ... I need the money now ...'

'Look, Rosa. I will not have a thief in the household. Did you or did you not take the camera? If you did, I will have to report you to the police, you know. And they will send you right back to the Philippines. You know that, don't you? You cannot stay here if you've committed a crime.'

'Just three months pay, ma'am, please ... I will work six months without pay afterwards.'

'Look, Rosa, if I don't have that video camera by tomorrow afternoon, I will report it as stolen to the police, do you understand?'

The voices were raised now, one in anger, the other in despair. In his bathtub, Billy had stopped playing with his rubber duck, and was whimpering.

'It's all right, child,' the Old One whispered soothingly. But Billy only whimpered more. 'Nai-nai will give you another toy,' she said, handing him a plastic shampoo bottle.

The boy flung it away. 'Rosa!' he wailed. 'Rosa!'

The noise from the living room stopped abruptly. Both women rushed into the bathroom, looking anxious.

'What's the matter, baby?' Beverly shouted, pushing the Old One away to get nearer the bathtub.

'Rosa!' Billy screamed. 'I want Rosaaaa!'

His mother tried to pick him up, then changed her mind as the soapsuds from his flailing arms splashed onto her silk blouse. Although she was on the board of several children's charities, she never seemed very interested in her own child, unless it was to dawdle him for the requisite few minutes in front of her dinner guests. With no audience before her, and with her silk blouse splattered, she was only too eager to step aside. 'All right, you deal with him, Rosa,' she snapped, and stalked out of the bathroom.

Rosa pulled a towel from the rack and deftly wrapped Billy up in it before picking him up. She sat on the edge of the bathtub, and cradled the boy in her lap, and rocked him to and fro, cooing at him.

The boy quieted down, and snuggled against Rosa. Discreetly, so quickly that the Old One wondered if she had imagined it, Rosa bent down and wiped her own tears away with the edge of the towel. Then the towel was wrapped snugly around Billy, and the two of them snuggled together.

The next morning, the Old One couldn't find her joss sticks. She pulled out the drawer where she usually kept them, and rummaged through the scraps of paper, matchboxes and candles looking for them. 'I know there were a few more in that packet,' she murmured to herself. 'My memory isn't that bad, is it?'

She looked up at the statuette of the Goddess of Mercy that was perched on the altar. 'Wasn't I saying just yesterday, that I'd have to go down to Chinatown soon to get some more? But for this week, we had enough, didn't we?' She looked into the calm face of Kuan Yin for confirmation, then shook her head. 'Maybe my memory is getting bad …'

Then she smelt the familiar scent of sandalwood—it was not drifting up from the small bronze urn heaped high with ashes of past joss sticks, but from outside her room. But where?

Nobody else in the apartment ever lit them, in fact Beverly had wrinkled her nose up in disdain at the smell, and pointedly suggested that her mother-in-law light her joss sticks only after they had left for the office. Wordlessly, the Old One had demurred; just as wordlessly, she had moved the entire altar from the living room into her own bedroom after Beverly had wanted their new CD player and amplifiers installed there. What was the point of arguing? Her son had taken it upon himself, either out of a sense of filial piety for his mother or personal distaste at yet another sign of conspicuous consumption by his wife, to argue against the Kuan Yin altar being moved. 'She has always occupied a central place wherever we lived,' Ah Liong had said to Beverly. 'It seems, I don't know, ungrateful somehow to move her into some small back room when we finally have a nice living room.'

'Really, Leon, you talk as if it was a real woman, for god's sake. With feelings that can be hurt!'

There was an awkward silence. Ah Liong had been caught off-guard by his wife again, the Old One realised. His working-class, Chinese, 'superstitious' background had been showing again.

'Well, my mother is a real woman,' he finally countered. 'And her feelings might be hurt if that statue is moved.'

At that point the Old One had stepped in. Quietly, murmuring in Cantonese that it'd be more convenient to have the Kuan Yin Pusa in her room anyway, she had gently taken the statuette down from the altar, and walked away with it. It wasn't worth yet another argument between her son and his wife, she thought—their arguments flared up far too often as it was. Besides, the Old One didn't think that Kuan Yin Pusa would mind the changes. She was, after all, the Goddess of Compassion: she should understand and forgive the Old One for moving her.

And in a way, having the statuette in her own room did prove more convenient. She could see Her and pray to Her even lying in bed, in the pale light of the candles as she dozed off at night. And in the mornings, she could light the incense without having to worry so much about whether the fragrance would permeate the whole apartment.

She followed the scent of the incense now, out to the living room and across the kitchen to the maid's room. The door to it was ajar, and the Old One peered in. Rosa was down on her knees, her hands clasped in prayer before a small ceramic statue of the Madonna and Child. Neatly arranged before the statue were two candles and a bouquet of joss sticks, the tendrils of smoke twisting up towards the open doorway.

For a moment the Old One felt as if she was looking into a mirror, so reminiscent was this scene of her own past. How often had she been like that, murmuring desperately to an impassive goddess for some sign of the compassion that was carved on her smooth features. When her young husband had suddenly died from a heart attack; when she had lost her first job as a washing woman trying to support her infant son; when Ah Liong had been suspended from school for drinking and smoking cigarettes; when he had written back from London saying he was in love with a British girl and might settle down there …. The Old One sighed. Kuan Yin had been good to her.

Startled, Rosa swivelled around, and saw her standing in the doorway. She clambered to her feet, wiping her tear-stained cheek with one hand. 'I … Is Billy awake already?' she asked.

The Old One shook her head. 'He still napping. No, I look for them …' she said, pointing to the joss sticks. 'No more.'

Rosa looked stricken. 'I'm sorry … I thought you'd have another packet. Here …' She snatched the joss sticks, and tried to press them into the Old One's hands.

'No, no. You keep them,' she said, backing away. 'I don't need. You need more.' On an impulse, she went over to the kumquat bush at the balcony, and picked a handful of the little oranges. 'Here,' she said, holding them out to Rosa, 'for her …' she nodded at the statue of the Madonna.

When Rosa, surprised and confused, didn't take them, the Old One hobbled into the room and carefully placed the kumquats in front of the candles. She looked at Rosa, 'What her name?' she asked.

'Holy Mary, Mother of God,' Rosa answered.

'Holy Mary,' the Old One said, switching to Cantonese, 'You help Rosa, please. She's a good girl. Her children need her. You have to help them, too.' In quick succession, she bowed her head three times, then backed away.

'What did you say?' Rosa asked.

'I ask her to help you. And help your children. She understand Chinese?'

Rosa smiled. 'She understands my Tagalog. I think she understands whatever is spoken to her from the heart,' she said.

The Old One smiled back. 'Same as my Kuan Yin Pusa,' she replied.

It was strange and yet oddly natural, that the two of them could communicate so easily in a language that was so foreign to both of them. In a way, it was perhaps because they spoke English in defence, as the enemy tongue, that the sense of sympathy arose.

'Better that my husband die, like yours, than smoke this white powder,' Rosa was saying. 'For almost seven months now, he spends the money I send back on cocaine, when I thought he was paying for the house we had bought.'

'Men,' the Old One agreed. 'Not much use.'

'And my children—where will they live now, if the bank takes away the house? What will they do? Where can they go? I try to tell Madam, try to borrow money, try to ask for three months' salary ahead of time—but she doesn't hear.'

The Old One snorted. 'She not like your Mary or my Kuan Yin. She not hear, she not help.'

'It's not her fault. She wouldn't understand,' Rosa said softly. 'Madam—she has never needed help,' Rosa said.

The Old One lifted her eyebrows, surprised at the maid's generosity. Rosa was, she decided, a better woman than her daughter-in-law.

'And so you took her camera-thing,' she said.

'Borrowed,' Rosa amended quickly. 'I only pawned it, so I could send the money to the bank, so my children wouldn't be turned out of our home. Next month, I would have saved up enough to buy the video camera back, except …'

'Except Beverly wants it now.'

'Tonight,' Rosa said miserably.

'And what you will do?'

'What can I do? I have no money to buy back the camera. And Madam, she said if there is no camera tonight, she will dismiss me.' She sucked in her breath and moaned. 'Oh Mary, Mother of God, please help me.'

They both turned toward the statuette. The joss sticks had burnt out, but thin wisps of smoke still curled upwards. Mary-Mother-of-God gazed blankly at the smoke.

'If she not help you,' the Old One said. 'I help you.'

Her jade bracelet had cost Ah Liong three thousand dollars, but the pawnshop broker had only given her nine hundred dollars for it, and that only grudgingly. She remembered how Ah Liong had escorted her to the biggest goldsmith shop in People's Park, sat her down on a stool, then asked—no, demanded—to see the most expensive jade bracelet in the shop. Oh, that was a day to remember! So proud she had been, not just of her grown son with his clipped British accent, but of the respect he was showing her, in front of the world. 'My son, just back from London,' she had said to the jeweller, 'and now he has started his first job, a very good job …'

'Ah Mah,' he had said, embarrassed.

'With the big law firm, Low, Li and Li.'

'Enough, Ah Mah!'

The man behind the counter had smiled ingratiatingly, then brought out a tray of jade. 'This is the best quality jade we have,' he had said, carefully holding up a bracelet. See how pure and clear the green is?'

'How much?' the Old One had asked.

'Three thousand eight hundred dollars, *Tai-tai*.'

The Old One beamed. No one had ever called her 'tai-tai' before.

'Do you like it, Ah Mah?'

'*Too* expensive,' she said, for form's sake.

'The price is negotiable, of course,' the jeweller said. 'If the Tai-tai likes, she could try it on. '

It had felt cool and solid on her arm. Encircling her wrist the way Ah Liong used to do with his hand, when he was learning to roller-skate. She sighed. How the time had flown!

Ah Liong heard her sigh, and smiled. 'We'll take it,' he said. The Old One rubbed her bare wrist now, and sighed again. She looked out the bus window, and watched the streets of Chinatown slip past. It wasn't too late, she thought—if she got off at the next bus-stop, she could probably still claim her bracelet back. She had worn the bracelet for so many years that her arm felt strangely light now, without it.

As if sensing her thoughts, Rosa nudged her gently. '*Ayah*,' she said, 'I will buy your bracelet back for you, I promise. Soon.'

'No need,' the Old One said. What she meant was that, in a way, the bracelet had outlived its purpose anyway. She had wanted one all those years that she was washing clothes and scrubbing floors for other people, because it would have been a sign of luxury, that she had enough, and a little extra besides. Even after Ah Liong was getting a steady paycheck, and bought a HUDC flat, she had thought of the bracelet as an additional security. Not that Ah Liong didn't take care of all her needs, but it had never occurred to him that she might like a savings account of her own, just in case there might be, say, an earthquake someday or, even worse, if he were to suddenly die. But the sense of impending catastrophe which had haunted her as a young widow had gradually receded as she became older and more secure, so that today, she suddenly realised, she no longer needed the security her jade bracelet had once provided her.

'You are so kind, ayah,' Rosa was saying now. 'From my heart I thank you,' and quickly, so suddenly that the Old One could not restrain her, Rosa had knelt down beside her, took her hand in both of hers, and kissed it.

'Rosa, Rosa, what're you doing?' Billy demanded, loud enough so that the couple seated in the aisle across from them looked up and stared.

'Shush,' the Old One said, and reaching into her pocket, held out a kumquat to him.

Billy took the miniature orange and bit into it, then grimaced, his mouth screwing up into a pucker. 'I want candy!' He wailed.

Rosa unwrapped a chocolate bar and broke off a piece for him. When he had calmed down, she took the kumquat away and started nibbling at it herself.

'Sour!' she said, taking another delicate bite.

'You like?' Rosa nodded.

'I like sour.'

'I like skin best ,' the Old One said, taking out another kumquat from her pocket and nibbling at it.

'It's bitter, but that makes the inside taste sweeter,' Rosa agreed.

Like life, the Old One thought, like our lives, she glanced over at Billy as he ate another piece of chocolate—too bad the youngsters nowadays didn't understand that.

In companionable silence, the two women nibbled at their kumquat as the bus approached their stop.

They hadn't really worked it out, but it was understood that Rosa would be the one to slip the video camera back into Mr Tan's study, since she would know exactly where she had taken it from. But by the time they got back to the apartment, it was much later than they had expected, and a distraught Beverly was waiting for them at the door.

'Where on earth have you all been?' she demanded, then, without giving them a chance to reply, she launched into a long series of chores for Rosa to do before the guests were due to arrive.

The Old One had given Billy his bath, and changed him into the outfit that his mother had selected for him—a miniature suit complete with a clip-on bowtie which made him look like a circus midget rather than a child—and still Rosa was busy scrubbing the sinks, while Beverly hovered around supervising.

It was only when Leon arrived back from the office, and Beverly went off to greet him, that the Old One was able to manage a brief exchange with Rosa.

'I put the camera-thing back?' she whispered.

Rosa nodded. 'It's in my room now, under the bed. Put it back in Mr Tan's desk drawer. The top one.'

'I do it now,' the Old One said, and moved off in search of the video camera. She had no trouble finding it under Rosa's narrow bed, nor even slipping into her son's study without anyone noticing, but once there, she stared in perplexity at the large wooden desk. Had Rosa said the drawer on the left, or the right? Or maybe it was the one in the middle? She had said the top drawer, didn't she? But which one?

In confusion she looked up at the small bronze paperweight that stood on a corner of the desk. It was of a young woman in a long loose robe, blindfolded, holding aloft a set of scales in one hand, and a sword in the other. Which goddess she was, the Old One had never understood, especially when her son had denied that the statue was a goddess at all. She was not to be found in any temple, he had told her, but rather in front of many of the courts of justice where trials were held, so the Old One assumed that lawyers might pray to her to win their case.

She had never seen her son pray to this blinded statue, but that he did pray, she was sure of, because didn't he win most of his legal cases—even those when he defended the poor and the powerless, like that homeless alcoholic who had accidentally knocked a display of crystalware over in some boutique, or that unwed teenage mother who begged for custody of her child? With her intuition and her English, she had understood enough that Ah Liong had won these cases against heavy odds, and she had been doubly proud of him, proud that he had won, but deeper than that, prouder that he had undertaken to represent these people at all. They had been through enough hard times, she and her son, that together they had come to respect the hardships borne by others, so that for all the things that she was grateful to Kuan Yin about, she often felt that perhaps the most important gift of all was that Ah Liong had been imbued with a sense of compassion too.

The Old One looked at this blindfolded goddess now, and wished that she knew how to pray to it. Holding up the video camera to it, she mumbled to the statuette, 'Please, which one? Which drawer does this go into? Can't you please tell me?'

But if that strange goddess gave a sign, the Old One couldn't see it. 'How would you know anyway, your eyes all wrapped up?'

she murmured. She pulled open the right-hand drawer, but it was crammed with documents. No way a camera would fit in there.

Hurriedly she shut it, then pulled at the drawer on the other side. The doorbell rang, and voices from the first guests wafted in, punctuated by light laughter and exclamations of 'Happy Birthday!' The Old One knew she didn't have much more time. Soon the party would be in full swing, and Beverly would be demanding the video-camera, issuing her ultimatum to Rosa in a dark corner somewhere. This left-hand drawer was not nearly as full as the other one.

Hurriedly, the Old One pushed a few pens and diskettes further into the drawer, then put the video-camera into it.

'No, it goes into the middle drawer!'

With a gasp, the Old One looked up. Her son was staring at her from the open doorway, a strange look on his face.

'The … middle drawer?' she repeated stupidly.

'Where did it come from?' he asked, walking towards her. He was holding a pile of giftwrapped presents in his hands, evidence that several guests had already arrived.

'I … I found it,' she said.

'Where?'

'In … in the closet. Of the front hall.'

'Ah Mah,' he said quietly. 'You don't have to lie to me.'

The Old One took a deep breath. 'All right, then. I bought it back. From the pawnshop.' Nervously she rubbed the wrist where the bracelet had been.

He glanced at her bare wrist. 'With your jade bracelet?' He sounded shocked.

'I didn't need it as much as …' she paused, confused.

'As much as Rosa?'

The Old One refused to answer. She didn't, she thought grimly, have to be a trained lawyer to know when the best answer was none at all.

'Ah Mah, that wasn't right,' her son was saying now. 'It wasn't right for Rosa to take the camera without asking us. And it isn't right for you to try and cover up for her.'

'Oh yes?' The Old One took a deep breath. 'Who are you, Ah Liong, to tell me what is right and wrong, when I have spent the last thirty years teaching you? Does that British law school tell you it's right for you to spend more on one party that what your maid earns in a year? Did your wife insist it's right for you to get more toys—things you don't even need,' she gestured to the stack of gifts he was holding, 'when Rosa can't even provide a home for her own children?'

'Ah Mah, you don't understand,' Ah Liong mumbled. 'The legal system has to do with justice, not equality ...'

'Oh I understand,' the Old One retorted. 'I understand that in the last thirty years that I have raised you, you think you've become stronger and smarter and richer than your old mother. You think ...'

Just then the door swung open again, and Beverly came in, bearing another armful of presents. 'Leon! There you are! Just about everyone's here—and look at all these things!' She deposited the presents on the desk, knocking over the statue of the blindfolded goddess in the process.

'More things,' the Old One said. 'When you have everything you need already.' Pointedly she held out the video camera and handed it to him. 'Everything, Ah Liong, except a kind heart.' She had used the Cantonese term, *liong-sum*, literally a kind heart: "liong" as kind, the same word that his name was based on. She reached over to the fallen statuette, and set it upright again. 'This goddess of yours, this one that you lawyers worship, has she no *liong-sum*?'

For a long moment her son did not say anything.

Beverly glanced sharply at the two of them. 'What's going on?' she said, 'And my video-camera—where did it suddenly come from?'

'Tell her,' the Old One said. She put the video camera on the desk, next to the fallen statuette. 'This goddess you worship, Ah Liong, has she no *liong-sum* either?'

Ah Liong bit his lower lip. Just the way he used to do as a little boy, his mother realised, watching him, just the way he did when he was thinking hard. Then his mouth relaxed, and broadened into a shy smile.

'Yes, she does have *liong-sum*, Ah Mah,' he said. He reached out and set the statuette upright again. 'I'm glad you've reminded me of it.'

Turning to his wife, he said in English, 'That video camera was in my desk drawer all along, dear.'

'But you said you looked there!' Beverly protested.

'I looked in the side drawers. I must have forgotten to look in the middle one. Come along; if the guests are all here, you can start filming your party.' He put a practised arm around her waist, one of those suave gestures he had come back from London and so charmed Beverly with, and escorted her out of the room.

At the doorway, he paused briefly, and glanced back at his mother, one eyebrow lifted as if in search of her approval, an expression sweetly familiar to her.

The Old One smiled at him, a long proud smile. Thirty years, she thought, it had taken thirty years for her son to become a grown man, intelligent, rich—and compassionate. Yes, that strange blindfolded goddess must have a kind heart after all.

Glossary

The Glossary is divided into two sections: Abbreviations, and Colloquialisms and Non-English Words and Phrases. The meanings of colloquialisms and non-English words and phrases are generally those applicable to the contexts in which they appear in *More than Half the Sky*. As a rule, non-English words and phrases are italicised only when they first appear in the individual text (and not subsequently). In a small number of cases, certain words, contemporary names and titles which may not be readily recognisable to the non-Singaporean reader have also been included.

For other abbreviations and colloquialisms frequently used in Singapore, see the *Times-Chambers Essential English Dictionary* (Singapore: Federal, 1997; publ. by arr. with Chambers-Harrap Publ., Edinburgh), especially Appendix 1 ("Common borrowed words in colloquial Singaporean and Malaysian English"), pp. 1183–1185; and Appendix 4 ("Abbreviations"), pp. 1196–1202.

Abbreviations

CC   Community Centre
NTUC   National Trades Union Congress
SDU   Social Development Unit
SIM   Singapore Institute of Management
SSO   Singapore Symphony Orchestra
TCS   Television Corporation of Singapore

Colloquialisms and Non-English Words and Phrases

Abbreviations: C   Chinese
                  Ca   Cantonese
                  H   Hokkien
                  M   Malay
                  Ma   Mandarin

abang   (M) older brother. Also honorific for husband.
ah boy   common nickname or pet-name for young male children (as *ah girl* is for young female children). Term combines Chinese and English.
agar-agar   (M) jelly, made by boiling isinglass or various algae with sugar, and allowed to set at room temperature or in the refrigerator.

Ah Chim   (H) auntie. Also used to address a servant (considered more polite than addressing her by name).
Ah Phoh   (Ca) term of address for maternal grandmother. See *Po-po*.
Ah Soh   (Ca) auntie, as in Wong-*soh*, Lee-*soh*, where Wong and Lee are surnames.

aiyah (C) expression or exclamation of resignation or annoyance, usually used at the beginning of a sentence. Also *aiyoh, ayah.*

aiyoh see *aiyah.*

alamak (M) expression or exclamation of surprise or annoyance, usually used at the beginning of a sentence.

amah (C) female domestic. See *black-and-white Chinese amahs.*

ang pow (H) red packet (containing a gift of money).

ang mo (H); *hong-mo* (C); literally, red hair or red-haired. A white man.

ang mo kia white child, white children.

ang mo lau literally, white man's mansion; used for big bungalows/ houses.

ang mo towkay the white Master or Boss or Head of the House. See *towkay.*

Apa lah dia cakap? (M) What is he/she saying?

ayah (C) see *aiyah.*

baik (M) good.

bak kut teh (H) stew, more like Chinese soup than Western stew in consistency, cooked with pork ribs (*bak kut*), spices and garlic. *Teh*: tea.

bangun (M) rise; stand.

Band Two refers to a common system of classification of marks used in primary schools: Band 1: 85% and above; Band 2: 70–84%; Band 3: 50–69%; Band 4: under 50%.

black-and-white Chinese amahs Chinese female domestics (a rare breed today) distinguished by their black trousers and white Chinese-style blouses, worn effectively as a uniform.

buaya (M) crocodile.

chap-cheng kia (H) literally, child of ten breeds. Bastard, i.e., child born of a mixed marriage.

char-siew-pao (Ca) steamed bun with filling of (minced) roast pork. Euphemism for breast(s). See *pau.*

chepat lah (M) hurry up. See below for *lah.*

dai-koh (Ca) also *tai-kor.* Eldest brother.

deep-fried cuttlefish transliteration of a Chinese expression to suggest deep trouble. Cf in hot soup.

dim sum (Ca) also tim sum. Literally, touch the heart. An assortment of bite-size foods often served in the late morning for brunch.

enche cabin also *enche kebin*; a famous *nyonya* (Peranankan) dish made of previously deep-fried chicken and potatoes which are then added, together with peas, to a light stew of carrots and onions.

erhu (Ma) two-stringed Chinese fiddle, played in an upright position, with the base resting on the player's lap, and with the bow threaded between the strings.

fengshui (Ma) literally, wind-water. Chinese art of geomancy: the placement and location of buildings and man-made structures to harmonize with, as well as benefit from, the surrounding physical and man-made environment.

got head and got tail transliteration of Hokkien saying which means bringing matters which have been started to a proper end.

Gong-gong (Ca) term of address for maternal grandfather. Also *Ah Gong*.

guanxi (Ma) also *guangxi*. Business relationships and connections; networking.

hanyu pinyin (Ma) romanized system of representing Chinese characters, usually accompanied by tone marks above the vowels.

hoi toi (Ca) literally, open (the) table. Lay the table (implying that the food is ready).

hong-mo sek (Ca) literally, red-hair food. Western cuisine.

jianbizi (Ma) also *jiantizi*. Simplified Chinese characters, first introduced in China in the early fifties. Cf *fantizi*: non-simplified (classical) Chinese characters.

jie (Ma) elder sister.

James Lye Inspector Mike Chin in the popular TCS police and crime series, 'Triple Nine.'

kaki (M) literally leg or foot. Customary partner.

kampong (M) Malay village, comprising primarily wooden houses on stilts.

kaypoh (H) busybody. Cf *sam gu lok por*.

kiasu (H) literally, afraid of losing. Common Singaporean expression meaning fearful of losing out to others, or being got the better of.

kongsi (H) clan association.

kwei-lo (Ca) literally, devil-fellow. A foreigner, usually a white man.

kueh (M) cake(s), made with different kinds of flour like wheat, rice or mung bean, and using various methods of cooking: boiling, steaming, deep-frying, baking.

lah (M) particle, used for emphasis, as in *Apa lah dia cakap?* Or *chepat lah* and *Ask her to eat lah*.

lawah (M) attracting attention; showing off.

lelong (M) an impromptu sale, especially when the vendor wishes to dispose of many items quickly.

lor (H) particle, used to emphasise the self-evident nature of what is being said.

mee (H) noodles. Maggi mee is a popular brand of packet-noodles.

money face transliteration of Hokkien term which means a person who is obsessed with money.

nai-nai (Ca) term of address for paternal grandmother.

niaow (H) fussy and petty.
pau (C) steamed bun(s) made from rice flour and often with assorted fillings.
pontianak (M) female Malay spirit which sucks blood and preys on pregnant women.
Po-po (Ca) maternal grandmother. See *Ah Phoh.*
Pusa (Ca) *bodhisattva* (Sanskrit) or future Buddha. In Mahayana Buddhism, the bodhisattva indefinitely delays the attainment of Buddhahood so as to devote herself or himself to the welfare of all.
rice-bin transliteration of Chinese term which means a useless person (who functions only as a receptacle for food). See also *fan thong* (Ca), p.194
samsu (H) Chinese liquor made from fermented rice.
sabo sabotage.
sam gu lok por (Ca) literally, three aunts, six grandmothers. Busybody. Cf *kaypoh.*
sampan (Ca) literally, three planks. Small wooden boat, propelled by oars in the stern. Also used in Malay.
sien (H) tired, bored.
sini (M) here.
sua teng (H) literally, hilltop. A rural area.
suah-ku (H) also *sua-ku.* Literally, a hill tortoise. A naif or country bumpkin.
suay (H) bringing ill luck or misfortune.
su kia har (Hainanese) little squatter hut.
sup-sup-swee (Ca) literally, little bits. Nothing much; of little importance.
tai-kor see *dai-koh.*
tai-tai (Ca) a wealthy married woman, well dressed and with wealthy friends and time for leisure activities.
telima kasih (M) Corruption of *terima kaseh*: thank you.
tim sum see *dim sum.*
tongkang (H) barge. Sometimes refers to Chinese junk.
towkay (H) owner or head of a business; Master.
towkay neoh (H) mistress of the house.
towkay kiah (H) son of the Master; young master.
Triple Nine Popular TCS series on crime and the police. Singapore's version of *NYPD Blue.*
Wah liau (H) also *wah lau.* Exclamatory expression of surprise, wonder or annoyance, often occurring at the beginning of a sentence.
Wong-soh see *Ah Soh.*

Leong Liew Geok

Selected Bibliography

Publications on Women in Singapore

Alputharajah, V. *Sexual Behaviour of Women in Singapore.* Singapore: PG Publ., 1990.

Association of Women for Action and Research (AWARE). *Declaration and Constitution.* Singapore: AWARE, 1986.

Ban, Kah Choon, Gopal Baratham & Janadas Devan, eds. *Commentary: Journal of the National University of Singapore Society.* Special Issue on Women. New Issue 5.1 (Oct. 1981).

Bartholomew, Geoffrey Wilson, & Lalith William Athulathmudali. 'Women's Charter.' *Malayan Law Review 3.2* (Dec. 1961), pp. 316–330.

Boey Chee Yin. 'Daughters and Working Mothers.' *The Contemporary Family in Singapore: Structure and Change.* Eds. Eddie C Y Kuo and Aline K Wong. Singapore: Singapore University Press, 1979, pp. 62–87.

Chang, Cheng-tung. 'Nuptiality Patterns Among Women of Childbearing Age.' *The Contemporary Family in Singapore: Structure and Change.* Eds. Eddie C Y Kuo and Aline K Wong. Singapore: Singapore University Press, 1979, pp. 117–141.

Chang, Weining C, & Wong Wing Keung. 'Gender Differences in Achievement Motivation in Singapore.' Dept. of Social Work & Psychology, National University of Singapore, 1994. Dept. of Social Work & Psychology Working Paper No. 27.

Chew, Phyllis Ghim Lian. 'The Singapore Council of Women and the Women's Movement.' *Journal of Southeast Asian Studies* 25.1 (March 1994), pp. 112–140.

Chin, Woon Ping, ed. *Playful Phoenix: Women Write for the Singapore Stage* [six plays]. Singapore: TheatreWorks, 1996.

Chopard, Kelly. *A Helping Hand: The Asian Women's Welfare Association Story.* Singapore: Landmark (for AWWA), 1996.

Department of Statistics, Singapore. *Statistics on Marriages and Divorces;* 1996. Singapore: Department of Statistics, Ministry of Trade and Industry, 1997.

Selected Bibliography

Directory of Services for Women. Singapore: The Family and Women's Welfare Section, Ministry of Community Development, Feb. 1992.

Eng, Wee Ling. *A Woman's Place: The Story of Singapore Women.* Eds. Aline Wong and Leong Wai Kum. Singapore: PAP Women's Wing, 1993.

[The text is based on the research findings in *Singapore Women: Three Decades of Change,* see Aline K Wong and Leong Wai Kum, eds., below.]

Government of Singapore Women's Charter (Ch. 353); The Statutes of the Republic of Singapore. Singapore: Govt. Printers, 1985 (rev. ed.).

Goatly, Andrew. 'How Can an Educated Woman Know Her Place: An Analysis of a *Straits Times* "twentysomething" Column.' *awareness: A Journal of the Association of Women for Action and Research* 4.1 (Jan. 1997), pp. 30–47.

Heng, Geraldine. *The Sun in Her Eyes: Stories by Singapore Women* [twelve stories]. Singapore: Woodrose Publications, 1976.

Heng, Geraldine, & Janadas Devan. 'State Fatherhood: The Politics of Nationalism, Sexuality and Race in Singapore.' *Nationalisms and Sexualities.* Eds. Andrew Parker et al. New York: Routledge, 1992, pp. 343–364.

[Also publ. in *Bewitching Women, Pious Men: Gender and Body Politics in Southeast Asia.* Eds. Aihwa Ong & Michael G Peletz (see entry below), pp. 195–215.]

Koh, Tai Ann. 'Biographical, Literary Writings and Plays in English by Women from Malaysia and Singapore: A Checklist.' *Commentary* 7.2 & 3 (Dec. 1987), pp. 94–96.

————. 'History/His Story as Her Story: Chinese Women's Biographical Writing from Indonesia, Malaysia and Singapore.' *Southeast Asian Chinese: The Socio-Cultural Dimension.* Ed. Leo Suryadinata. Singapore: Times Academic Press [for Singapore Society for Asian Studies, Association of Nanyang University Graduates and Singapore Federation of Chinese Clan Associations], 1995, pp. 251–260.

————. 'Wandering Through the Minefield: Leading Who, Where to, and for What.' *awareness: A Journal of the Association of Women for Action and Research* 3.1. (Jan. 1996), pp. 23–30.

Koh, Tai Ann, & Vivienne Wee, eds. 'Women's Choices, Women's Lives.' Special issue on Women. *Commentary* 7.2 & 3 (Dec. 1987).

Kwa, Aileen, & Clare Lim. 'Beijing: A Woman's Conference on the World or a World Conference on Women?' *awareness: A Journal of the Association of Women for Action and Research* 3.1 (Jan. 1996), pp. 4–22.

Lam, Jenny, ed. *Voices and Choices: The Women's Movement in Singapore.* Singapore: Times Editions [for Singapore Council of Women's Organisations and Singapore Baha'i Women's Committee], 1993.

Leong, Wai Kum. *Family Law in Singapore: Cases and Commentary on the Women's Charter and Family Law.* Singapore & Kuala Lumpur: Malayan Law Journal Pte Ltd. & Malayan Law Journal Sdn Bhd., 1990.

_____. 'Turning Point in Singapore Family Law: Women's Charter (Amendment) Bill 1979.' *Malayan Law Review* 21.2 (Dec. 1979), pp. 327–350.

Lim, Catherine. *The Woman's Book of Superlatives* [ten stories]. Singapore: Times Editions, 1993.

_____. 'Oscar Doesn't Understand: Things are Changing too Fast for some Singaporean Men.' *Asia Magazine* 32.J23 (2–4 Sept. 1994), p. 30.

Lim, Joyce. 'The Write Way.' *Female* (May 1996), pp. 26–32. [Women writers in Singapore, with particular reference to Stella Kon, Catherine Lim & Tan Mei Ching.]

Lim, Linda C Y. 'Women in the Singapore Economy: A Four-Part Study on Female Participation in the Labour Force.' *Commentary* 5.1 (Oct. 1981), pp. 9–40.

Lim Seow Yoke. 'Women in Singapore Politics, 1945–1970.' 1984/1985 Academic Exercise. Dept. of History, National University of Singapore.

Low, Guat Tin. *Successful Women in Singapore.* Singapore: EPB Publishers, 1993.

Mehta, Kalyani. *Giving Up Hope: A Study of Attempted Suicide Amongst Indian Women.* Singapore: Times Books, 1990.

Ministry of Social Affairs. *Report on National Survey on Married Women, their Role in the Family and Society.* Singapore: Research Branch, Ministry of Social Affairs, 1984.

NTUC Legal Department and NTUC Women's Secretariat. *Legal Rights and Support Services for Women Workers.* Singapore: SNP Publ., 1994.

NTUC Women's Programme. *Seminar on the Responsibilities and Aspirations of Working Women in Singapore* [Proceedings]; 13–14 Jan. 1979.

PuruShotam, Nirmala. 'Women and Knowledge of Power: Notes on the Singaporean Dilemma.' *Imagining Singapore*. Eds. Ban Kah Choon, Anne Pakir & Tong Chee Kiong. Singapore: Times Academic Press, 1992, pp. 320–361.

Quah, Euston. *Value of Household Production in Singapore*. Singapore: Heinemann (for Centre for Advanced Studies, NUS), 1988.

Quah, Stella. *Between Two Worlds: Modern Wives in a Traditional Setting*. Singapore: ISEAS, 1988. [Field Report Series No. 19.]

_____. *Family in Singapore: Sociological Perspectives*. Singapore: Times Academic Press, 1994.

_____. *The Family as an Asset: An International Perspective on Marriage, Parenthood and Social Policy*. Singapore: Times Academic Press, 1990.

_____. 'Marriage and Family.' *Singapore Women: Three Decades of Change*. Eds. Aline K Wong & Leong Wai Kam. Singapore: Times Academic Press, 1993, pp. 28–85.

Report of the Select Committee on the Women's Charter (Amendment) Bill [Bill No. 23/79]. Presented to Parliament on 25 Feb. 1980.

Republic of Singapore: Reprint of *The Women's Charter* (Chapter 47 of the Revised Edition). Singapore: Attorney General's Chambers, 1981.

Singapore Association of Women Lawyers. *Legal Status of Singapore Women*. Singapore: Asiapac, 1986.

Singapore Council of Women's Organizations. *SCWO Salutes Singapore Women*; 1980–1990. 10th Anniversary Commemorative Publication of SCWO.

Singam, Constance, intro. *The Ties that Bind: In Search of the Modern Singapore Family*. Singapore: Armour (for AWARE), 1996.

'Stand Up and Be Counted.' Executive Lifestyle, *Business Times* Weekend edition, Mch. 8–9, 1997 [Special Feature on International Women's Day].

Tan. P C, and G W Jones. 'Malay Divorce in Peninsular Malaysia: The Near Disappearance of an Institution.' *Southeast Asian Journal of Social Science* 18.2 (1990), pp. 85–114.

Warren, James Francis. *Ah Ku and Karayuki-san: Prostitution in Singapore, 1870–1940*. Singapore: Oxford University Press, 1993.

Wong, Aline, and Eddie Kuo. *Divorce in Singapore*. Singapore: Graham Brash, 1983.

Wong, Aline. *Economic Development and Women's Place: Women in Singapore.* London: Change: International Reports: Women and Society, June 1980.

_____. 'Women as a Minority Group.' *Singapore: Society in Transition.* Ed. Riaz Hassan. Kuala Lumpur: Oxford University Press, 1976, pp. 290–314.

Wong, Aline, et al. *Women in Modern Singapore.* Singapore: University Education Press, 1975.

Wong, Aline. 'Women's Status and Changing Family Values.' *The Contemporary Family in Singapore :Structure and Change.* Eds. Eddie C Y Kuo & Aline K Wong. Singapore: Singapore University Press, 1979, pp. 40–61.

Wong, Aline K. 'Working Mothers and the Care of Pre–School Children in Singapore: A Research Report.' Singapore: The Singapore Girl Guides Assoc., Oct. 1980.

Wong, Aline, and Leong Wai Kum, eds. *Singapore Women: Three Decades of Change.* Singapore: Times Academic Press, 1993.

Zhang, Xina. *Singapore Women at the Helm.* Singapore: Asiapac, 1996. (Originally in Chinese; trans. Guan Libing.)

Publications on Women in the Asia–Pacific Region

Allen, Pamela, sel. & trans. *Women's Voices: An Anthology of Short Stories by Indonesian Women Writers.* Melbourne: Longman, 1995.

Ariffin, Jamilah. *Women and Development in Malaysia.* Petaling Jaya: Pelanduk, 1992.

_____, co–ord. *Reviewing Malaysian Women's Status: Country Report in Preparation for the Fourth UN Conference on Women.* Kuala Lumpur: Population Studies Unit, Faculty of Economics and Administration, University of Malaya, c. 1994.

Argawal, Bina, ed. *Structures of Patriarchy: State, Community and Household in Modernising Asia.* London: Zed Books; New Delhi: Kali for Women, 1988.
[Papers from the Regional Conference for Asia on Women and the Household, held in New Delhi, 27–31 Jan. 1985; sponsored by Commission on Women of the International Union of Anthropological and Ethnological Sciences, Research Committee 32 of the International Sociological Assoc., and the Indian Assoc. for Women's Studies.]

Selected Bibliography

Arkin, Marian, & Barbara Shollar. *Longman Anthology of World Literature by Women, 1875–1975.* New York & London: Longman, 1989.
[Section on 'Women's Literary Traditions: Regional Essays' includes Elizabeth Webby on Australia & New Zealand, pp. 1073–1079; Katherine Carlitz on China, pp. 1110–1115; Susie Tharu on India, pp. 1134–1142; Chieko Mulhern on Japan, pp. 1152–1162.]

Atkinson, Jane Monnig, & Sherry Errington, eds. *Power and Difference: Gender in Island Southeast Asia.* Stanford: Stanford University Press, 1990.

Blake, Myrna, & Hema Goonatilake. *Case Studies on Women in the Informal Sector.* Bangkok : Asian & Pacific Centre for Women and Development, June 1980.

Brill, Alida. *A Rising Public Voice: Women in Politics Worldwide.* New York: The Feminist Press, 1995.

Brinton, Mary C. *Women and the Economic Miracle: Gender and Work in Postwar Japan.* Berkeley: University of California Press, 1993.

Brooks, David, & Brenda Walker. *Poetry and Gender: Statements and Essays in Australian Women's Poetry and Politics.* St Lucia: University of Queensland Press, 1989.

Buckley, Sandra. *Broken Silence: Voices of Japanese Feminism.* Berkeley: University of California Press, 1997.

Bunkle, Phillida, and Beryl Hughes. *Women in New Zealand Society.* Sydney: George Allen and Unwin, 1980.

Catley, Christine Cole, ed. *Celebrating Women: New Zealand Women and Their Stories.* Whatamongo Bay: Cape Catley Ltd., 1984.

Chandler, Glen, Norma Sullivan & Jan Branson, eds. *Development and Displacement: Women in Southeast Asia.* Clayton, Vic.: Centre of Southeast Asian Studies, Monash University, 1991. [Monash papers on Southeast Asia: No. 18.]

Chatterjee, Partha. 'Colonialism, Nationalism and Colonized Women: The Context in India.' *American Ethnologist* 16.4 (1989), pp. 622–633.

Cheung, Angelica, et al. 'More than Just a Pretty Face.' *Asia Magazine* (cover story) 35.M11 (Mch. 7–9, 1997), pp. 10–14. [The sexploitation of women in advertising.]

Clark, Alice W. *Gender and Political Economy: Explorations of South Asian Systems.* Delhi: Oxford University Press, 1993.

Chlebowska, Krystyna. *Literacy for Rural Women in the Third World.* Paris: UNESCO, 1990.

Cohen, Colleen Ballerina, Richard Wilk & Beverly Stoeltje. *Beauty Queens on the Global Stage: Gender, Contests and Power.* New York & London: Routledge, 1996.

Conway, Jill Ker, & Susan C Bourke, eds. *The Politics of Women's Education: Perspectives from Asia, Africa, and Latin America.* Ann Arbor: University of Michigan Press, 1995.

Dancz, Virginia H. *Women and Party Politics in Peninsular Malaysia.* Oxford: Oxford University Press, 1987 [East Asian Social Science Monograph Series.]

Daud, Dr. Fatimah. *'Minah Karan': The Truth about Malaysian Factory Girls.* Kuala Lumpur: Berita Pub. Sdn. Bhd., for Dept. of Anthropology and Sociology, University of Malaya, 1985.

Else, Anne, & Heather Roberts, eds. *A Woman's Life: Writing by Women about Female Experience in New Zealand.* Auckland: Penguin Books, 1989.

Esterline, May Handy. *They Changed their Worlds: Nine Women of Asia.* Lanham, Maryland; & London: University Press of America, 1987. [Based on biographies publ. by Ramon Magsaysay Award Foundation, Manila, Philippines.]

Far Eastern Economic Review. Cover Story: 'Women in Society.' 121.1 (Jan. 5, 1984), pp. 26–40.

Fawcett, James T, Siew-Ean Khoo & Peter C Smith, eds. *Women in the Cities of Asia: Migration and Urban Adaptation.* Boulder, Colorado: Westview Press, 1984. [Publ. in co-operation with the East-West Population Inst., East-West Center, Honolulu.]

Filipino Women in Education. Manila: National Commission on the Role of Filipino Women, 1985.

Flemming, Leslie A., ed. *Women's Work for Women: Missionaries and Social Change in Asia.* Boulder, Colorado: Westview Press, 1989.

Fraser, Arvonne. 'The 1995 UN Conference on Women in Beijing.' *Women's Rights as Human Rights,* ed. Joanna Kerr. London: Zed Books [in assoc. with the North-South Inst.], 1993, pp. 153–156.

Friedlander, Eva. 'Inclusive Boundaries, Exclusive Ideologies: Hindu Fundamentalism and Gender in India Today.' *Feminism, Nationalism and Militarism.* Ed. Constance R Sutton. New York: Assoc. for Feminist Anthropology/American Anthropological Assoc. in collaboration with the International Women's Anthropology Conference, 1995, pp. 51–56.

Fujimura-Fanselow, Kumiko, & Atsuko Kameda, eds. Japanese *New Feminist Perspectives on the Past, Present and Future*. New York: The Feminist Press, 1995.
[Includes an Appendix, 'Significant Dates in the Recent History of Japanese Women,' pp. 407–414.]

Gelb, Joyce, & Marian Lief Palley, eds. *Women of Japan and Korea: Continuity and Change*. Philadelphia: Temple University Press, 1994.

Genovese, Michael A, ed. *Women as National Leaders*. Newbury Park, CA; London & New Delhi: Sage Publications, 1993.

Gerke, Solvay. *Social Change and Life Planning of Rural Javanese Women*. Saarbrücken & Fort Lauderdale: Breitenbach, 1992.

Gluckman, Ron. 'Women on Top.' *Asia Magazine* (cover story) 35.M10 (Feb. 21–23, 1997), pp. 10–14.

Grieve, Norma, and Ailsa Burns. *Australian Women: Contemporary Feminist Thought*. Melbourne: Oxford University Press, 1994.

Gurpreet, Mahajan. 'Gender Equality and Community Rights: Paradoxes of Liberal Democracy in India.' *Journal of Gender Studies* 5.2 (July 1996), pp. 169–176.

Haas, Robert, & Rahmah Hashim, eds. *Malaysian Women: Creating their Political Awareness*. Kuala Lumpur: Asian Inst. for Devt. Communication, in co-op. with the Malaysian Office of the Friedrich Naumann Foundation (Germany), 1994. [Papers presented at a seminar (n.d.).]

Hainsworth, G B. *Southeast Asia: Women, Changing Social Structure and Cultural Continuity*. Ottawa: University of Ottawa Press, 1981.

Hélie–Lucas, Marie Aimée. 'Women Living Under Muslim Laws.' *Ours by Right: Women's Rights as Human Rights*. Ed. Joanna Kerr. London: Zed Books [in assoc. with the North–South Inst.], 1993, pp. 52–64.

Helliwell, Christine. 'Women in Asia: Anthropology and the Study of Women.' *Asia's Cultural Mosaic: An Anthropological Introduction*. Ed. Grant Evans. New York: Prentice Hall, 1993, pp. 260–286.

Heyzer, Noeleen, ed. *A Commitment to the World's Women: Perspectives on Development for Beijing and Beyond*. New York: United Nations Development Fund for Women, 1995.

_____, ed. *Daughters in Industry: Work Skills and Consciousness of Women Workers in Asia*. Kuala Lumpur: Asia and Pacific Devt. Centre, 1988.

Heyzer, Noeleen, and Gita Sen, eds. *Gender, Economic Growth and Poverty: Market Growth and State Planning in Asia and the Pacific.* New Delhi: Kali for Women, and Utrecht, Netherlands: International Books, in collaboration with the Asian and Pacific Development Centre, Kuala Lumpur, 1994.

Heyzer, Noeleen. *Working Women in South-East Asia: Development, Subordination and Emancipation.* Milton Keynes; Philadelphia: Open University Press, 1986.

Hicks, George. *The Comfort Women: Sex Slaves of the Japanese Imperial Forces.* Singapore: Heinemann, 1995.

Hiraga, Masako K. 'Metaphors Japanese Women Live By.' *Working Papers on Language, Gender and Sexism* (AILA Commission on Language and Gender) 1.1, pp. 38–57.

Holmström, Lakshmi, ed. *The Inner Courtyard: Stories by Indian Women.* London: Virago, 1990.

Hong, Evelyn. *Malaysian Women: Problems and Issues.* Penang: Consumer Assoc. of Penang, 1983.

Howard, Keith, ed. *True Stories of the Korean Comfort Women.* London: Cassell [for the Korean Council for Women Drafted for Military Sexual Slavery in Japan], 1995.

Hunter, Janet, ed. *Japanese Women Working.* London & New York: Routledge, 1994.

Imamura, Anne E., ed. *Re-Imaging Japanese Women.* Berkeley: University of California Press, 1996.

International Conference on Women in the Asia–Pacific Region: Persons, Powers and Politics: 11–13 August 1997. [Jointly organised by the Dept. of Geography, S E Asian Studies Centre, Centre for Advanced Studies, National University of Singapore.] *Proceedings.*

International Federation of Commercial, Clerical & Technical Employees, FIET. Proceedings of Regional Women [sic] Conference: 'Equality for Women.' Penang, Malaysia; 12–16 Feb. 1979.

Iwao, Sumiko. The Japanese Woman: Traditional Image and Changing Reality. New York: The Free Press, 1993.

Jahan, Rounag, ed. *Women in Asia.* London: Minority Rights Group, 1992 [1980].
    [Reports on the position of women in Pakistan, India, Sri Lanka, Bangladesh, Philippines, Indonesia, S. Korea, Japan, China.]

Japan Echo. Vol 23 (1993). Special issue: The Graying Society. See Ashino Yuriko, 'Reproductive Rights: A Female View,' pp. 35–37; Yashiro Naohiro, 'Eliminating Institutional Bias Against Working Women,' pp. 43–47.

Jaschok, Maria, & Suzanne Miers, eds. *Women and Chinese Patriarchy: Submission, Servitude and Escape.* London & New Jersey: Zed Books, & Hong Kong: Hong Kong University at Pokfulam, 1994.

Jayawardena, Kumari. *Feminism and Nationalism in the Third World.* London: Zed Books; New Delhi: Kali for Women, 1986.

Jeffs, Angela. 'Land of the Rising Daughter.' *Asia Magazine* 28.F–2 (Oct. 19–21, 1990), pp. 6–16.

Jones, Gavin M. *Marriage and Divorce in Islamic South-East Asia.* Kuala Lumpur: Oxford University Press, 1994. [South-East Asian Social Science Monograph.]

Kanematsu, Elizabeth. *Women in Society: Japan.* Singapore: Times Books, 1993.

Katrak, Ketu H. 'Indian Nationalism, Ghandian "Satyagraha," and Representations of Female Sexuality.' *Nationalisms and Sexualities.* Ed. Andrew Parker, et al. New York & London: Routledge, 1992, pp. 392–406.

Kepner, Susan Fukop, ed. & transl. *The Lioness in Bloom: Modern Thai Fiction about Women.* Berkeley: University of California Press, 1996.

Khan, Nighat Said, ed. *Voices Within: Dialogues with Women on Islam.* Lahore: ASR Publications, 1993.

Kim, Kyung-Ai. 'Nationalism: An Advocate of, or a Barrier to Feminism in South Korea.' *Women's Studies International Forum* 19.1 & 2 (Jan.–April 1996), pp. 65–74. [Special issue: 'Links Across Differences: Gender, Ethnicity and Nationalism.']

Kim, Young-Chung. *Women of Korea: A History from Ancient Times to 1945.* Seoul: Ewha Women's University Press, 1976.

Kittredge, Cherry. *Womansword: What Japanese Words Say about Women.* Illus. Taro Higuchi. New York: Kodansha Int'l, 1987.

Kono, Taeko. *Toddler Hunting and Other Stories.* Transl. Lucy North; add. transl. Lucy Flower. New York: New Directions, 1996. [Ten stories about unhappy women in post-war Japan.]

Lebra, Joyce, and Joy Paulson. *Chinese Women in South East Asia.* Singapore: Times, 1980.

Lie, Merete, & Ragnhild Lund. *Renegotiating Local Values: Working Women and Foreign Industry in Malaysia*. Richmond, Surrey: Curzon Press, 1994.

Lim, Shirley Geok-lin. *Among the White Moon Faces: Memoirs of a Nyonya Feminist*. Singapore: Times Editions, 1996.

Liu, Nienling, et al., trans. *The Rose Colored Dinner: New Works by Contemporary Chinese Women Writers*. Hong Kong: Joint Publ. Co. Ltd., 1988.

Matsui, Yayori. *Women's Asia*. Trans. Mitsuko Matsuda. London & New Jersey: Zed Books, 1989 [orig. pub. in Japan, 1987].

McGranahan, Carole. 'Miss Tibet or Tibet Misrepresented?: The Trope of Woman-as-Nation in the Struggle for Tibet.' *Beauty Queens on the Global Stage: Gender, Contests and Power*. Eds. C B Cohen, R Wilk & B Stoeltje. New York & London: Routledge, 1996, pp. 161–184.

Mi, Mi Khaing. *The World of Burmese Women*. Singapore: Times Books International, 1986.

Minamoto, Junko. 'Buddhism and the Historical Construction of Sexuality in Japan.' *US–Japan Women's Journal: A Journal for the International Exchange of Gender Studies*. English Supplement 5 (1993), pp. 87–115.

Mohanty, Chandra Talpade, & Satya P. Mohanty, intro. *The Slate of Life: More Contemporary Stories by Women Writers of India*. Ed. by Kali for Women. New York: Feminist Press, 1994.

Momsen, Janet Henshall. *Women and Development in the Third World*. London & New York: Routledge, 1991.

Moy, Joyce. 'Jobs for the Boys.' *The Asia Magazine* (cover story) 35.M13 (4–6 Apr. 1997), pp. 10–14.

Mukhopadhyay, Carol Chapnick, & Susan Seymour. *Women, Education, and Family Structure in India*. Boulder: Westview Press, 1994.

Murray, Alison J. *No Money, No Honey: A Study of Street Traders and Prostitutes in Jakarta*. New York: Oxford University Press, 1991.

Murray, Alison, & Tess Robinson. 'Minding Your Peers and Queers: female sex workers in the AIDS discourse in Australia and South-east Asia.' *Gender, Place and Culture: A Journal of Feminist Geography* 3.1 (March 1996), pp. 43–60.

Nagata, Judith, & Janet W. Salaff, eds. 'Strategies for Survival: Lives of Southeast Asian Women.' *Southeast Asian Journal of Social Science* [Special Issue] 24.1 (1996).

Selected Bibliography

The New Zealand Journal of History 27.2 (Oct. 1993). Guest ed. Raewyn Dalziel. [Special issue marking centennial of women's franchise in New Zealand.]

Ong, Aihwa. 'Colonialism and Modernity: Feminist Re-presentations of Women in Non-Western Societies.' *Inscriptions* [No.] 3/4 (1988), pp. 79–93.

_____. 'Postcolonial Nationalism: Women and Retraditionalization in the Islamic Imaginary, Malaysia.' *Feminism, Nationalism and Militarism.* Ed. Constance R Sutton. New York: Assoc. for Feminist Anthropology/ American Anthropological Assoc., in collaboration with the International Women's Anthropology Conference, 1995, pp. 43–50.

_____. *Spirits of Resistance and Capitalist Discipline: Factory Women in Malaysia.* Albany: State University of New York Press, 1987. [State University of New York Series in the anthropology of work.]

_____. 'State versus Islam: Malay Families, Women's Bodies and the Body Politic in West Malaysia.' *American Ethnologist* 17.2 (1990), pp. 258–276.

Ong, Aihwa, & Michael G Peletz, eds. *Bewitching Women, Pious Men: Gender and Body Politics in Southeast Asia.* Berkeley, Los Angeles, London: University of California Press, 1995. [Papers from conference on gender in Southeast Asian cultures, held at the University of California, Berkeley, in the winter of 1992. Includes two previously published papers not presented at conference.]

Orr, Robert, & Pauline Whyte. *The Women of Rural Asia.* Boulder, Colorado: Westview Press, 1982. [Westview special studies on women in contemporary society.]

Patel, Rashida. 'Challenges Facing Women in Pakistan.' *Ours by Right: Women's Rights as Human Rights.* Ed. Joanna Kerr. London: Zed Books (in assoc. with the North–South Inst.), 1993, pp. 32–39.

Petersen, Kirsten Holst, & Anna Rutherford, eds. *A Double Colonization: Colonial and Post-Colonial Women's Writing.* Mundelstrup, Denmark: Dangaroo Press, 1986.

Petrie, Barbara, ed. Kiwi and Emu: *An Anthology of Contemporary Poetry by Australian and New Zealand Women.* Springwood: Butterfly Books, 1989.

Pettman, Jane. *Living in the Margins: Racism, Sexism and Feminism in Australia.* Sydney: Allen and Unwin, 1992.

Pietila, Hilkka, & Jeanne Vickers. *Making Women Matter: The Role of the United Nations.* New Jersey: Zed Books, 1990.

'Reflections on the Fourth World Conference on Women and NGO Forum 1995.' *Signs: Journal of Women in Culture and Society* 22.1 (Autumn 1996), pp. 181–226.

[Includes Jian Guan, 'Review of (three) UN Reports (*Women in a Changing Global Economy: 1994 World Survey on the Role of Women in Development; From Nairobi to Beijing: Second Review and Appraisal of the Implementation of the Nairobi Forward-Looking Strategies for the Advancement of Women; and Women: Looking Beyond 2000*), pp. 222–226; Aruna Rao, 'Engendering Institutional Change,' pp. 218–221; Charlotte Bunch & Susana Fried, 'Beijing '95: Moving Women's Human Rights from Margin to Center,' pp. 200–204; Esther Ngan-ling Chow, 'Making Waves, Moving Mountains: Reflections on Beijing '95 and Beyond,' pp. 185–192; Wang Zheng, 'A Historic Turning Point for the Women's Movement in China,' pp. 192–199.]

Reynolds, Margaret. 'Women.' *Australian Civilisation.* Ed. Richard Nile. Melbourne: Oxford University Press, 1994, pp. 125–140.

Roy, Manisha. *Bengali Women.* Calcutta: Stree, 1993

The Slate of Life: An Anthology of Stories by Indian Women. New Delhi: Kali for Women, 1990..

Sheridan, Susan. *Along the Faultlines: Sex, Race and Nation in Australian Women's Writing; 1880's–1930's.* St Leonards, NSW: Allen & Unwin Pty Ltd., 1995.

Shimizu, Yasuko. 'Asian Perspective – Asian Brides for Rural Japan.' *Japan Christian Quarterly* 54.3 (1988), pp. 179–181.

Sieh Lee, Mei Ling, et al. *Women Managers of Malaysia.* Kuala Lumpur: Faculty of Economics and Administration, University of Malaya, 1991.

Sonbol, Amira. 'Changing Perceptions of Feminine Beauty in Islamic Society.' *Ideals of Feminine Beauty: Philosophical, Social and Cultural Dimensions.* Ed. Karen A Callaghan. Westport, Connecticut: Greenwood, 1994 (Contrib. in Women's Studies, No. 141), pp. 53–66.

Stevens, Maila. *Why Gender Matters in Southeast Asian Politics.* Clayton, Victoria: Centre of Southeast Asian Studies, Monash University, 1991. [Monash Papers on Southeast Asia: No. 23.]

Tama, Yasuko. 'The Logic of Abortion: Japanese Debates on the Legitimacy of Abortion as Seen in Post-World War 2 Newspapers.' *US–Japan Women's Journal: A Journal for the International Exchange of Gender Studies.* English Supplement 7 (1994), pp. 3–30.

Tan, Joo Ean. 'The Effect of Development on the Decline of Universal Marriage in Thailand, 1970–1990.' *Southeast Asian Journal of Social Science* 24.2 (1996), pp. 70–83.

Tang, David. 'Mighty Aphrodite.' *Asia Magazine* 36.N11 (6–8 Mch. 1998), p. 30.

Tharu, Susie, & K Lalita, eds. *Women Writing in India: 600 B.C. to the Present.* New York: Feminist Press at CUNY, 1990.

Thorbek, Susanne. *Voices from the City: Women of Bangkok.* London & New York: Zed Books, 1987.

Thorbek, Susanne. *Gender and Slum Culture in Urban Asia.* Trans. Brian Fedsfod. London & New York: Zed Books, 1994.

Tyner, James A. 'Constructions of Filipina Migrant Entertainers.' *Gender, Place and Culture: A Journal of Feminist Geography* 3.1 (March 1996), pp. 77–94.

Ueda, Makoto. *The Mothers of Dreams and Other Short Stories: Portrayals of Women in Modern Japanese Fiction.* Tokyo: Kodansha International, 1987.

van Bemmelen, Sita, et al., eds. *Women and Mediation in Indonesia.* Leiden: KITLV Press, 1992.

van Esterik, Penny. 'The Politics of Beauty in Thailand.' *Beauty Queens on the Global Stage: Gender, Contests and Power.* Ed. C B Cohen, R Wilk & B Stoeltje. New York & London: Routledge, 1996, pp. 203–216.

Ward, B E. *Women in the New Asia: the Changing Social Roles of Men and Women in South and South-east Asia.* Paris: UNESCO, 1963.

Wee, Vivienne, Noeleen Heyzer, et al. *Gender, Poverty and Sustainable Development: Towards a Holistic Framework of Understanding and Action.* Singapore: Centre for Environment, Gender and Development [ENGENDER], with assist. from UNDP, 1995.

Wever, Lydia, sel. *Yellow Pencils: Contemporary Poetry by New Zealand Women.* Auckland & New York: Oxford University Press, 1988.

Wolf, Margery, & Roxane Witke. *Women in Chinese Society.* Stanford: Stanford University Press, 1975.

Women in Development in the South Pacific: Barriers and Opportunities. Canberra: Development Studies Centre, Australian National University, 1985. [Papers presented at a Conference held in Vanuatu from 11–14 August 1984.]

Women in Politics in Asia and the Pacific: Proceedings of the Seminar on the Participation of Women in Politics as an Aspect of Human Resources Development, 18–20 Nov. 1992; Seoul. New York: United Nations, 1993.

Women Social Scientists: Asia-Pacific. Bangkok: Regional Unit for Social and Human Sciences in Asia and the Pacific, UNESCO Principal Regional Office for Asia and the Pacific, 1987.

Women's Economic Participation in Asia and the Pacific. Bangkok: UN Economic and Social Commission for Asia and the Pacific, 1987. [Contributions from Australia, India, Indonesia, Japan, Korea, Singapore and Thailand.]

Writing for Women: Civic Education. Bangkok: UNESCO Principal Regional Office for Asia and the Pacific, 1990.

Zacharias, Usha. 'The Sita Myth and Hindu Fundamentalism: Masculine Signs of Feminine Beauty.' *Ideals of Feminine Beauty: Philosophical, Social and Cultural Dimensions.* Ed. Karen A Callaghan. Westport, Connecticut: Greenwood, 1994 (Contrib. in Women's Studies, No. 141), pp. 37–52.

Zapanta-Manlapez, Edna, ed. *Songs of Ourselves: Writings by Filipino Women in English.* Manila: Anvil Publishing, 1994.

Leong Liew Geok

The Contributors

Abbreviations

ASEAN	Association of Southeast Asian Nations
AWARE	Association of Women for Action and Research
HDB	Housing and Development Board
ISEAS	Institute for Southeast Asian Studies
MOE	Ministry of Education
NAC	National Arts Council
NBDCS	National Book Development Council of Singapore
NTUC	National Trades Union Congress
NUS	National University of Singapore
PAP	People's Action Party
RELC	Regional English Language Centre
SBC	Singapore Broadcasting Corporation
SRT	Singapore Repertory Theatre
STARS	Singapore Theatre American Repertory Showcase
TCS	Television Corporation of Singapore
TESOL	Teaching of English to Speakers of Other Languages
UNESCO	United Nations Educational, Scientific and Cultural Organization

 REBECCA CHUA (b. 1953) won the Rotary Award for Journalism in 1979–80. She has participated in Writing Programmes at the Vermont Studio Center, Banff Fine Arts Centre and South-East Asia Writers' Conference in Bali. She has taught journalism at NUS and Creative Writing at the University of Toronto. She teaches creative writing and storytelling at various schools and colleges across Ontario. *The Newspaper Editor and Other Stories* (1981) received a Commendation Award from NBDCS in 1982. Her short stories have been anthologised in *Singapore Short Stories* (1989), *The Fiction of Singapore* (1990) and *Tapestry: A Collection of Short Stories* (1992), and published in Singapore and Malaysia, Hong Kong, Japan, Canada, USA and UK. Her work has been translated into Malay, Chinese and Japanese, and broadcast in Singapore, Canada and by the BBC. She also writes poetry and plays. Presently, she divides her time among Canada, the United States, Singapore and Southeast Asia.

ENG WEE LING (b. 1962) wrote her first play, 'Woman,' when she was a final year Law student living in Sheares Hall at NUS. It was a project born out of frustration with the lack of good, meaty female roles in Singapore drama. After the success of 'Woman' (in which she acted, as well as directed) in 1985, she devised and acted in 'Confessions of Three Unmarried Women' (1987) for ACTION! Theatre. A revised version became the first play to be staged at Chijmes Hall in 1996. She was ACTION! Theatre's resident playwright from 1987–91, when her plays, 'Party Animals,' 'Graveyard Shift,' 'Wing Tips and Shoulder Pads,' and 'Second Home' were staged. 'Quarter to Midnight' (1987) and 'Death at the Drama Centre' (1989) were produced by STARS (now SRT). She is the author of a commissioned work, *A Woman's Place: The Story of Singapore Women* (1993), a PAP Women's Wing publication. Once a litigation lawyer, she is currently a domestic CEO with two small children to care for. She has been on the NAC's Drama Review Committee since 1996.

HENG SIOK TIAN (b. 1963) is a Programme Officer with the School Libraries Unit; Languages and Library, Curriculum Planning and Development Division, Ministry of Education. *Crossing the Chopsticks and Other Poems* was published in 1993. Yin-ly was shortlisted for the 1995 Singapore Literature Prize (Poetry). Her poems have appeared in *Words for the 25th* (1990); *New Voices in Southeast Asia* (1991); *Singapore: Places, Poems, Paintings* (1993); *The Calling of Kindred* (1993); and *Journeys: Words, Home and Nation: Anthology of Singapore Poetry, 1984–1995* (1995). A short play, 'The Lift,' was staged in 1991 at the Substation's Guinness Theatre, and selected for a 15-minute reading at the Third International Women Playwrights' Conference in Adelaide, in 1994. Her short stories have appeared in various publications, including *The Fiction of Singapore* (1990).

MINFONG HO (b. 1951) was born in Burma, raised in Thailand, and educated in Taiwan and the United States. Her writings have been published in the United States and Singapore, and translated into Japanese, Chinese, French, Thai and Tagalog. Her semi-autobiographical first novel, *Sing to the Dawn* (1975), was awarded first prize by the Council on Interracial Books for Children in New York. It was recently adapted and made into a musical, which launched the 1996 Singapore Festival of Arts. Her second novel, *Rice Without Rain* (1986), based on the student movement in northern Thailand, where she taught in the early 70's, won the NBDCS Fiction Award in 1988, and was the Best Book for Young Adults from the American Library Association. After working as a nutritionist on the Thai-Cambodian border, she wrote *The Clay Marble* (1992), a novel about Cambodian refugees. This book was an American Bookseller Pick of the List, and a Notable Book in the Field of Social Studies. She helped compile and edit her father's memoirs, *Eating Salt* (1990). Her short stories have been widely anthologised, among them, 'Tanjong Rhu,' 'Birds of Paradise,' and 'The Winter Hibiscus.' She recently produced several picture books, *Hush! A Thai Lullabye* (1997 Caldecott Honor award from the American Library Assoc.); *The Two Brothers*, and *Maples in the Mist: A Translation of Tang Dynasty Poems.* Ho was a recipient of the (1996) South-East Asia Write Award in Bangkok, the 1997 Cultural Medallion (Singapore) and the 1997 Mont Blanc-NUS Centre for the Arts Literary Award. With her husband and three children, she lives in New York state where, instead of the water buffaloes of her childhood, she watches herds of wild deer grazing from her desk window.

HO POH FUN (b. 1946) teaches at Raffles Junior College and runs its Creative Writing Club which taps the talents of its young writers; the Club is responsible for the College's annual Afternoon of Poetry and Music. A recent Club publication, *Tributaries: Convergence on an Afternoon of Poetry and*

Music (1995), features works by some of Singapore's most promising writers nurtured by the Creative Arts Programme of which she is mentor and workshop instructor. Her poems have appeared in *Focus, Singa, The Straits Times, Words for the 25th* (1990); *Singapore: Places, Poems, Paintings* (1992); and Journeys: Words, Home and Nation (1995). Her short stories, several of which have won prizes in national short story competitions, have appeared in *Singa, Tanjong Rhu and Other Stories* (1983), *The Fiction of Singapore* (1990) and *Singular Stories: Tales from Singapore* (1993). Her first collection, *Katong and Other Poems* (1994), secured a Commendation Award for Poetry in the NBDCS Book Awards in 1996. 'Guest,' a short story featuring voice-play on the rhythms of migration, settlement and resettlement in northern Thailand, will be appearing in a regional prose collection to be published by the ASEAN Committee on Culture and Information.

GERALDINE KAN (b. 1967) was formerly a *Straits Times* journalist who covered the social services beat and wrote a lighthearted column, 'twentysomething.' Her play, 'The Trial,' won third prize in the 1989 NUS-Shell Short Play Competition; it was staged at Nanyang Technological University the following year. While an undergraduate at UCLA, she spent her free time watching movies in Westwood, and cycling at Santa Monica and Venice beaches. She also wrote for the UCLA *Daily Bruin,* a university paper that gave her her first real immersion in American life. *Somersaults and Pirouettes* (1994), her book of short stories, was started in graduate school in Northwestern University, and written in between hanging out at museums, cafes and jazz clubs. She currently works in media relations for a large information technology company, and is addicted to mocha and cappuccino.

STELLA KON (b. 1944) is of Peranakan descent (both her parents were born in Emerald Hill Road). Born in Edinburgh and educated in Singapore, she lived for many years in Malaysia, but now lives in Singapore. Divorced, she has two sons, a surgeon and an orthodontist, who live in London, and two grandchildren. She has won first prize on three occasions in the Singapore National Playwriting Competition: for 'The Bridge' in 1977; for 'Trial' in 1983; and for 'Emily of Emerald Hill' in 1985. The latter, a one-woman drama about a Peranakan matriarch, has been staged in Malaysia, Singapore, Honolulu, and at the 1986 Edinburgh Festival of Arts, and is now widely known. In recent years, Kon has also tried her hand at prose fiction; her novel, *Eston* (1995), won a Merit Award in the 1994 Singapore Literature Prize (Fiction) Competition.

LAI AH ENG (b. 1954) is an anthropologist who has worked as an education officer in consumer education (Consumers' Association of Penang, Malaysia); a tutor in development studies (Universiti Sains Malaysia) and sociology (NUS), a research officer on public housing and community issues (HDB) and a researcher with the Singapore National Heritage Board. Currently with ISEAS, she is the author of *Peasants, Proletarians and Prostitutes: A Preliminary Investigation into the Work of Chinese Women in Colonial Malaya* (1986) and *Meanings of Multiethnicity : A Case Study of Ethnicity and Ethnic Relations in Singapore* (1995), originally a doctoral dissertation for Cambridge University. It was Highly Commended (Non-fiction) in the 1996 NBDCS Book Awards. A founding member of AWARE, she co-authored several of its early works on the position of women in Singapore. Her current projects include oral histories of older women's economic and family lives in Singapore, and the experiences and contributions of ethnic minorities in Singapore's development. In between working and mothering, she writes the occasional short story. Her first, 'Gods, Ghosts and Germs,' won third prize in the 1989 Singapore National Short Story Writing Competition. She is working on her third book, *Travels in the Neighbourhood*, based on her observations and experiences of local public housing communities in Singapore, and *A Coffeeshop in Sentul*, based on her childhood experiences of living in one.

AGNES SHUN-LING LAM (b. 1954) was born and initially educated in Hong Kong. After graduating from the University of Singapore in 1977, she tutored in the Department of English before completing her TESOL Certificate and doctorate in linguistics at the University of Pittsburgh in 1984. She was a lecturer in NUS until 1990. A Singaporean by naturalisation, she is now Associate Professor and Associate Director at the English Centre, University of Hong Kong. She has held visitorships at the University of Pittsburgh, the Ontario Institute for Studies in Education, the Chinese Academy of Sciences, the Central University of Nationalities and the University of Cambridge. Her poetry has appeared in *Commentary*, *Focus*, *Singa*, *Westerly* and *Hong Kong Papers for Linguistics and Language Teaching*. Her first collection of poems, *Woman to Woman* (1997), was published by Asia 2000 in Hong Kong.

LEE TZU PHENG (b. 1946) is a Senior Lecturer in the Department of English Language and Literature, NUS. Born and educated in Singapore, her poetry has appeared in anthologies and journals in Singapore, Malaysia, the Philippines, Hong Kong, Japan, India, the United Kingdom, Australia and the United States. Several of her poems are taught in college and university courses in Australia, Canada, the United States and Singapore. Three earlier collections, *Prospect of a Drowning* (1980), *Against the Next Wave* (1988), and *The Brink of an Amen* (1991), all won NBDCS awards for Poetry; she received the Singapore Cultural Medallion for Literature in 1985, and the SEA Write Award in 1987. Known for her interest in children's literature, Lee has contributed to journals and conferences on the subject. She wrote *Growing Readers* (1987), and has done story-telling on television. For her poetry and contribution to the promotion of children's reading, she was presented by the Government of Chile with the Gabriela Mistral Award in 1996, named after the Chilean poet and educationist who was Nobel Laureate in 1945. Recently appointed a Member of the NAC, Lee also received the 1996 Mont Blanc-NUS Centre for the Arts Literary Award for her services to literature. Her fourth collection of poems, *Lambada by Galilee and Other Surprises*, was published in 1997.

 **LEONG LIEW GEOK** (b. 1947) is a Senior Lecturer in the Department of English Language and Literature, NUS. Born in Penang and educated in Malaysia, Australia, England and the United States, her poetry has appeared in various journals, including *awareness, Commentary, Focus, The Malahat Review, Phoenix: Sri Lanka Journal of English in the Commonwealth, Singa* and *Solidarity*, and has been anthologised in *Critical Engagements: Singapore Poems in Focus* (1986), *Singapore: Poems, Places, Paintings* (1993), *Voices 4: Readings by Singapore Writers* (1995), *Journeys: Words, Home and Nation* (1995) and the forthcoming *Memories and Desires: A Poetic History of Singapore* (1998). The author of *Love is Not Enough* (1991), she is working on a second collection of poems, *Women Without Men*, and is currently preparing a book of essays on the Literature in English of the Pacific War in Malaysia and Singapore. Married, and with three children, she is a plant addict, and a rabid trial-and-error gardener.

SUCHEN CHRISTINE LIM (b. 1948) was born in Perak and was educated in the Convent of the Holy Infant Jesus in Penang, Kedah and Singapore. At the age of fifteen, she moved with her family to Singapore. She began writing fiction when she returned to NUS for an Honours year in Literature after some years of teaching in Catholic Junior College. The result was *Ricebowl* (1984). In 1986, she co-authored with Ophelia Ooi 'The Amah: A Portrait in Black and White,' which won the merit prize in the 1986 NUS-Shell Short Play Competition. In 1989, while studying for a post-graduate Diploma in Applied Linguistics, she co-edited a literature series for secondary schools, *Mosaic Books 1 and 2*, and completed her second novel, *Gift from the Gods* (1990). She was the first writer to win the Singapore Literature Prize for her third novel, *Fistful of Colours* (1993). A recently completed novel, *Bit of Earth*, is due for publication shortly. She recently attended the International Writers' Program at the University of Iowa on a Fulbright Scholarship. A curriculum specialist with MOE, she has been writing language curriculum materials for more than a decade, for pre-primary to pre-university levels. She also writes stories for children; several like 'Granny,' 'Roti Prata,' and 'Woo Won Ton,' are used in schools.

LIN HSIN HSIN (b.****) is an information technologist, artist and poet, who speaks sixteen computer languages besides Chinese, English, French and Japanese. To date, she has published more than a hundred papers on Information Technology. She has held fifteen solo exhibitions in Singapore, Amsterdam and San Jose, and has participated in more than 170 group exhibitions in forty-nine cities throughout Asia, Europe and North America. The winner of several art awards in Singapore and Paris, Lin was a Visiting Fellow with the Institut für Auslandsbeziehungen, Federal Republic of Germany, in 1988, and a Japan Foundation Fellow in 1990. Her art-works are in private, public and museum collections in Asia, Europe and North America. The Java-powered and Shockwave-staged *Lin Hsin Hsin Art Museum* (<http://www.lhham.com.sg>) on the Internet, the first of its kind in Asia, has been visited by more than 380,000 visitors from ninety-one countries since its inauguration in April 1995. It was recognised as among the 'Top 5% of All Web Sites' by Point Communication, USA, in September 1995, and received the 'Virtuocity Award' from VXR Corporation, USA, in July 1996. Her latest exhibition, '.@rt: a Cyberart Show,' featured still and animated digital art-works created with a two-button mouse and a 16.7 million digital palette. Lin has published five collections of poetry: *take a word for a walk* (1989); *from time to time* (1991); *Love @ 1st Byte* (1992); *sunny side up* (1994) and *in Bytes we tr@v@l* (1997). Her poems have been published in Singapore, Switzerland, Japan and the United States.

 **MARY LOH CHIEU KWUAN** (b. 1959) co-authored *Mistress and Other Creative Take-Offs* (1990) with Desmond Sim and Ovidia Yu, and wrote 'Fast Cars and Fancy Women' which was first staged by TheatreWorks in 1991. She seeks time and opportunity to write her first solo book, which was supposed to have come out several years ago and which she promises will come out ... er, soon. She has taught in Catholic Junior College, and was Manager of Jubilee Hall and General Manager of The Really Useful Company (Singapore). Now a managing consultant building her own Empire, a marketing and communications consultancy, she finds alternative solace in cookie and cake baking, collecting antique ethnic recipes, amateur videography and plant hydration experiments (*au contraire*, Mary's garden doth not too well grow). She also conducts workshops in playwriting for participating students of the Creative Arts Programme, run by MOE and NUS.

NIRMALA PURUSHOTAM (b. 1951) is a Senior Lecturer in the Department of Sociology, NUS. She teaches in and writes on various fields, including race relations, gender issues, and phenomenological sociology. Her publications include *Singapore's Little India: Past, Present and Future* (1982; 2nd rev. ed., 1990), which won the NBDCS Award for the Best Book (Non-fiction) in 1984, and *Negotiating Language, Constructing Race: Disciplining Difference in Singapore* (forthcoming). Poetry, photography and cooking, combined with the challenge of raising an avidly inquiring son in a patriarchal world she cannot accept, help maintain her sociological imagination. Sociological field work has provided rich materials which have metamorphosed into embryonic novel ideas, short stories, gender-free children's books and poetry. Thus far, she has only consented to publish her poems, which have appeared in *awareness, Moving Colours* (1992), in which she explored the use of poetry to explicate the whispers that one can hear in abstract paintings, *Singapore: Places, Poems, Paintings* (1993) and *Journeys: Words, Home and Nation* (1995). She is currently writing a series of poem-songs on the Women's Charter, which she hopes to convert into a musical celebrating women's rights, won by women for themselves.

ROSALY PUTHUCHEARY (b. 1936) teaches English Literature and the General Paper at Anglo-Chinese Junior College. Born in Johor Baru where she received her early education, she has lived in Singapore since 1974. A Bachelor's and Master's graduate in English Literature from NUS, she holds a Diploma in Applied Linguistics from RELC. She has published three volumes of poetry: *Pillow your Dreams* (1978), *The Fragmented Ego* (1978) and *Dance on His Doorstep* (1992). A critical study of the Indian poet, Parasathy, was published in *The Journal of Indian Writing in English* (1980). A fourth volume of poems, *Dance with Leaves and Other Poems*, and a collection of short stories, *Slings and Arrows of Love*, are ready for publication. She is currently working on a second volume of short stories.

RASIAH HALIL @ Rashidah bte Shaik Abdul Halim (b. 1956) was a lecturer at the University of Brunei, NUS and the National Institute of Education. She received a Fulbright Scholarship to do research and to attend the International Writing Programme at the University of Iowa in 1995. A bilingual poet and author, her publications include two collections of poetry, *Perbualan: Buku Catatan Seorang Gipsi* (*Conversations: Notebook of a Gypsy*; 1988), *Sungai dan Lautan* (*The River and the Ocean*; 1995), and a collection of short stories, *Orang Luar* (*The Outsider*; 1991). Conversations received an NBDCS Commendation Award for Poetry in 1992. Her writings have been anthologised in *Puisi-Puisi Nusantara* (*The Poetry of the Malay Archipelago*; 1981), *The Poetry of Singapore* (1981), *The Fiction of Singapore* (1990), and *Journeys: Words, Home and Nation* (1995). She translated Yuksel Soylemez's poems in *Love is a Cup of Chicken Soup* into Malay (*Cinta Adalah Secangkir Sup Ayam*; 1992) and edited *Brunei Darussalam* (1993). She has received several literary awards since the 1980's. Her work has been published in Singapore, Malaysia and Brunei. She is currently pursuing doctoral studies in Malay Literature at the University of Malaya.

AMY SOBRIELO (b. 1938) is a former lecturer in the School of Arts, National Institute of Education. Born and educated in Singapore, she has contributed short stories to *Singa*, and written children's stories for the Longman's Quest Graded Readers Series and for an Asian Copublication Programme Series sponsored by the Asian Cultural Centre for UNESCO in Tokyo. She has also co-authored a series of English textbooks for secondary schools, called *Forte* (Longman), and co-edited *Potpourri* (Longman), two volumes of short stories for secondary school students. She recently completed two sets of activity sheets, 'Book Trails' and 'Book Adventures,' for use by teachers and students involved in enrichment reading programmes in both primary and secondary schools.

ELIZABETH SU (b. 1957) taught English Language and Literature in NUS for several years and served as Assistant Director, Master in Public Policy Programme (MPP), NUS Centre for Advanced Studies, from 1994–96. She recently graduated (Class of '97) from the Master in Public Administration Program at Harvard. Three short plays of hers which focussed on the idea of the family, 'The Clown,' 'A Woman's Right,' and 'The Shadow Master,' won merit prizes in the 1978, 1989 and 1991 Shell National Short Play Writing Competitions organised by Shell and the (then) Ministry of Culture. Married to a Norwegian, Su lived for four years along the Sognefjord, the longest fjord in Norway. Her experience of Norwegian culture enabled her to write *Culture Shock! Norway* (1995). A year's stint as a research officer at the National Museum in the early 1980's awakened her interest in history and culture. She speaks Cantonese, English, Japanese, Malay, Mandarin and Norwegian. A mother of four, Su has to juggle her time judiciously between looking after her family, scripting, broadcasting for Radio Singapore International, and occasional writing.

TAN MEI CHING (b. 1970) graduated from Willamette University, Oregon, and the University of Washington. Her entry was judged the Outstanding Entry in the Western Regional Honors Conference Writing Contest (1991); she won first prize in the *Just a Moment Writing Contest* (1991) and was again placed first in *The Jason Writing Contest* (1991). Her winning stories were published in 1991 in *The University of New Mexico Honors Review: Western Forum*

for the Arts and Sciences, and the journals, *Just a Moment* and *The Jason* respectively. Her one-act play, 'Water Ghosts,' was awarded first prize in the 1992 NUS-Shell Short Play Competition, and subsequently published in *Beyond the Footlights: New Play Scripts in Singapore Theatre* (1992). Another one-act play, 'The Can-Opener,' was staged by TheatreWorks as part of Singapore Press Holdings' Young Playwrights' Series III in 1995. *Beyond the Village Gate,* a novel, received a Commendation Award in the 1992 Singapore Literature Prize (Fiction) Competition, and was one of the texts in the Contemporary Literature class at Willamette University in Spring, 1996. *Crossing Distance* (1995), a collection of short stories, was awarded a Merit Prize in the 1994 Singapore Literature Prize (Fiction) Competition, and was Commended in the 1996 NBDCS Book Awards. 'Quiet the Gorilla' was performed by TheatreWorks in the 1996 SPH Festival of New Writing, and was published in *Playful Phoenix: Women Write for the Singapore Stage* (1996). Tan received the 1997 NAC Young Artist Award for Literature. A writer/producer in multimedia games, she is currently working on her next novel and play.

NALLA TAN, nee Navarednam (b. 1923) was born in Ipoh, Malaya, and educated at the Methodist Girls' School, Ipoh. She went on to read Medicine at the University of Singapore, married fellow physician, Tan Joo Liang, and made Singapore her home. After a stint with the Ministry of Health, she joined the NUS Faculty of Medicine and was in due course appointed Associate Professor of Medicine. In 1984, she was elected a Fellow of the Faculty of Community Medicine of the Royal Colleges of the United Kingdom. She started writing in the late '60's. A short story, 'The Goddess of Mercy,' was read over the BBC World Service in 1975. Her first collection of poems, Emerald Autumn (1976) was followed by a second, *The Gift* (1978), and a collection of short stories, *Hearts and Crosses* (1989). For four and a half years, she penned a weekly column, 'You,' covering a spectrum of social and other issues, sometimes controversial, in *The Sunday*

Times. She later wrote for the *New Nation* and the *Monitor.* Her short story, 'What You Asked,' was placed second in the *Asiaweek* Short Story Competition of 1990. 'Heat Wave' is included in *The Fiction of Singapore* (1990). In the pipeline are a trilogy of fiction, and a collection of poems, old and new.

THERESA TAN (b. 1967) is currently the cheerfully-married Editor of *Female* magazine. 'Kaleidoscope Eyes,' a play-in-progress, has been in the making for over two years. She is thinking very hard about a book she has been meaning to write before she turns thirty. Educated entirely in Singapore, and with an Honours degree in English Language from NUS, she stumbled upon drama at the age of nineteen while writing a Neil Simon-style comedy to cheer herself up. Several plays have been particularly popular with college drama societies: 'Pistachios and Whipped Cream,' which won first prize in the 1989 NUS-Shell Short Play Competition, was staged (for the umpteenth time) in 1996, this time by her alma mater, Catholic Junior College. 'Bra Sizes' (first performed by TheatreWorks in 1992) and 'Dirty Laundry,' her first full-length play (first performed by TheatreWorks in 1993) were staged by Temasek Junior College, also in 1996. Her favourite experience with the stage remains The Necessary Stage's ''Scuse Me While I Kiss the Sky' (1994), a workshopped piece about suicidal teenagers. She hopes to be able to put together another workshopped play within the next five years.

VERENA TAY SIEW HUI (b. 1965) has freelanced for local magazines, worked in the Ministry of Defence (Public Affairs), and as a marketing executive in publishing. She has been fascinated by theatre for as long as she can remember. Since 1986, she has been involved in all aspects of English language theatre in Singapore, working with companies such as Practice Theatre Ensemble, ACTION! Theatre, TheatreWorks and The Necessary Stage. Her acting credits include 'Mama Looking for her Cat' (1988), 'The Silly Little Girl and the Funny Old Tree' (1989), 'The Caucasian Chalk Circle' (1989), 'Exit' (1990), 'Macbeth' (1993), 'Under the Bed' (1993) and 'Lao Jiu' (1994). Her better known directorial credits include devised plays like 'Second Home' (ACTION! Theatre, 1991) 'Best Foot Forward' (ACTION! Theatre, 1995), and 'Love, Food & Babies' (The Necessary Stage, 1995), which she also scripted. A member of TheatreWorks' Writers' Laboratory from 1992–94, she contributed the skit, 'The Space Traveller's Guide to Singapore (Abridged)' to the company's New Year comedy review (1992/1993), and wrote 'The Story of Bukit Merah' (1992) for The Necessary Stage's Theatre-in-Education programme. 'Love, Food and Babies' won a Merit Prize in the Open Category of TheatreWorks' Twenty-four Hour Playwriting Competition (1996). 'Prosperity' was originally an entry for ACTION! Theatre's first Ten-Minute Play Competition (1994). She is currently working fulltime as an Actor-Facilitator in The Necessary Stage's Theatre for Youth Branch.

CLAIRE THAM (b. 1967) was educated in the Convent of the Holy Infant Jesus, Hwa Chong Junior College and Oxford University. A lawyer by profession, she started writing at a very young age. She won two second prizes in the 1984 National Short Story Writing Competition, for 'Homecoming' and 'Fascist Rock.' *Fascist Rock: Stories of Rebellion* (1990) secured a Commendation Award for Fiction from NBDCS in 1992. *Saving the Rainforest and other Stories* (1993) won a Highly Commended Award for Fiction from NBDCS in 1995. She is currently working on her first novel.

 **DENYSE TESSENSOHN** (b. 1950) practised law for eight years before starting the first school in executive and personal grooming in the region in 1983. The author of *Modern Manners* (1992; rpt. 1992, 1995) and *Excel in Oral English* (1995; rpt. 1996, 1997), she is Director of Clea Consultants Pte Ltd. and The Finishing School Pte Ltd., and has taught thousands the finer points of personal presentation and grooming since 1988. She began writing fiction, songs and poetry in 1988. *Feel*, a collection of ten short stories about people confronted with difficult decisions, won a Commendation Prize in the 1994 Singapore Literature Prize (Fiction) Competition. She teaches speech improvement in local schools and colleges, and continues to teach executive grooming and phonetics in the region. A sickeningly incurable optimist, she is trying to put pain into her writing.

 **WEE KIAT** (b. 1947) graduated from the University of Singapore with an Honours degree in Social Sciences. Formerly a senior consultant in an international public relations firm, she is now with the University Liaison Office, NUS. Although she had always wanted to pursue a career which involved writing, she had to devote the earlier part of her working life to helping in the family business. Nevertheless, she freelanced for magazines like *Her World, Calibre* and *Golf*. Taking the plunge in mid-life, she became editor of a trade journal, *Singapore Air Cargo*, and contributing editor to ACCENT. Her first novel, *Women in Men's Houses*, was published in 1992. A second, Eat *Company Sleep Bunk Berth*, was published in 1997. She hopes to write a children's book, and a book on cats so that Singaporeans will take ownership of 'longkang' cats. Her two children remain her greatest achievement.

ELEANOR WONG (b. 1962) is a lawyer with an international law firm specialising in regional finance transactions. Her first play, 'Peter's Passionate Pursuit,' won first prize (jointly with 'Ash and Shadowless' by Chua Tze Wei) in the first NUS National Short Play Writing Competition in 1985. 'Peter's Passionate Pursuit' has been performed by several theatre groups over the ensuing decade. It was staged during the 1988 Singapore Festival of Arts, and represented Singapore at the first ASEAN Theatre Festival in Manila in 1988. It has also been performed at the Five Arts Centre, Kuala Lumpur. The success of 'Peter' led to the following ACTION! Theatre productions of her plays: 'Touch the Soul of a God' (1987), 'Real Life?' (1988), 'Exit' (1990), 'The Joust' (1991) and 'Block Sale' (1996). Other plays of hers have been performed by TheatreWorks: 'Jackson on a Jaunt' (1989), 'Mergers and Accusations' (1993), and 'Wills and Secession' (1995). 'Mergers and Accusations' won an NBDCS award (jointly with 'Undercover' by Tan Tarn How and 'Cetecea' by Otto Fong) in 1996. These plays are collected in *Dirty Laundry, Mergers & Undercover: Plays from TheatreWorks' Writers' Lab* (1995). She has also written musical numbers for *Pop Sparks I* (1988) and *II* (1989), featuring original popular music written by Singaporean composers, and for several privately-staged musicals.

ANGELINE YAP (b. 1959) is a lawyer by profession. She, her husband and their three children are addicted to print, but not their pet hamster. She started writing poetry in her childhood. Her poems and short stories have won prizes in various competitions organised by the Southeast Asian Ministers of Education Organisation, Shankar's International Children's Art Competition, NBDCS, the NUS Literary Society, etc. She has contributed to various publications, from school yearbooks, newspapers and student magazines to *Saya, New Directions, Focus* and *Singa* as well as written articles for various law publications. Her poems have been anthologised in *But We Have No Legends* (1978), *The Poetry of Singapore* (1985), *Words for the 25th* (1990), *Journeys: Words, Home and Nation* (1995) and *Memories and Desires: A Poetic History of Singapore* (forthcoming). *Home and Beyond* was a finalist in the 1997 Singapore Literature Prize (Poetry) Competition. Her poems have been performed over radio and television. *Collected Poems* was published in 1985. 'Song of a Singaporean' was translated into Tamil by K Elangovan in 1989; 'Nightmare' and 'Blue,' set to music by Leong Yoon Pin and Assoc. Prof. Bernard Tan respectively, have been sung at choral competitions in Singapore and Finland. In writing as in design, she likes simple, uncluttered lines. Many of her poems are specifically written to be read aloud.

LESLEY YEOW, nee Gan (b. 1965) has enjoyed writing ever since she was introduced to compositions in primary school. Her poems and short stories have won prizes in Temasek Junior College and in NUS from which she graduated with an Honours degree in English Literature. She now writes for her own pleasure while professionally, she is a book editor who helps others with their writing. Two things keep her writing: encouragement from friends and family, which acts as a nudge in the right direction; and the fear that as one becomes preoccupied with the obligations of living, one neglects what is truly important to the extent of losing the ability to do it. Her journal, short stories, personal newsletters and scripts for church services are the products of the cultivation of that discipline she disdained to exercise in the heady days of inspiration.

 **OVIDIA YU TSIN YUEN** (b. 1961) started writing while at Methodist Girls' School. Her first stage piece was performed when she was in Anglo-Chinese Junior College. Arguably the most prolific and versatile of Singaporean playwrights, she was in the International Writers' Program at the University of Iowa in 1990/1991. Some two dozen plays have been performed or given dramatised readings by various companies in Singapore. They include 'Dead on Cue' (1987), ''Cupboards' (1990) and 'Round and Round the Dining Table' (1988, for [then] SBC 12) by The Necessary Stage; 'Face Values' (1988) and 'Family Affairs' (1989) by The Shell Players; 'Mistress' (1990), 'Imagine' (1991), 'Six Lonely Oysters' (1994; 1996), 'Hokkien Mee' (1995) and 'Playing Mothers' (1996) by ACTION! Theatre; 'Ja' (1991; 1993) by Music and Movement; 'Three Fat Virgins' (1992), 'Wife and Mother' (1992), 'Be the Food of Love (Play On ...)' (1993), by TheatreWorks; 'Three Fat Virgins Unassembled' (1995) by WOW Theatre; 'The Land of a Thousand Dreams' (1995) by NTUC; and 'Every Day Brings its Miracles' (1996) by the Singapore General Hospital Company. They have also been performed abroad, in Hong Kong, Kuala Lumpur, Glasgow, Edinburgh. 'The Woman in a Tree on a Hill' (produced by TheatreWorks and the Wayang Wayang Theatre Company in 1992, 1993 and 1996) won an Edinburgh Fringe First at the 1992 Edinburgh Arts Festival. The editor of a book on Girl Guides, *Guiding in Singapore: A Chronology of Guide Events; 1917–1990* (1990), she has written three works of fiction: *Miss Moorthy Investigates* (1989); together with Mary Loh Chieu Kwuan and Desmond Sim, *Mistress and Other Creative Takeoffs* (1990), and *The Mouse Marathon* (1993). 'A Dream of China' won the *Asiaweek* Short Story Competition in 1984. Her fiction has appeared in *The Original Singapore Sling Book* (1986), *The Fiction of Singapore* (1990) and *Tales of the Living, Tales of the Dead* (1990). In 1996, she received the Japan Chamber of Commerce and Industry Young Artist Award as well as the NAC Young Artist Award (for Drama and Fiction), and in 1997, the Singapore Youth Award (for Arts and Culture). *Breast Issues*, her latest play, was staged in November 1997 by SRT.